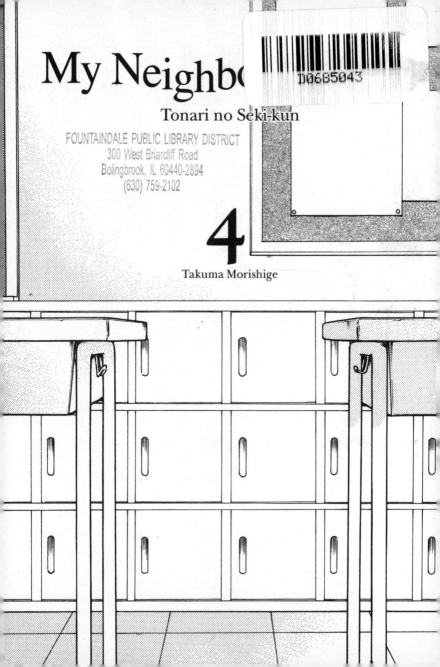

My Neighb...

Tonari no Seki-kun

4

Takuma Morishige

Schedule

43rd Period ③	44th Period ⑬	45th Period ㉓	46th Period ㉟
47th Period ㊺	48th Period ㊻	49th Period ㊼	50th Period ㊽
51st Period ㊾	52nd Period ⑩⑨	53rd Period ⑪⑨	54th Period ⑭①
55th Period ⑮①	Bonus ① ⑯②	Bonus ② ⑯⑤	Bonus ③ ⑯⑥

My
Neighbor
Seki

4

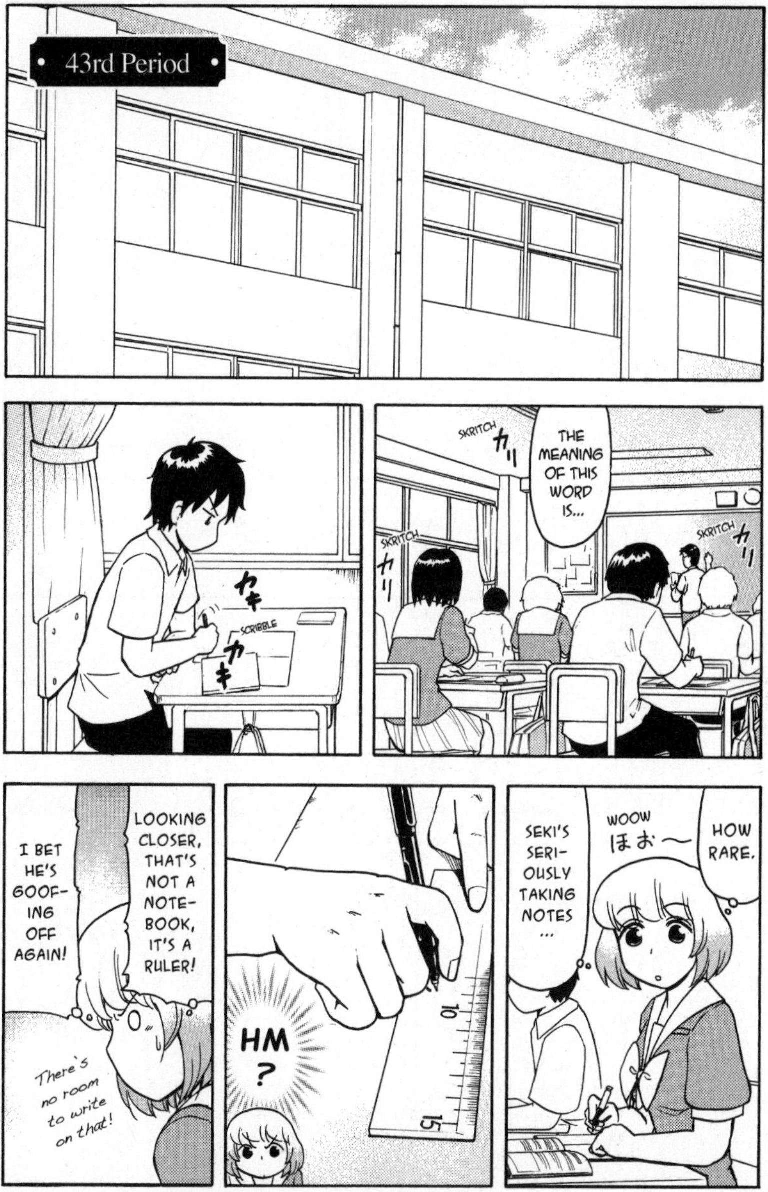
• 43rd Period •
SKRITCH カリ
THE MEANING OF THIS WORD IS...
SKRITCH カリ
SKRITCH カリ
カキ
SCRIBBLE
カキ
HOW RARE.
WOOW ほお～
SEKI'S SERIOUSLY TAKING NOTES...
HM?
LOOKING CLOSER, THAT'S NOT A NOTEBOOK, IT'S A RULER!
I BET HE'S GOOFING OFF AGAIN!
There's no room to write on that!
10
15

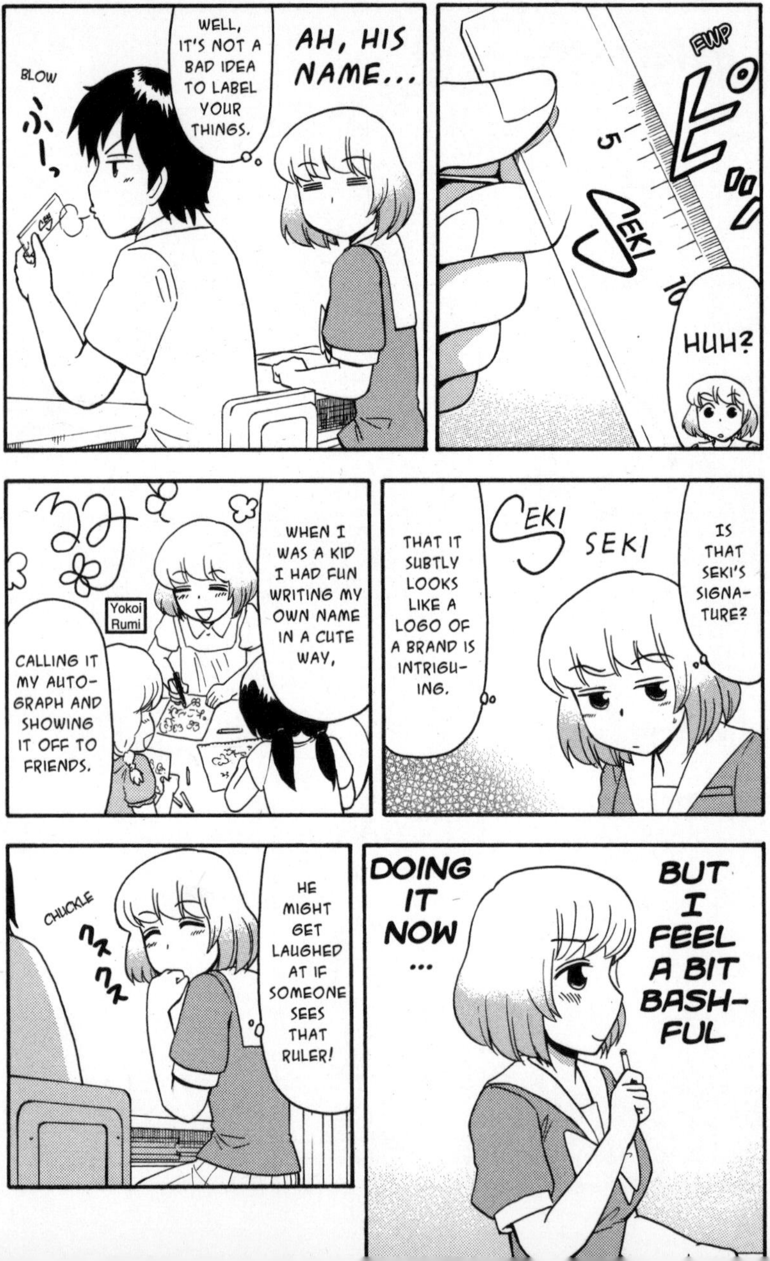
FWP
SEKI
HUH?
AH, HIS NAME...
WELL, IT'S NOT A BAD IDEA TO LABEL YOUR THINGS.
BLOW
IS THAT SEKI'S SIGNATURE?
SEKI
SEKI
THAT IT SUBTLY LOOKS LIKE A LOGO OF A BRAND IS INTRIGUING.
WHEN I WAS A KID I HAD FUN WRITING MY OWN NAME IN A CUTE WAY,
Yokoi Rumi
CALLING IT MY AUTOGRAPH AND SHOWING IT OFF TO FRIENDS.
BUT I FEEL A BIT BASHFUL
DOING IT NOW...
HE MIGHT GET LAUGHED AT IF SOMEONE SEES THAT RULER!
CHUCKLE

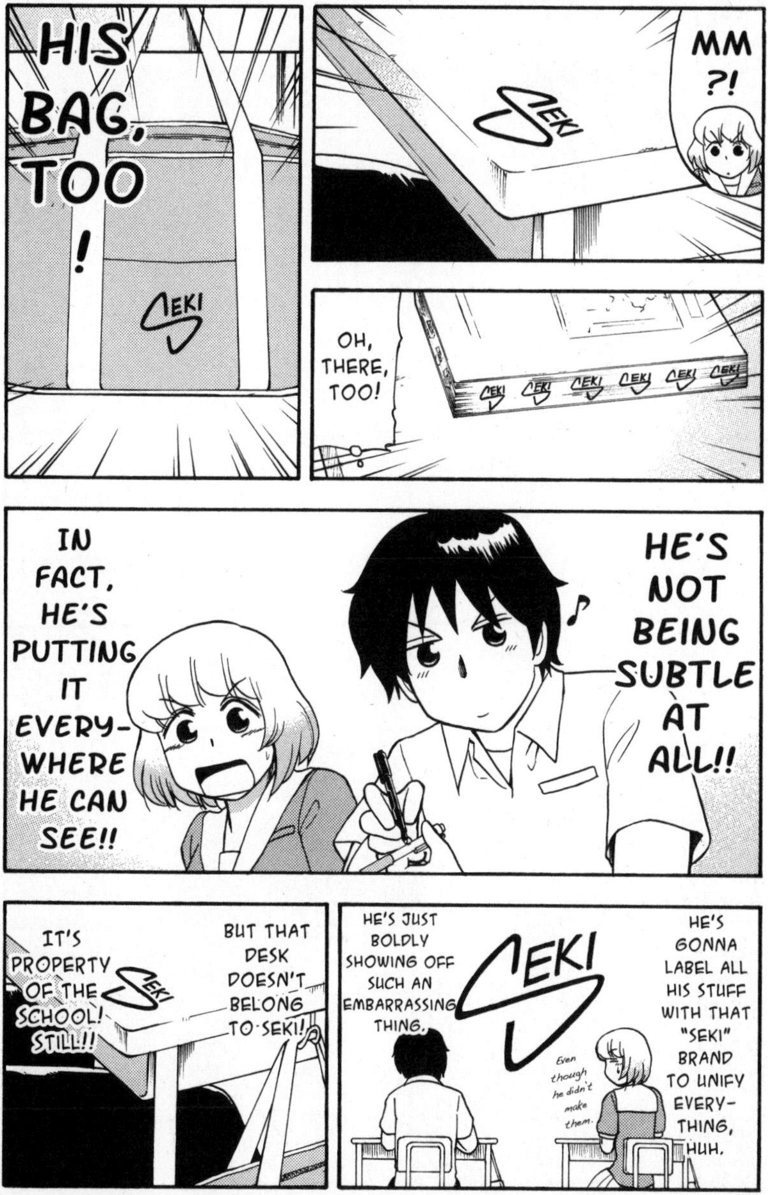
MM ?!
SEKI
OH, THERE, TOO!
HIS BAG, TOO!
SEKI
HE'S NOT BEING SUBTLE AT ALL!!
IN FACT, HE'S PUTTING IT EVERY-WHERE HE CAN SEE!!
HE'S GONNA LABEL ALL HIS STUFF WITH THAT "SEKI" BRAND TO UNIFY EVERY-THING, HUH.
SEKI
Even though he didn't make them.
HE'S JUST BOLDLY SHOWING OFF SUCH AN EMBARRASSING THING.
BUT THAT DESK DOESN'T BELONG TO SEKI!
SEKI
IT'S PROPERTY OF THE SCHOOL! STILL!!

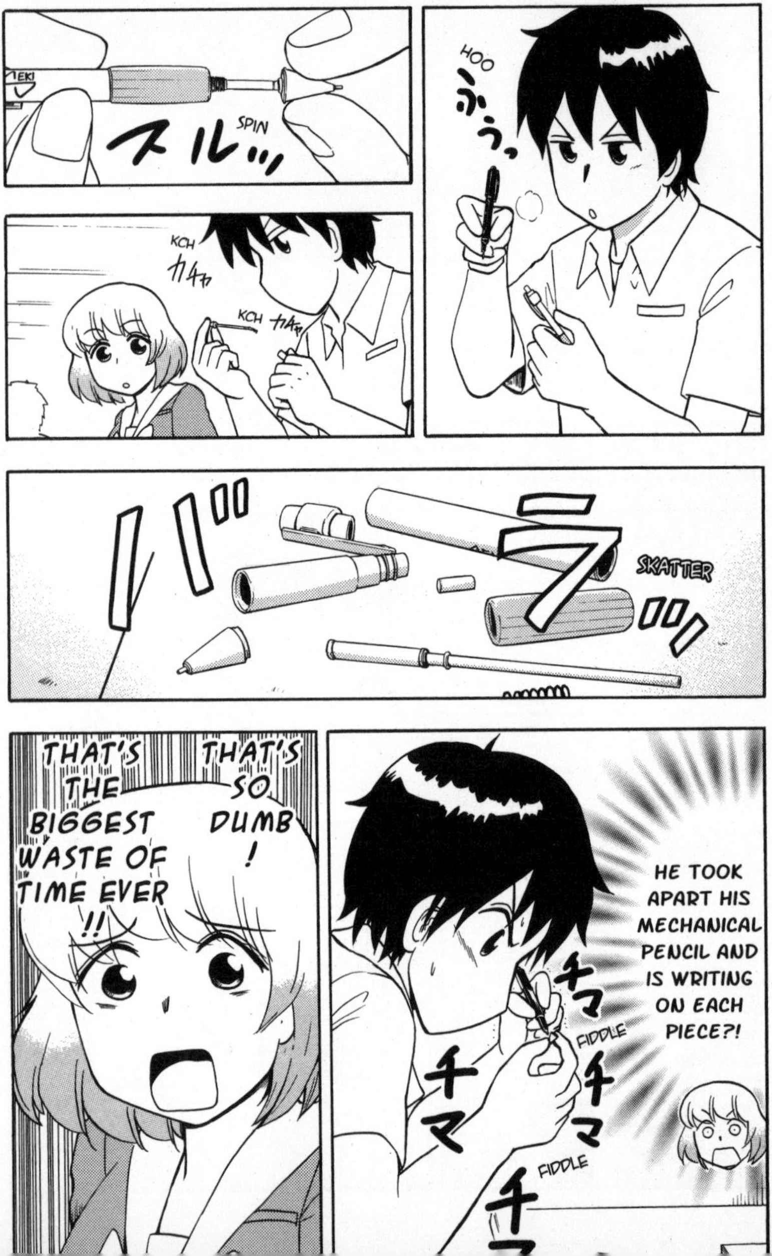
HOO
ふうっ
SPIN
スルッ
KCH
カチャ
KCH
カチャ
バラッ
SKATTER
HE TOOK APART HIS MECHANICAL PENCIL AND IS WRITING ON EACH PIECE?!
チマ
FIDDLE
チマ
チマ
FIDDLE
THAT'S SO DUMB!
THAT'S THE BIGGEST WASTE OF TIME EVER!!

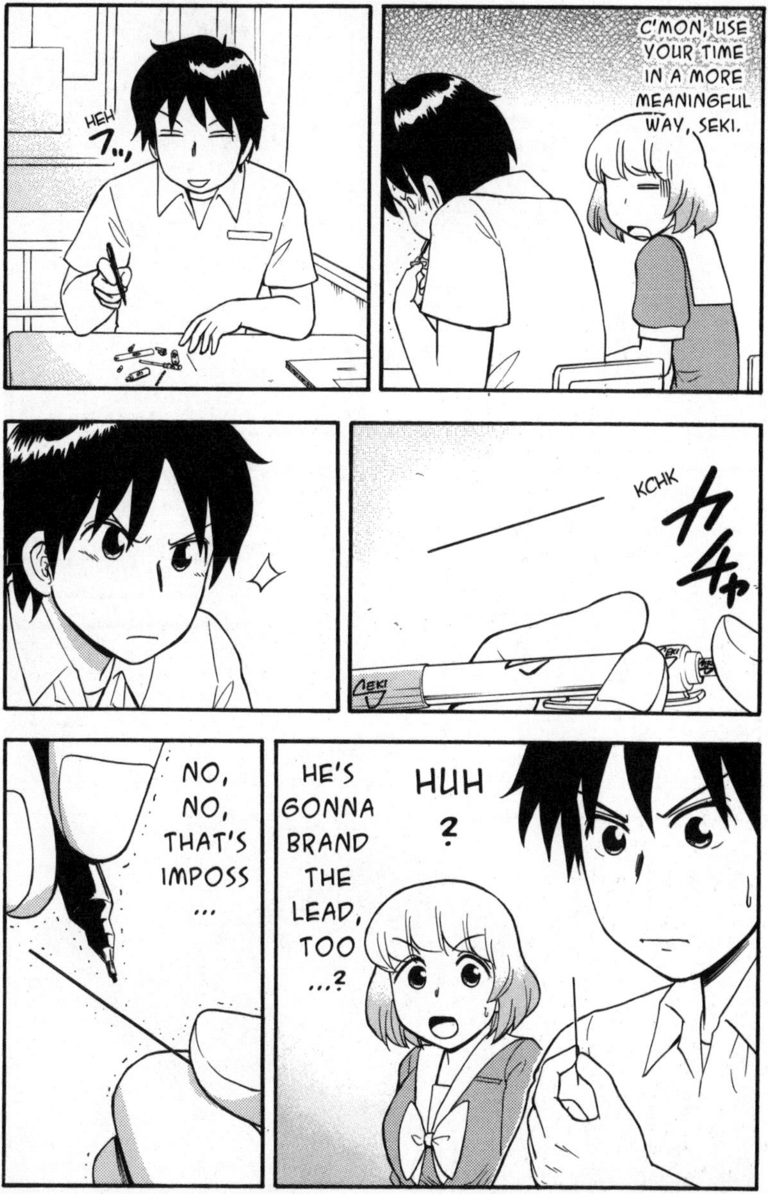
C'MON, USE YOUR TIME IN A MORE MEANINGFUL WAY, SEKI.
HEH
KCHK
SEKI
SEKI
HUH ?
HE'S GONNA BRAND THE LEAD, TOO ...?
NO, NO, THAT'S IMPOSS ...

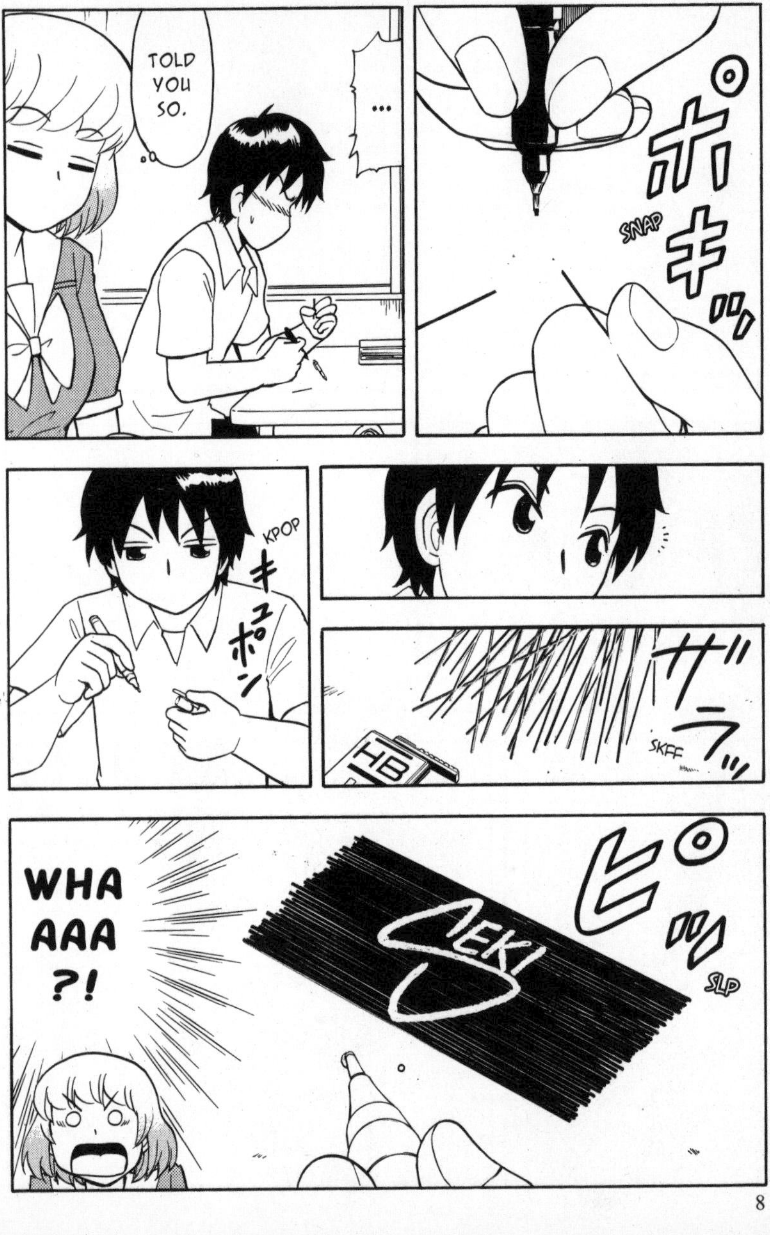
ポキッ
SNAP
...
TOLD YOU SO.
ザラッ
SKFF
キュポン
KPOP
ピッ
SLP
SEKI
WHAAAA?!

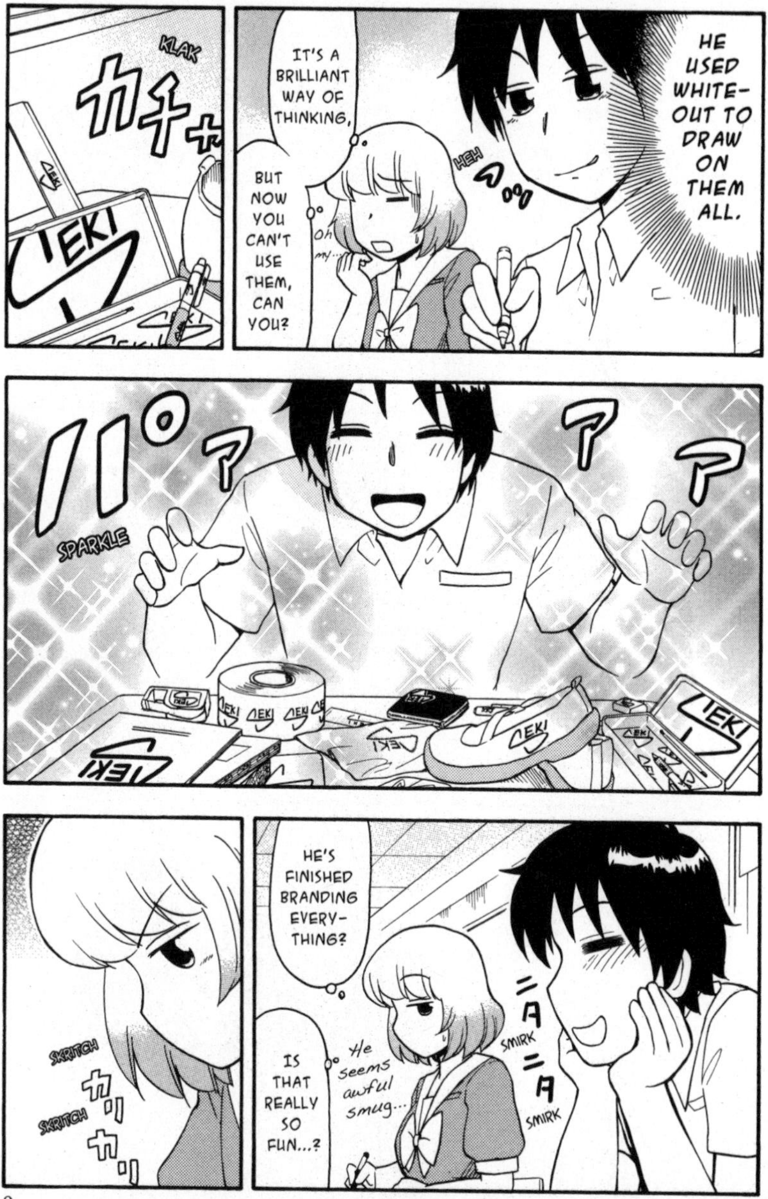
HE USED WHITE-OUT TO DRAW ON THEM ALL.
HEH
IT'S A BRILLIANT WAY OF THINKING,
BUT NOW YOU CAN'T USE THEM, CAN YOU?
Oh my...
KLAK
カチャ
パァアア
SPARKLE
HE'S FINISHED BRANDING EVERY-THING?
ニタ
SMIRK
ニタ
SMIRK
He seems awful smug...
IS THAT REALLY SO FUN...?
SKRITCH
カリ
SKRITCH
カリ

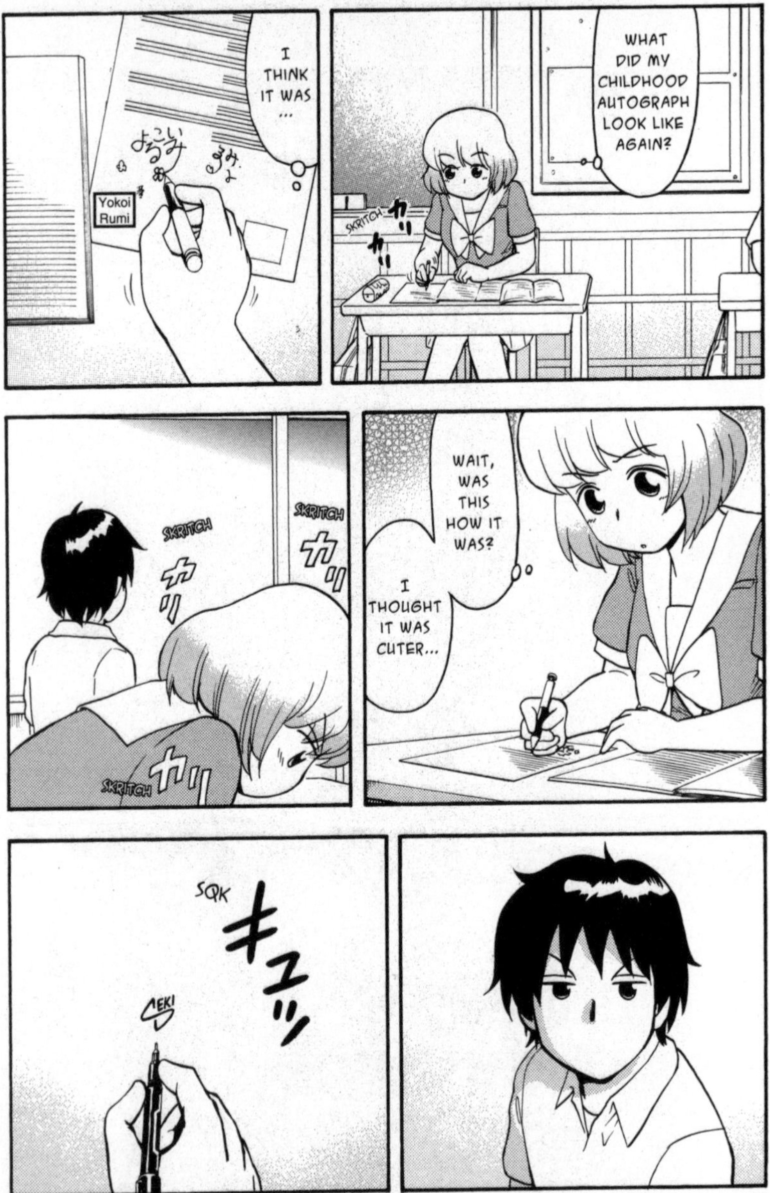
WHAT DID MY CHILDHOOD AUTOGRAPH LOOK LIKE AGAIN?
SKRITCH
I THINK IT WAS ...
Yokoi Rumi
WAIT, WAS THIS HOW IT WAS?
I THOUGHT IT WAS CUTER...
SKRITCH
SKRITCH
SKRITCH
SQK
SEKI

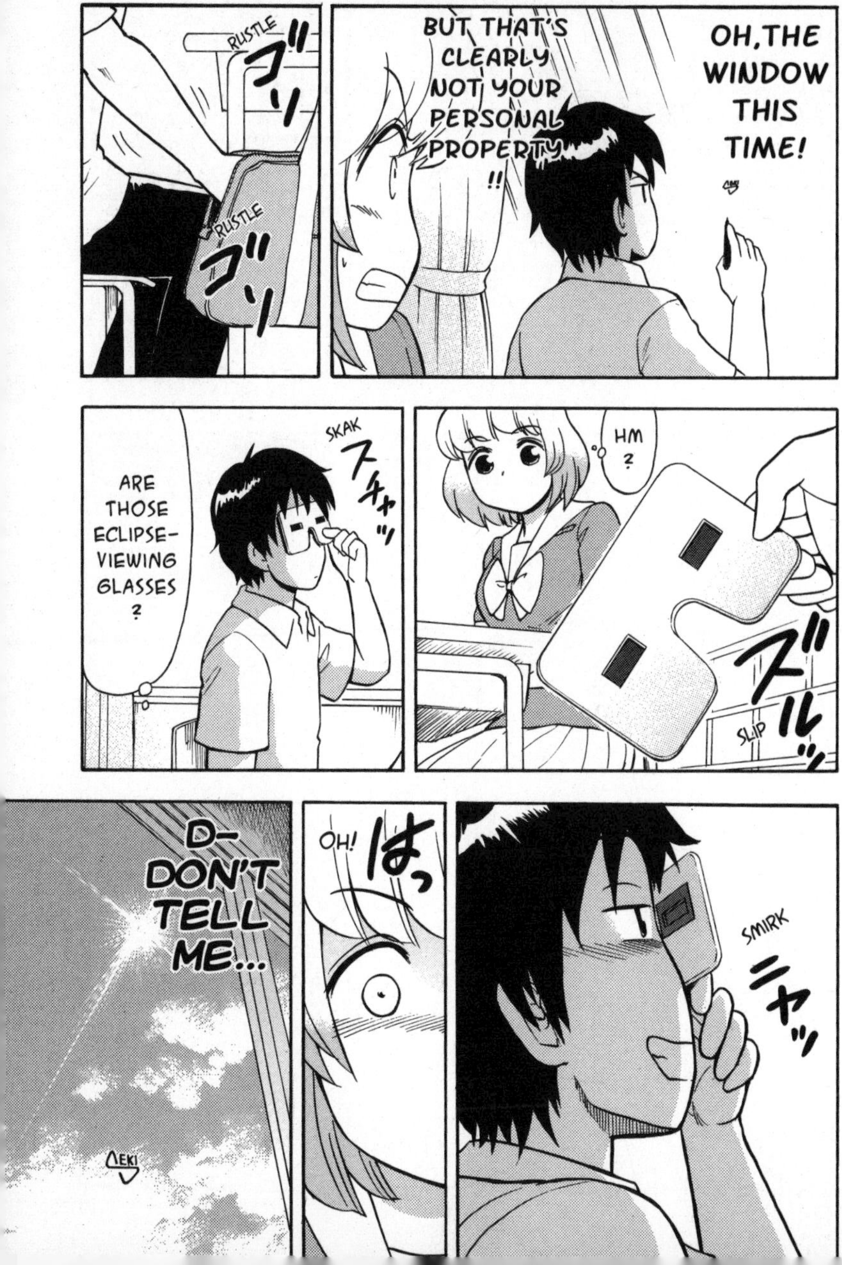
OH, THE WINDOW THIS TIME!
BUT THAT'S CLEARLY NOT YOUR PERSONAL PROPERTY!!
RUSTLE
ゴソ
RUSTLE
ゴソ
HM?
SLIP
ズルッ
SKAK
スチャッ
ARE THOSE ECLIPSE-VIEWING GLASSES?
SMIRK
ニヤッ
OH!
はっ
D-DON'T TELL ME...

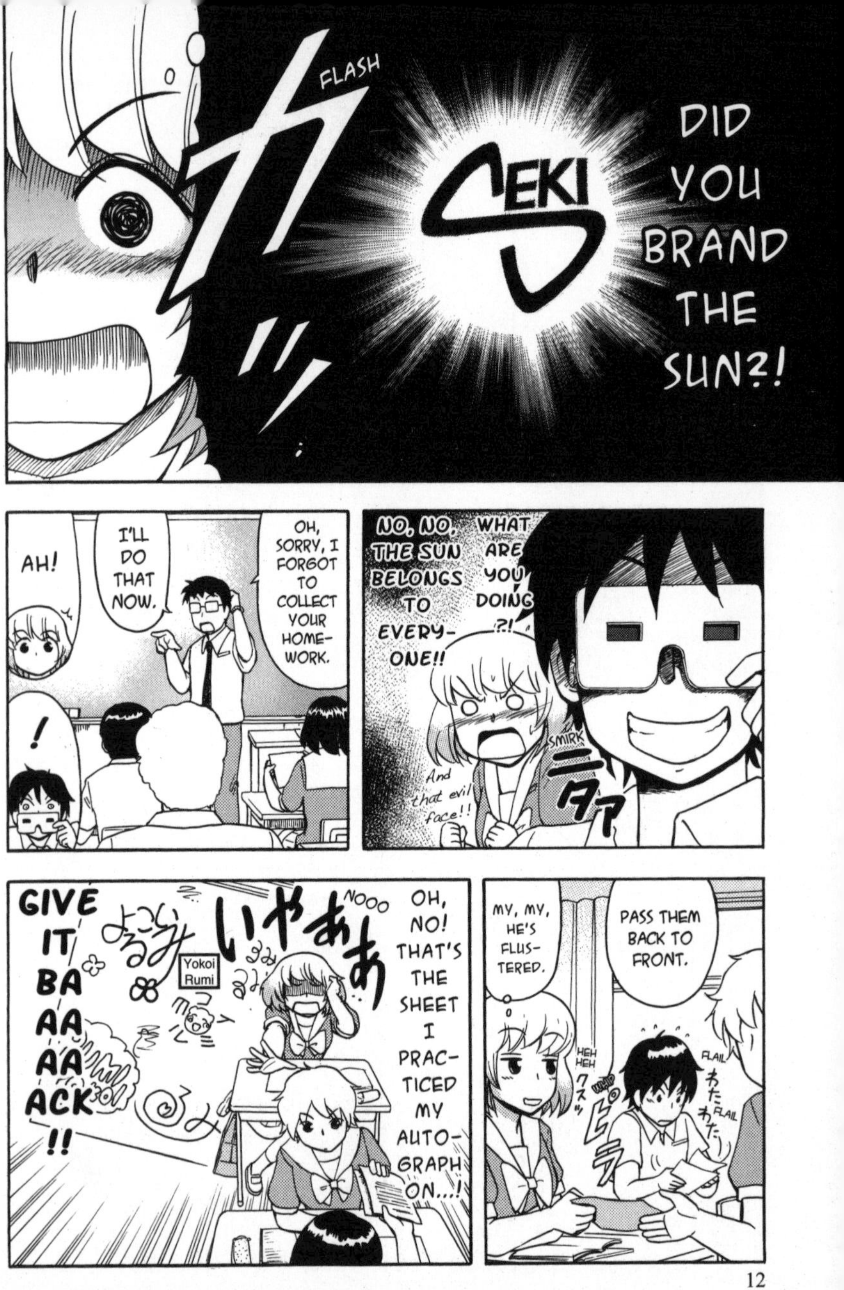
DID YOU BRAND THE SUN?!
FLASH
SEKI
WHAT ARE YOU DOING ?!
NO, NO, THE SUN BELONGS TO EVERY-ONE!!
SMIRK
And that evil face!!
OH, SORRY, I FORGOT TO COLLECT YOUR HOME-WORK.
I'LL DO THAT NOW.
AH!
!
PASS THEM BACK TO FRONT.
MY, MY, HE'S FLUS-TERED.
FLAIL
HEH HEH
WHIP
FLAIL
OH, NO! THAT'S THE SHEET I PRAC-TICED MY AUTO-GRAPH ON...!
NOOO
Yokoi Rumi
GIVE IT BAAAAAACK!!

44th Period

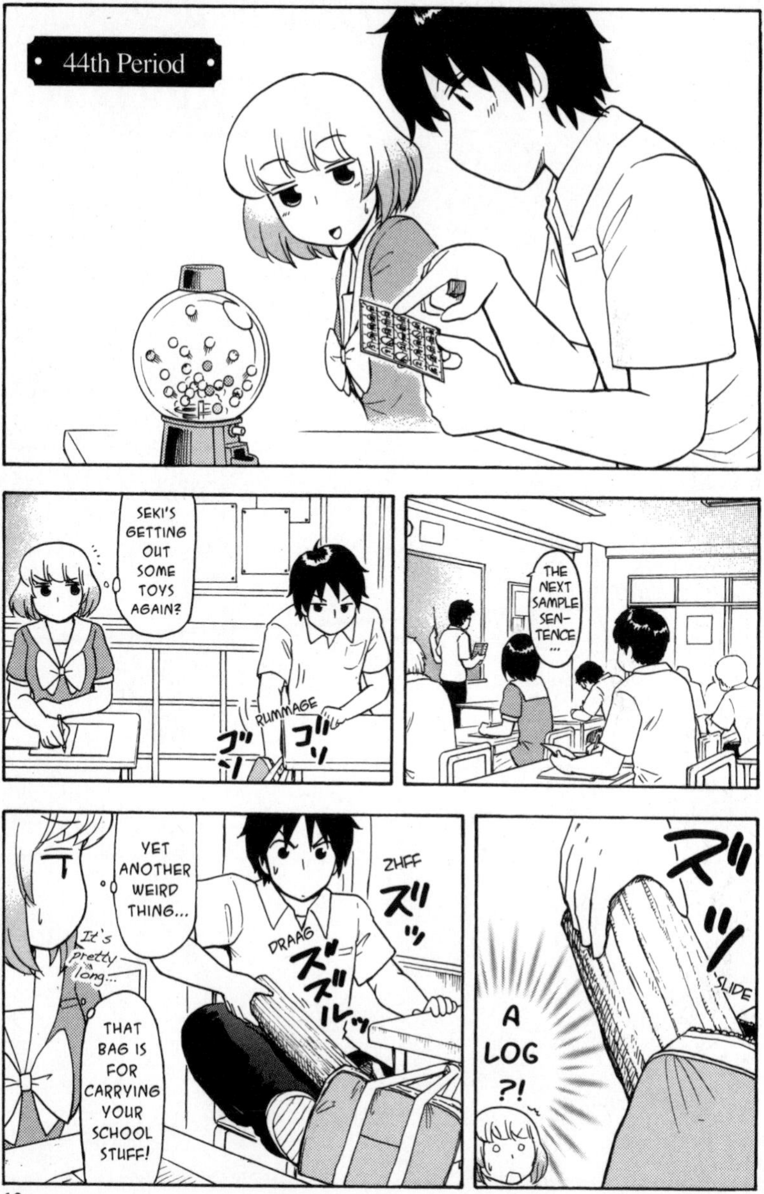

THE NEXT SAMPLE SENTENCE...
SEKI'S GETTING OUT SOME TOYS AGAIN?
RUMMAGE
SLIDE
A LOG ?!
YET ANOTHER WEIRD THING...
ZHFF
DRAAG
It's pretty long...
THAT BAG IS FOR CARRYING YOUR SCHOOL STUFF!

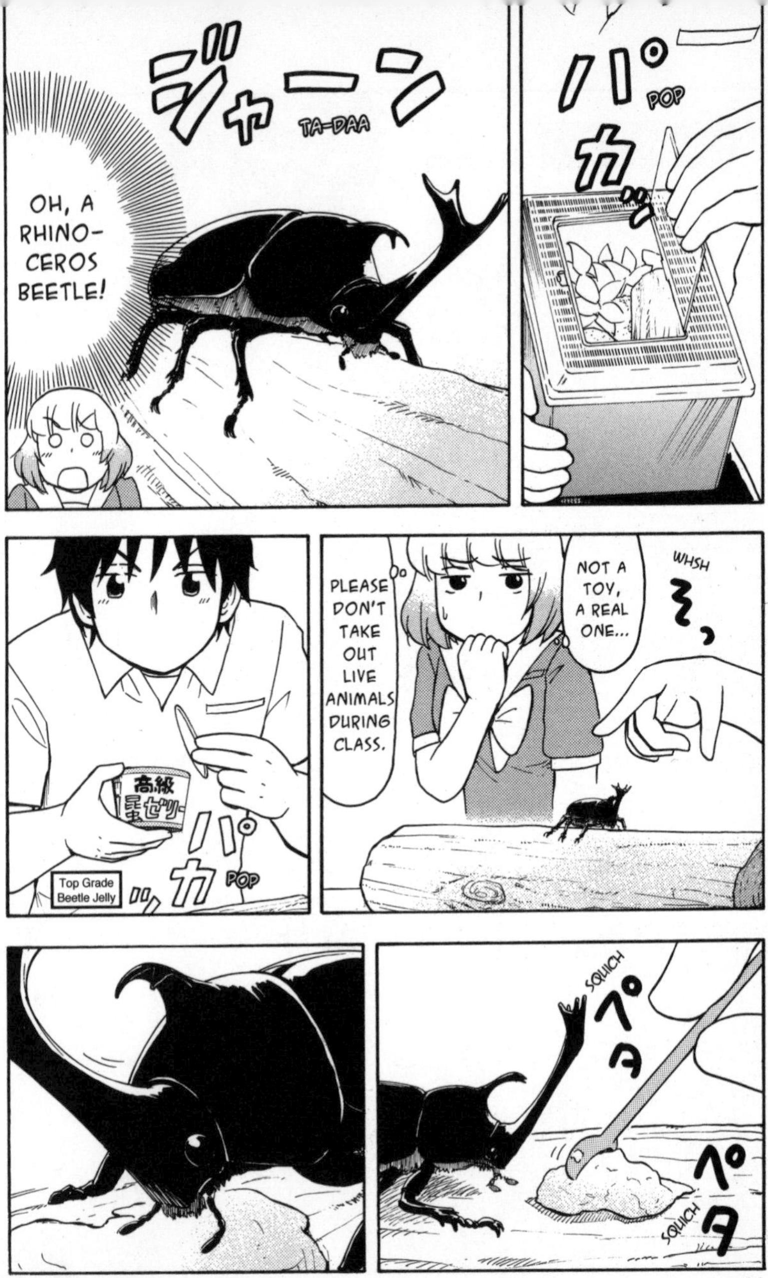
パカッ
POP
ジャーン
TA-DAA
OH, A RHINO-CEROS BEETLE!
NOT A TOY, A REAL ONE...
WHSH
PLEASE DON'T TAKE OUT LIVE ANIMALS DURING CLASS.
高級昆虫ゼリー
Top Grade Beetle Jelly
パカッ
POP
ペタ
SQUICH
ペタ
SQUICH

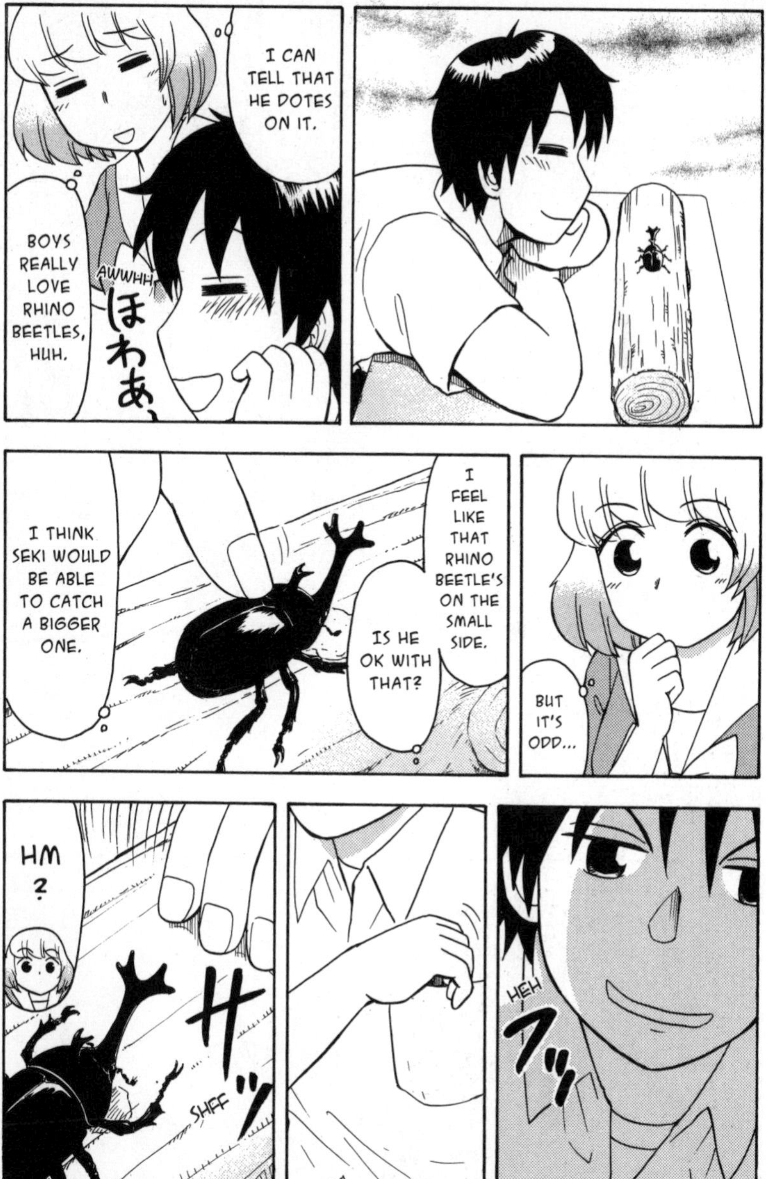
I CAN TELL THAT HE DOTES ON IT.
BOYS REALLY LOVE RHINO BEETLES, HUH.
AWWHH
ほわあ
BUT IT'S ODD...
I FEEL LIKE THAT RHINO BEETLE'S ON THE SMALL SIDE.
IS HE OK WITH THAT?
I THINK SEKI WOULD BE ABLE TO CATCH A BIGGER ONE.
HEH
フッ
HM?
SHFF
サッ

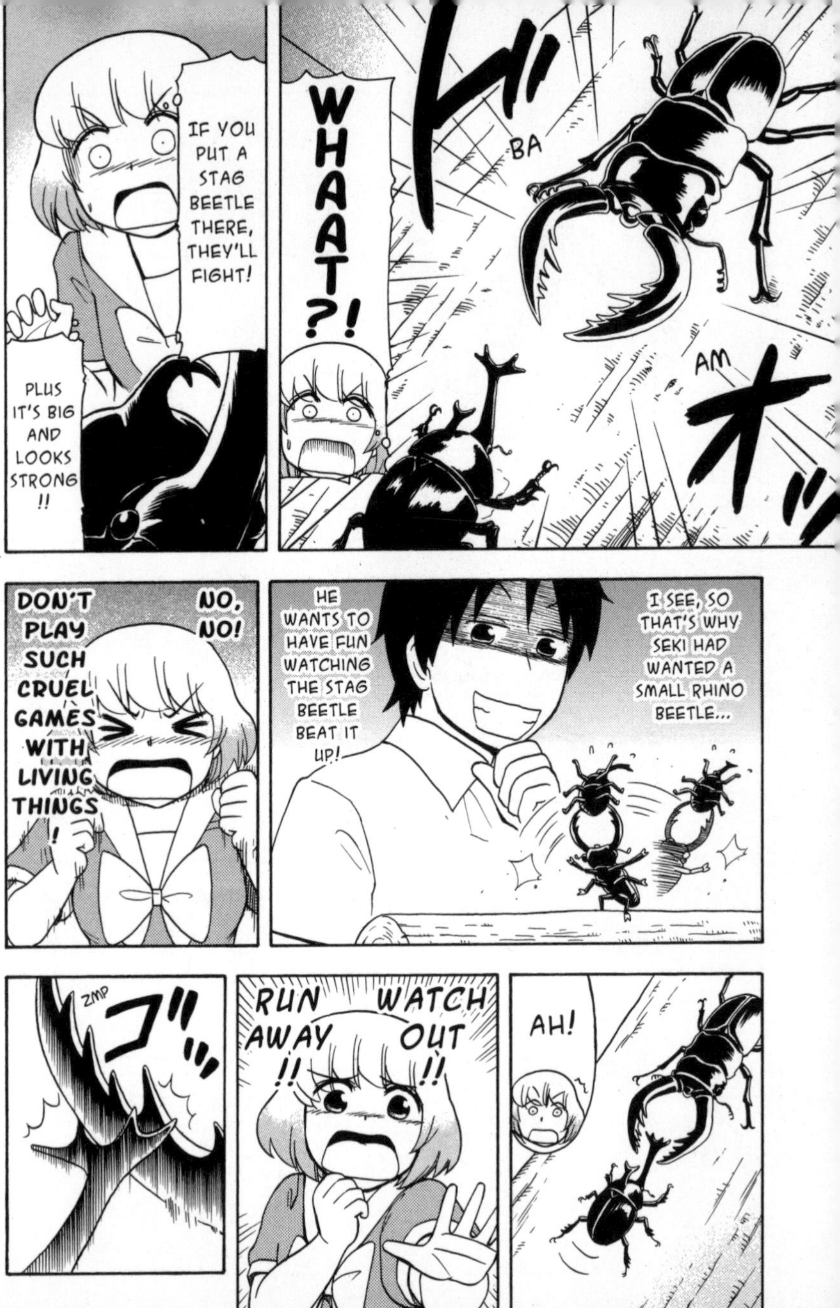
BA
WHAAT?!
AM
IF YOU PUT A STAG BEETLE THERE, THEY'LL FIGHT!
PLUS IT'S BIG AND LOOKS STRONG!!
I SEE, SO THAT'S WHY SEKI HAD WANTED A SMALL RHINO BEETLE...
HE WANTS TO HAVE FUN WATCHING THE STAG BEETLE BEAT IT UP!
NO, NO!
DON'T PLAY SUCH CRUEL GAMES WITH LIVING THINGS!
AH!
WATCH OUT!!
RUN AWAY!!
ZMP

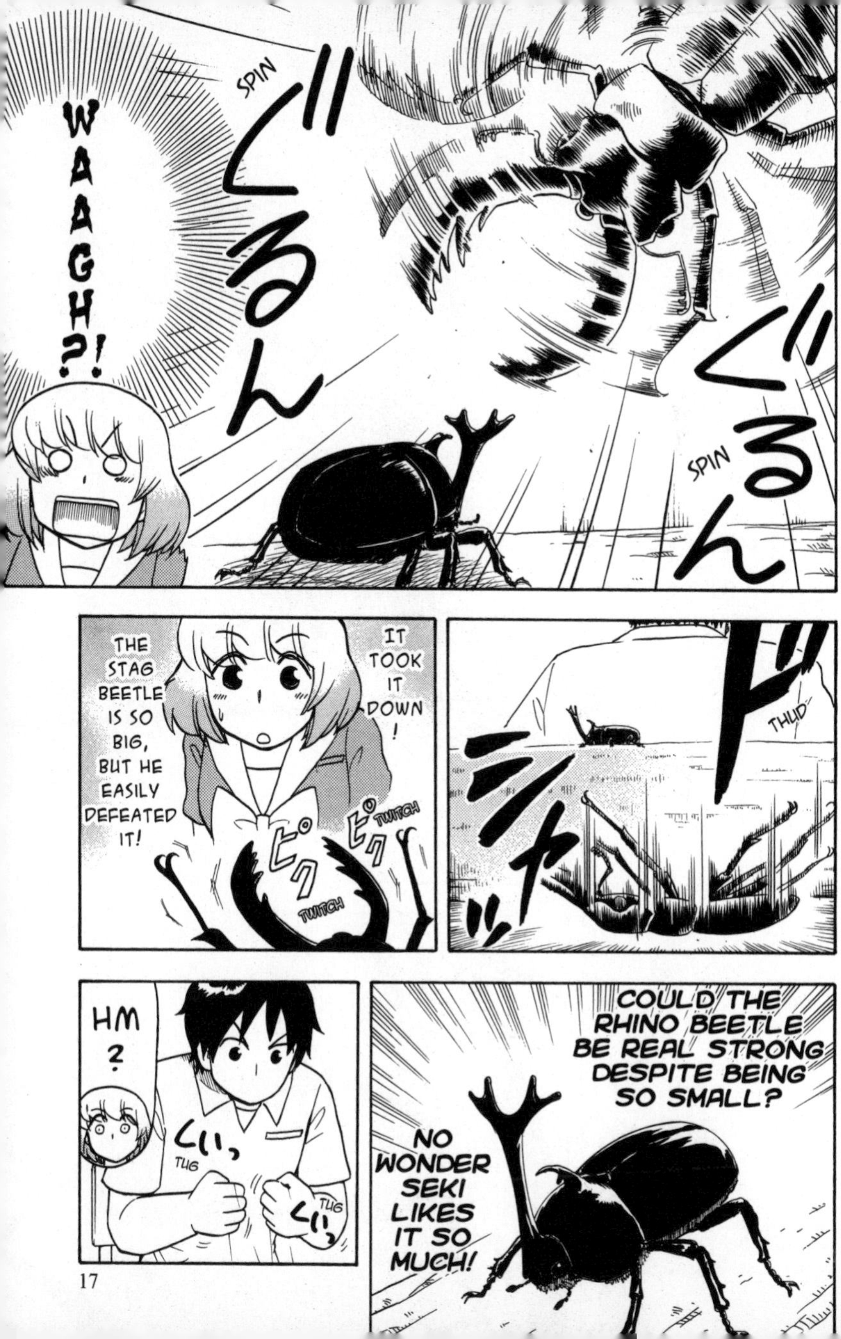
ぐるん
SPIN
ぐるん
SPIN
WAAGH?!
ドシャッ
THUD
IT TOOK IT DOWN!
THE STAG BEETLE IS SO BIG, BUT HE EASILY DEFEATED IT!
ピクピク
TWITCH
TWITCH
COULD THE RHINO BEETLE BE REAL STRONG DESPITE BEING SO SMALL?
NO WONDER SEKI LIKES IT SO MUCH!
HM?
くい、
TUG
くい、
TUG

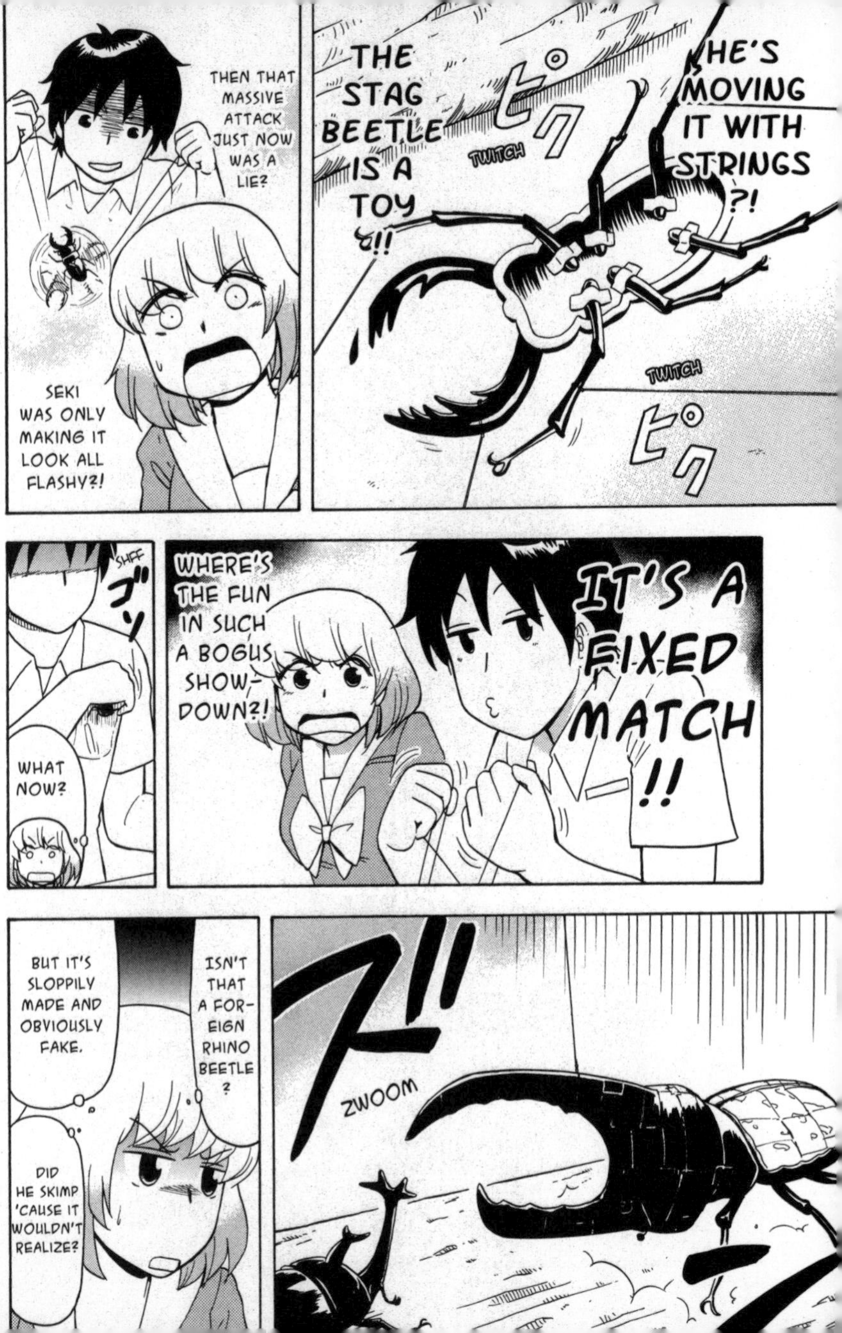

HE'S MOVING IT WITH STRINGS?!
THE STAG BEETLE IS A TOY?!!
ピク
TWITCH
TWITCH
ピク
THEN THAT MASSIVE ATTACK JUST NOW WAS A LIE?
SEKI WAS ONLY MAKING IT LOOK ALL FLASHY?!
IT'S A FIXED MATCH!!
WHERE'S THE FUN IN SUCH A BOGUS SHOW-DOWN?!
SHFF
WHAT NOW?
ZWOOM
ISN'T THAT A FOR-EIGN RHINO BEETLE?
BUT IT'S SLOPPILY MADE AND OBVIOUSLY FAKE.
DID HE SKIMP 'CAUSE IT WOULDN'T REALIZE?

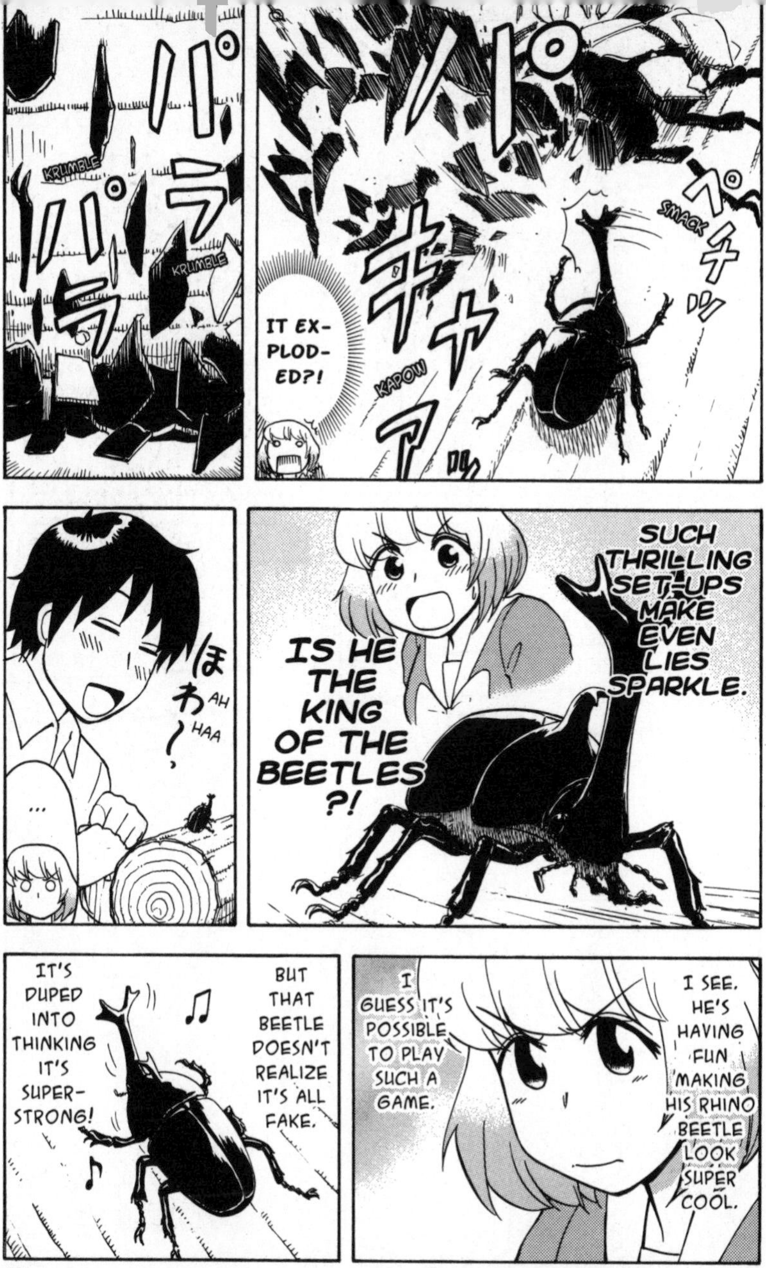
SMACK
KAPOW
IT EXPLODED?!
KRUMBLE
KRUMBLE
SUCH THRILLING SET-UPS MAKE EVEN LIES SPARKLE.
IS HE THE KING OF THE BEETLES?!
AH HAA
...
I SEE. HE'S HAVING FUN MAKING HIS RHINO BEETLE LOOK SUPER COOL.
I GUESS IT'S POSSIBLE TO PLAY SUCH A GAME.
BUT THAT BEETLE DOESN'T REALIZE IT'S ALL FAKE.
IT'S DUPED INTO THINKING IT'S SUPER-STRONG!

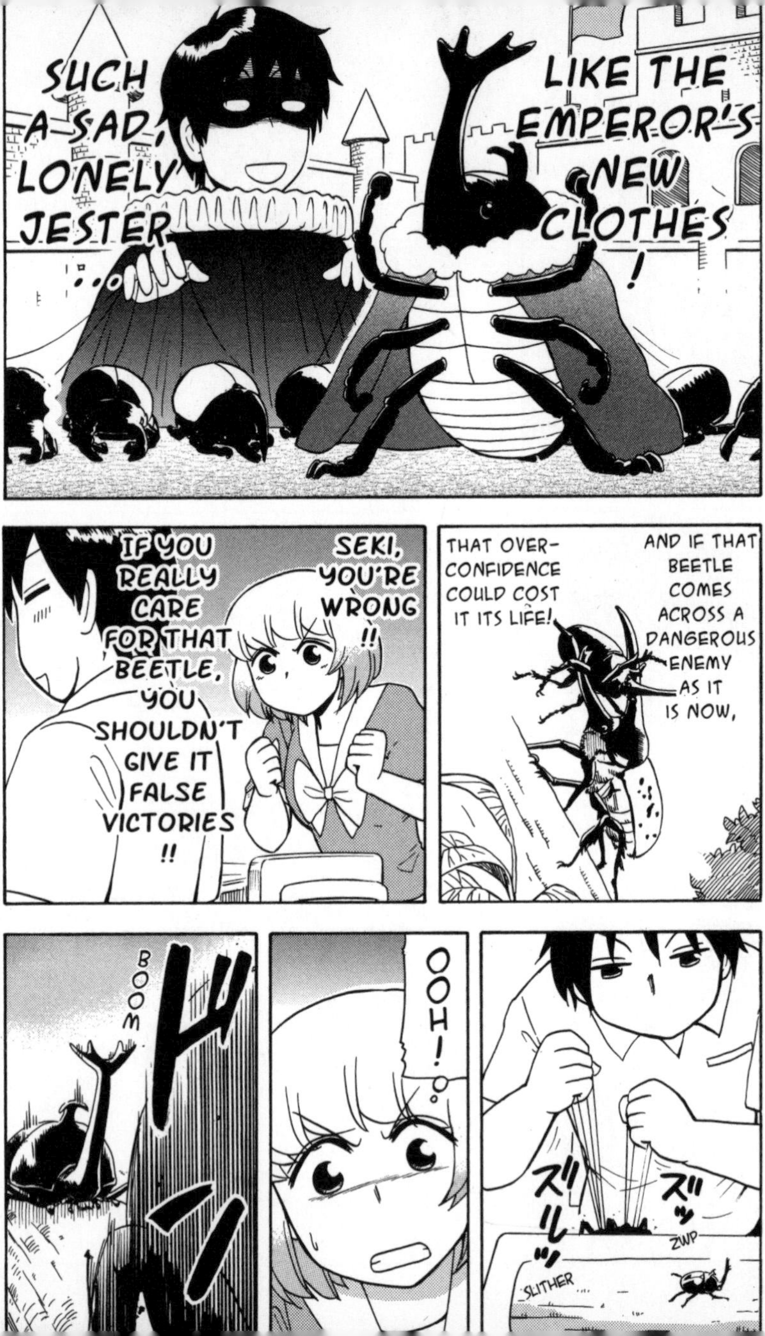
LIKE THE EMPEROR'S NEW CLOTHES!
SUCH A SAD, LONELY JESTER...
AND IF THAT BEETLE COMES ACROSS A DANGEROUS ENEMY AS IT IS NOW,
THAT OVER-CONFIDENCE COULD COST IT ITS LIFE!
SEKI, YOU'RE WRONG!!
IF YOU REALLY CARE FOR THAT BEETLE, YOU SHOULDN'T GIVE IT FALSE VICTORIES!!
ZWP
SLITHER
OOH!
BOOM

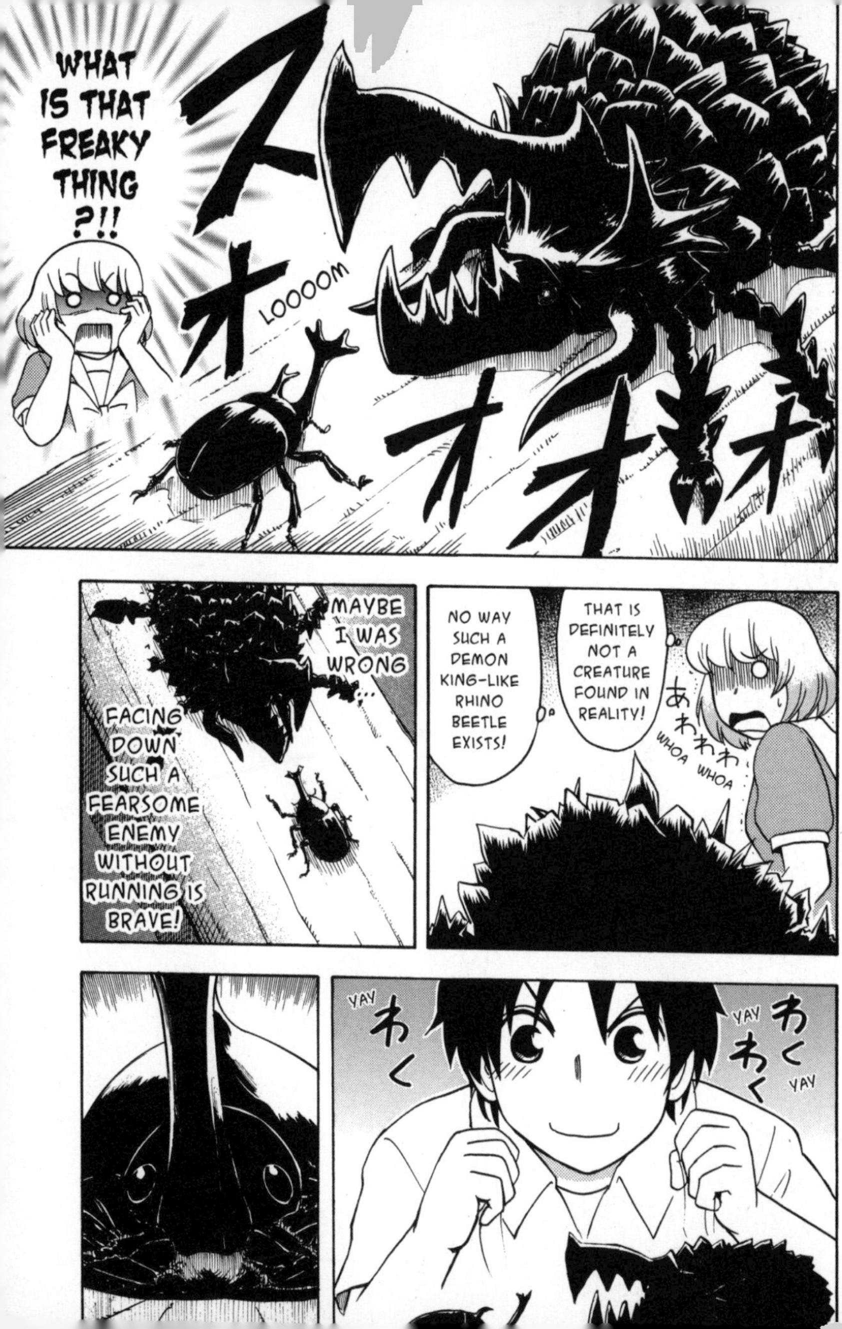
ズオオオオ
LOOOOM
WHAT IS THAT FREAKY THING?!!
あわわわ
WHOA WHOA
THAT IS DEFINITELY NOT A CREATURE FOUND IN REALITY!
NO WAY SUCH A DEMON KING-LIKE RHINO BEETLE EXISTS!
MAYBE I WAS WRONG...
FACING DOWN SUCH A FEARSOME ENEMY WITHOUT RUNNING IS BRAVE!
わくわく
YAY YAY
わく
YAY
わく
YAY

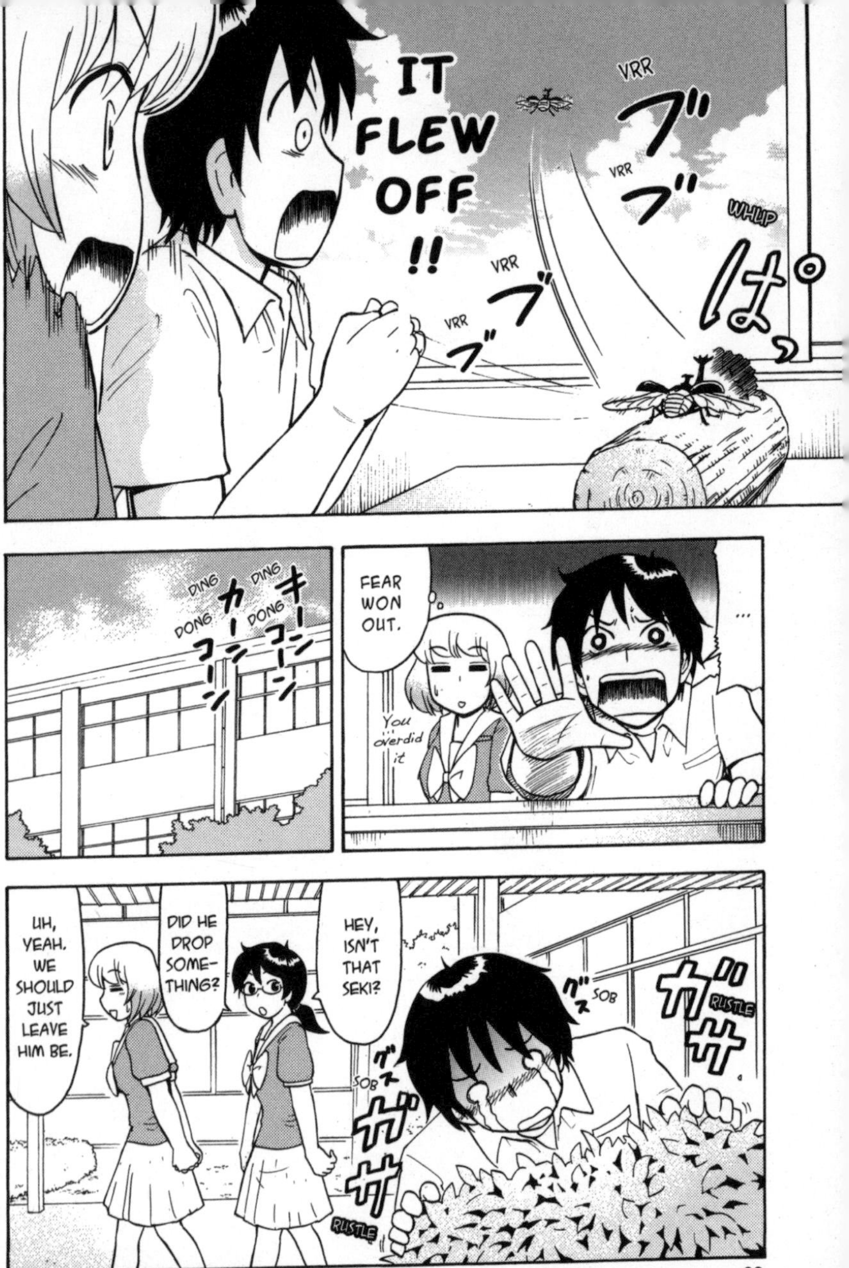
WHUP
ぱっ
VRR
ブ
VRR
ブ
IT FLEW OFF!!
VRR
ブ
VRR
ブ
FEAR WON OUT.
...
You overdid it
DING DONG
キーンコーン
DING DONG
カーンコーン
RUSTLE
ガサ
SOB
グス
HEY, ISN'T THAT SEKI?
DID HE DROP SOME-THING?
UH, YEAH. WE SHOULD JUST LEAVE HIM BE.
SOB
グス
ガサ
RUSTLE

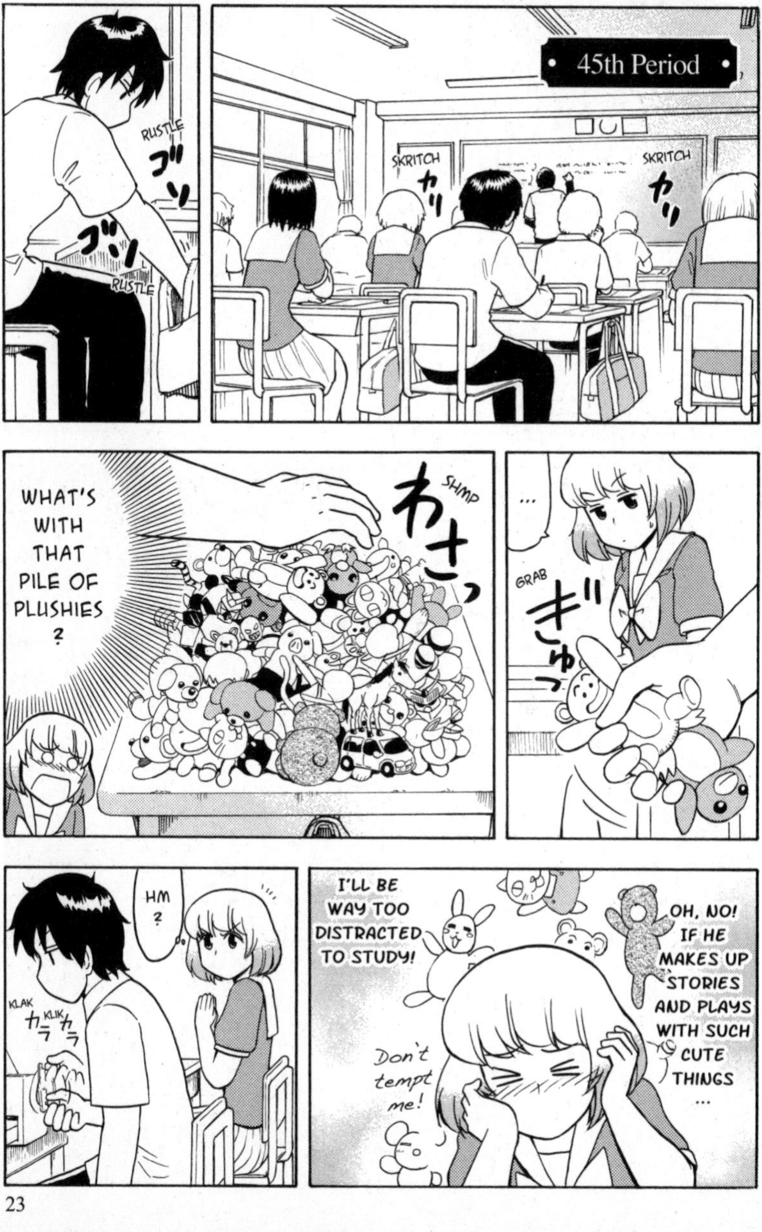

45th Period
SKRITCH
カリ
SKRITCH
カリ
RUSTLE
ゴソ
ゴソ
RUSTLE
...
GRAB
ぎゅっ
SHMP
わさっ
WHAT'S WITH THAT PILE OF PLUSHIES?
OH, NO! IF HE MAKES UP STORIES AND PLAYS WITH SUCH CUTE THINGS ...
I'LL BE WAY TOO DISTRACTED TO STUDY!
Don't tempt me!
HM?
KLAK
KLIK
カラカラ

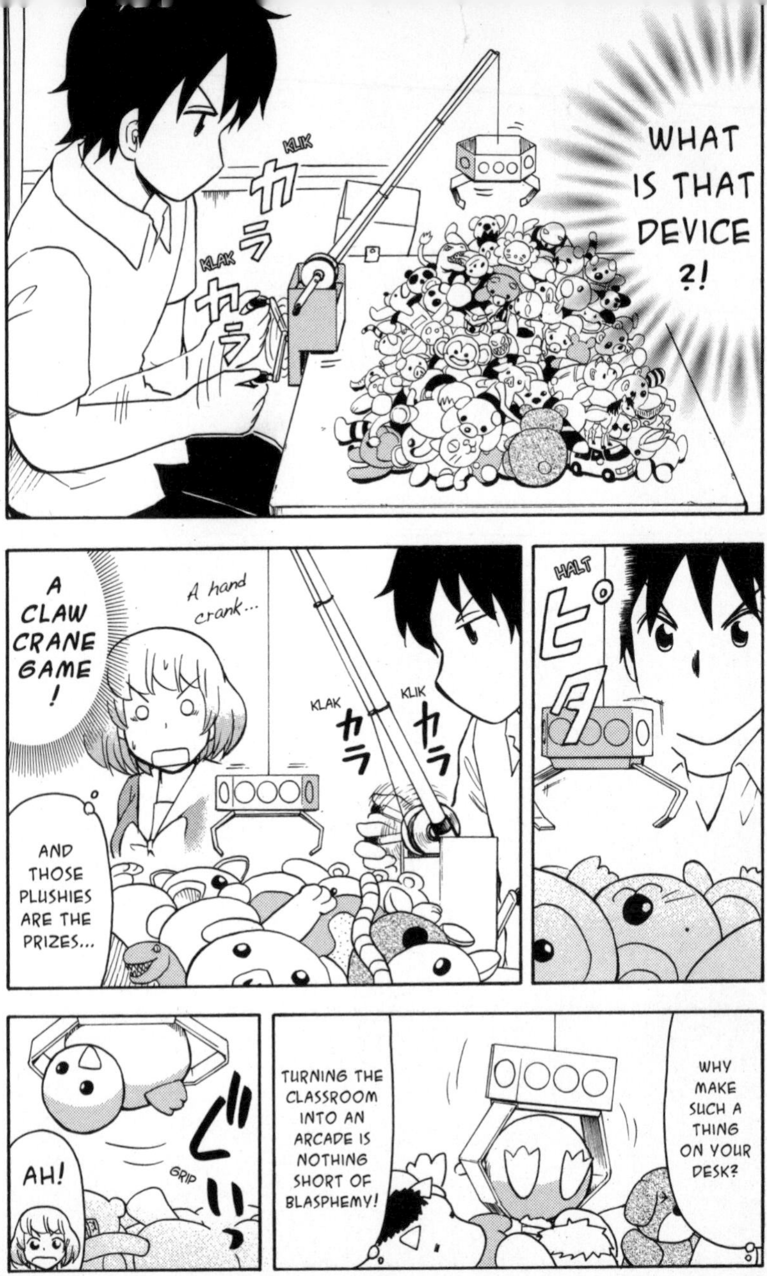
WHAT IS THAT DEVICE ?!
KLIK
カラ
KLAK
カラ
HALT
ピタ
A hand crank...
A CLAW CRANE GAME!
KLIK
カラ
KLAK
カラ
AND THOSE PLUSHIES ARE THE PRIZES...
WHY MAKE SUCH A THING ON YOUR DESK?
TURNING THE CLASSROOM INTO AN ARCADE IS NOTHING SHORT OF BLASPHEMY!
GRIP
ぐいっ
AH!

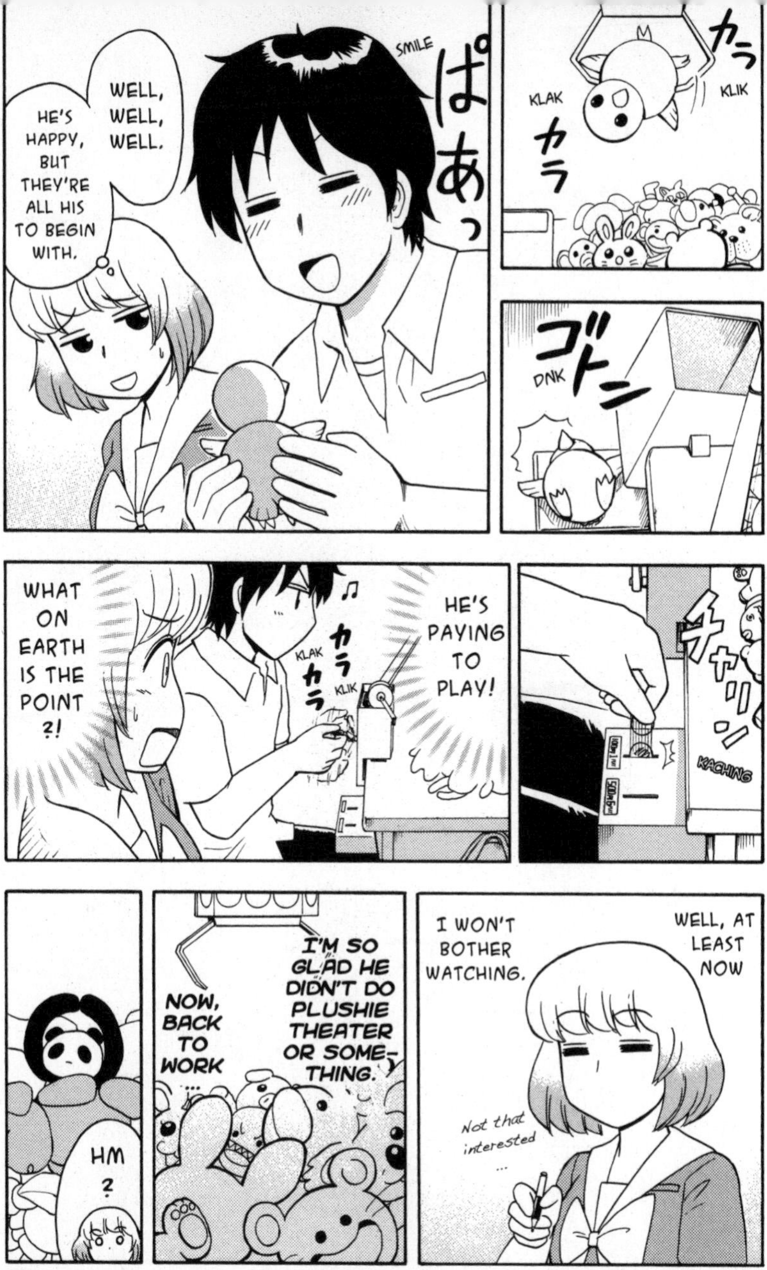

カラ
KLIK
KLAK
カラ
ゴトン
DNK
ぱあっ
SMILE
WELL, WELL, WELL.
HE'S HAPPY, BUT THEY'RE ALL HIS TO BEGIN WITH.
チャリーン
KACHING
HE'S PAYING TO PLAY!
カラ
KLAK
カラ
KLIK
WHAT ON EARTH IS THE POINT?!
WELL, AT LEAST NOW
I WON'T BOTHER WATCHING.
Not that interested ...
I'M SO GLAD HE DIDN'T DO PLUSHIE THEATER OR SOMETHING.
NOW, BACK TO WORK ...
HM?

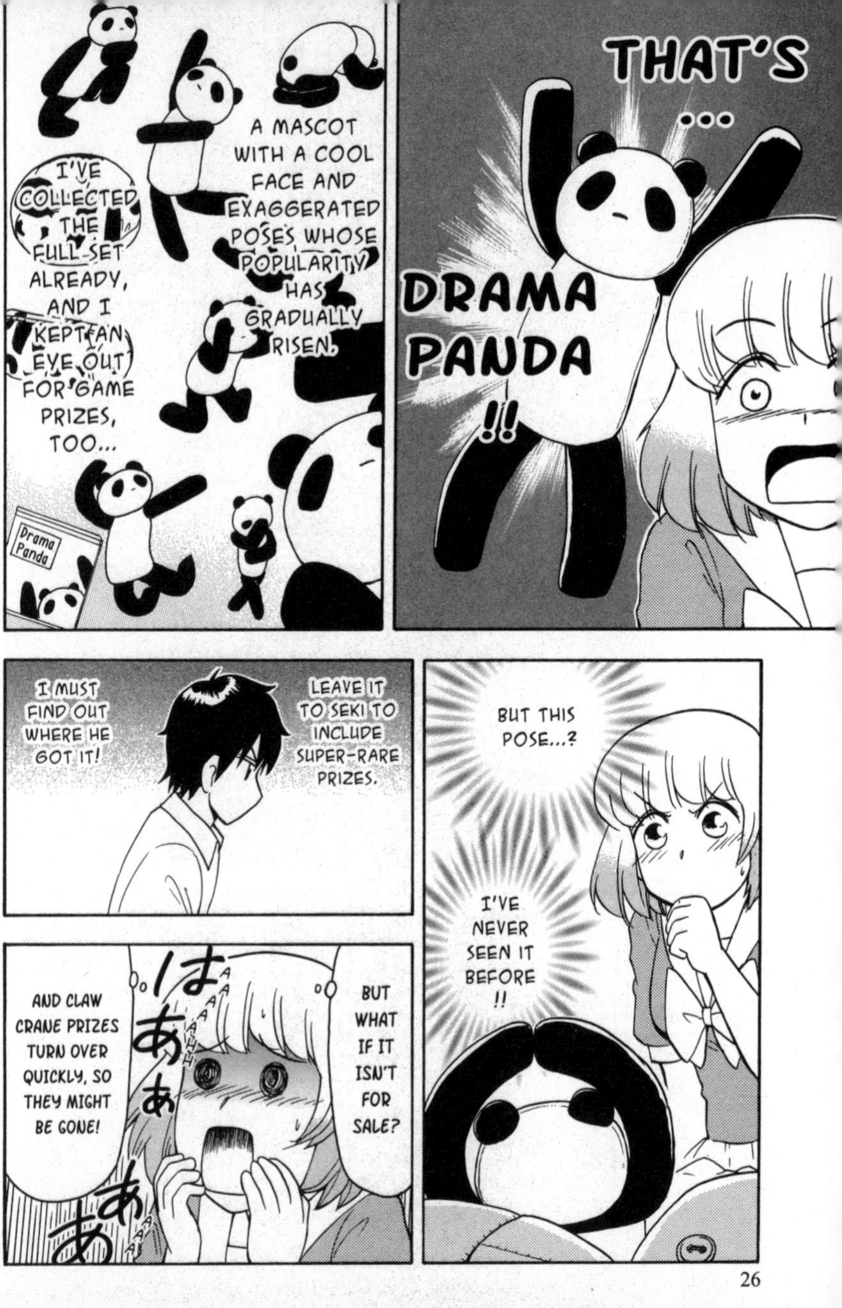
THAT'S ...
DRAMA PANDA !!
A MASCOT WITH A COOL FACE AND EXAGGERATED POSES WHOSE POPULARITY HAS GRADUALLY RISEN.
I'VE COLLECTED THE FULL SET ALREADY, AND I KEPT AN EYE OUT FOR GAME PRIZES, TOO...
Drama Panda
BUT THIS POSE...?
I'VE NEVER SEEN IT BEFORE !!
LEAVE IT TO SEKI TO INCLUDE SUPER-RARE PRIZES.
I MUST FIND OUT WHERE HE GOT IT!
BUT WHAT IF IT ISN'T FOR SALE?
はあぁ
AAAAHH
AND CLAW CRANE PRIZES TURN OVER QUICKLY, SO THEY MIGHT BE GONE!
ああ
AAA

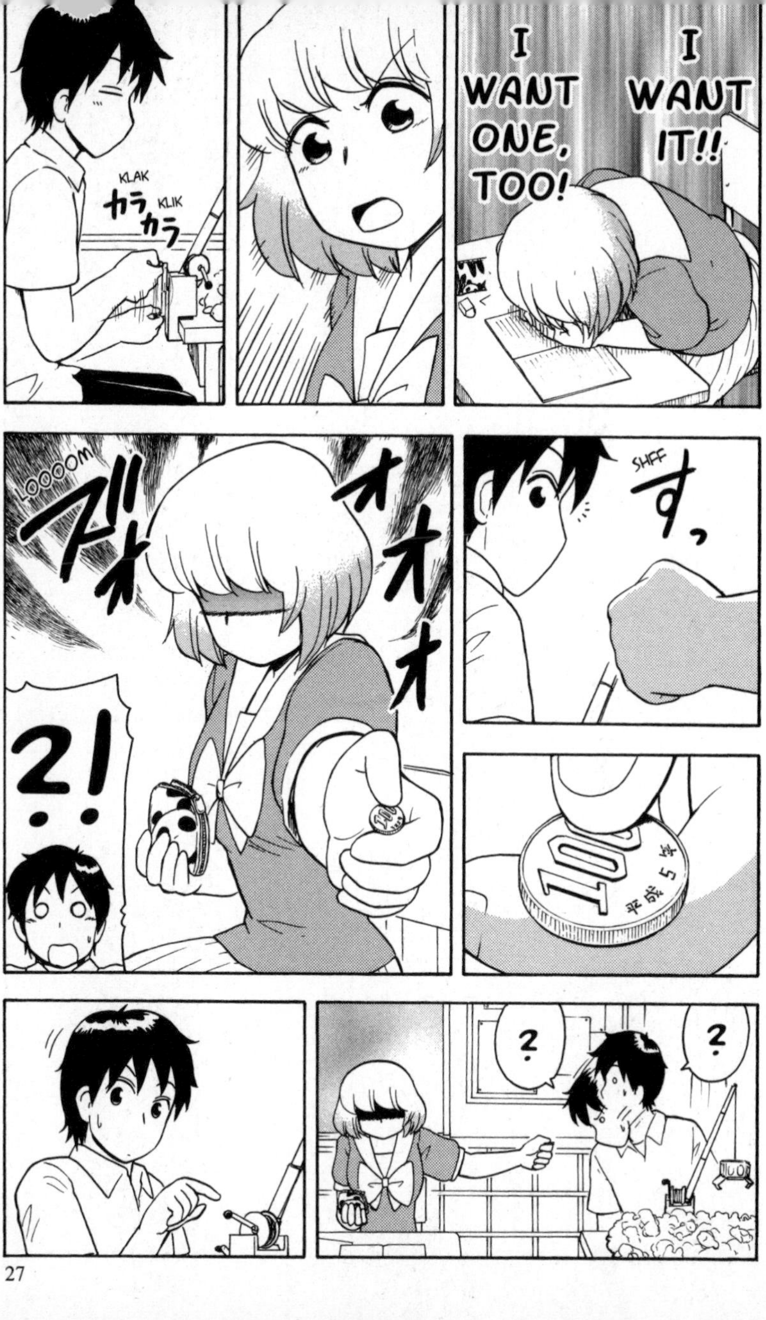

I WANT IT!!
I WANT ONE, TOO!
KLAK
カラ
KLIK
カラ
SHFF
すっ
LOOOOM
ズオオオオ
?!
?
?

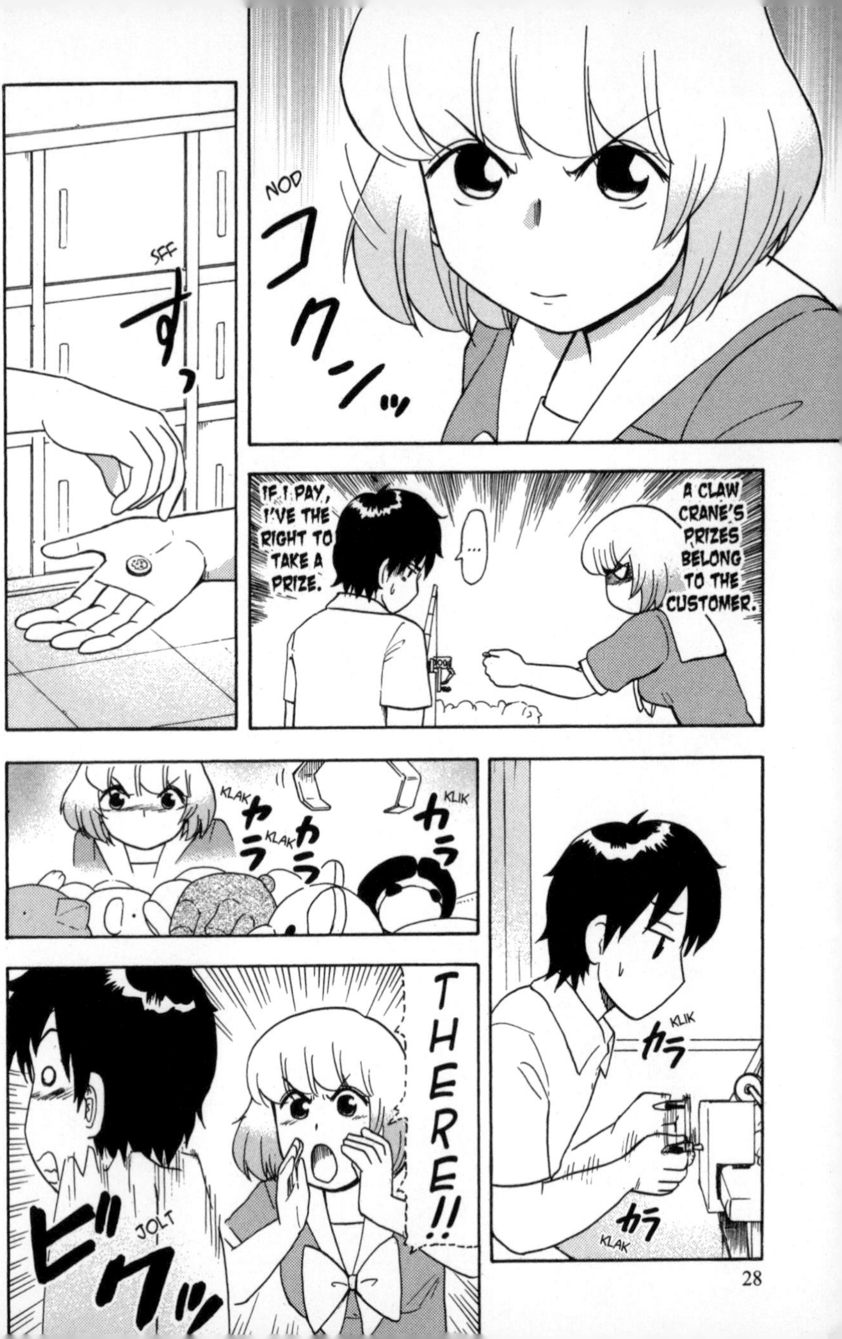
NOD
コクンッ
A CLAW CRANE'S PRIZES BELONG TO THE CUSTOMER.
...
IF I PAY, I'VE THE RIGHT TO TAKE A PRIZE.
SFF
すっ
KLIK
カラ
カラ
KLAK
KLIK
カラ
KLAK
カラ
KLAK
カラ
THERE!!
ビクッ
JOLT

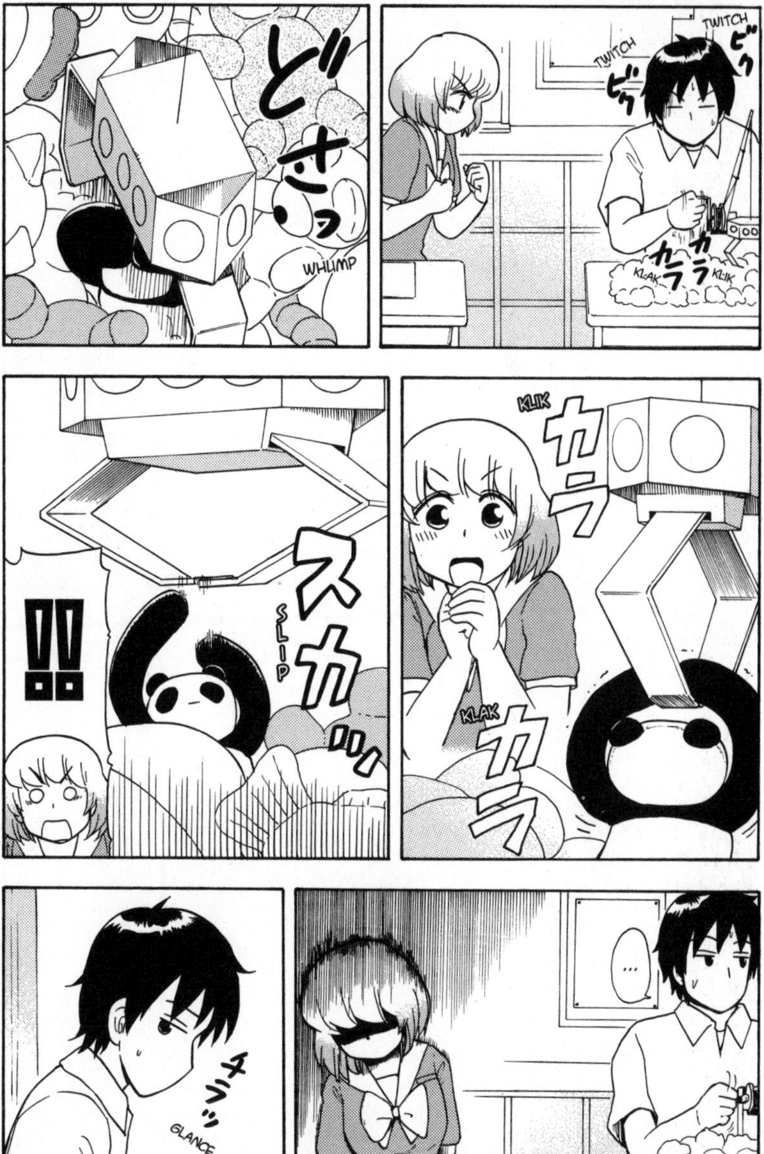
TWITCH
ビク
TWITCH
ビク
カラ
KLAK
カラ
KLIK
どさっ
WHUMP
KLIK
カラ
KLAK
カラ
スカッ
SLIP
!!
...
チラッ
GLANCE

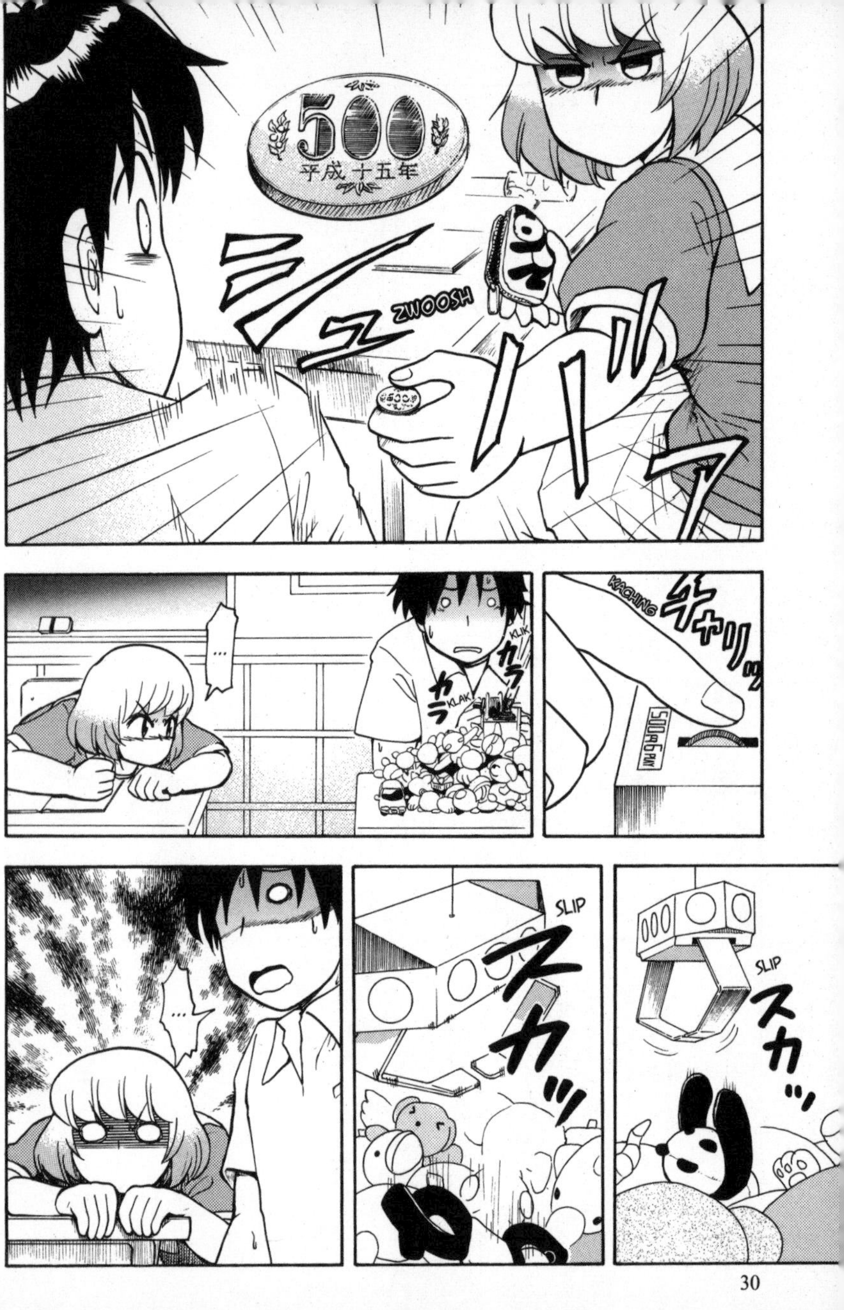

500
平成十五年
ZWOOSH
KACHING
チャリッ
500円6PLAY
KLIK
カラ
KLAK
カラ
...
SLIP
スカッ
SLIP
スカッ
...

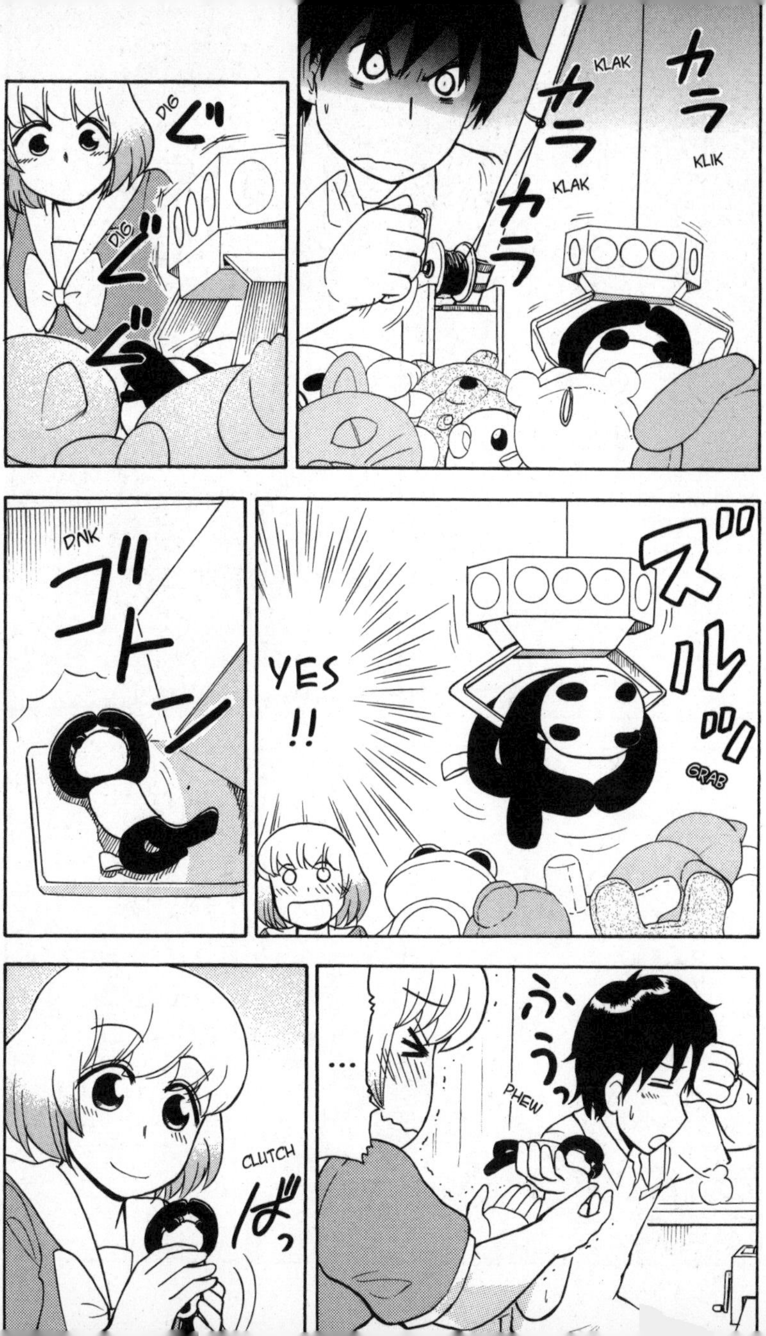
カラ
KLIK
KLAK
カラ
KLAK
カラ
DIG
ぐ
DIG
ぐ
ぐ
ズル
GRAB
YES !!
DNK
ゴトーン
ふうっ
PHEW
...
CLUTCH
ぱっ

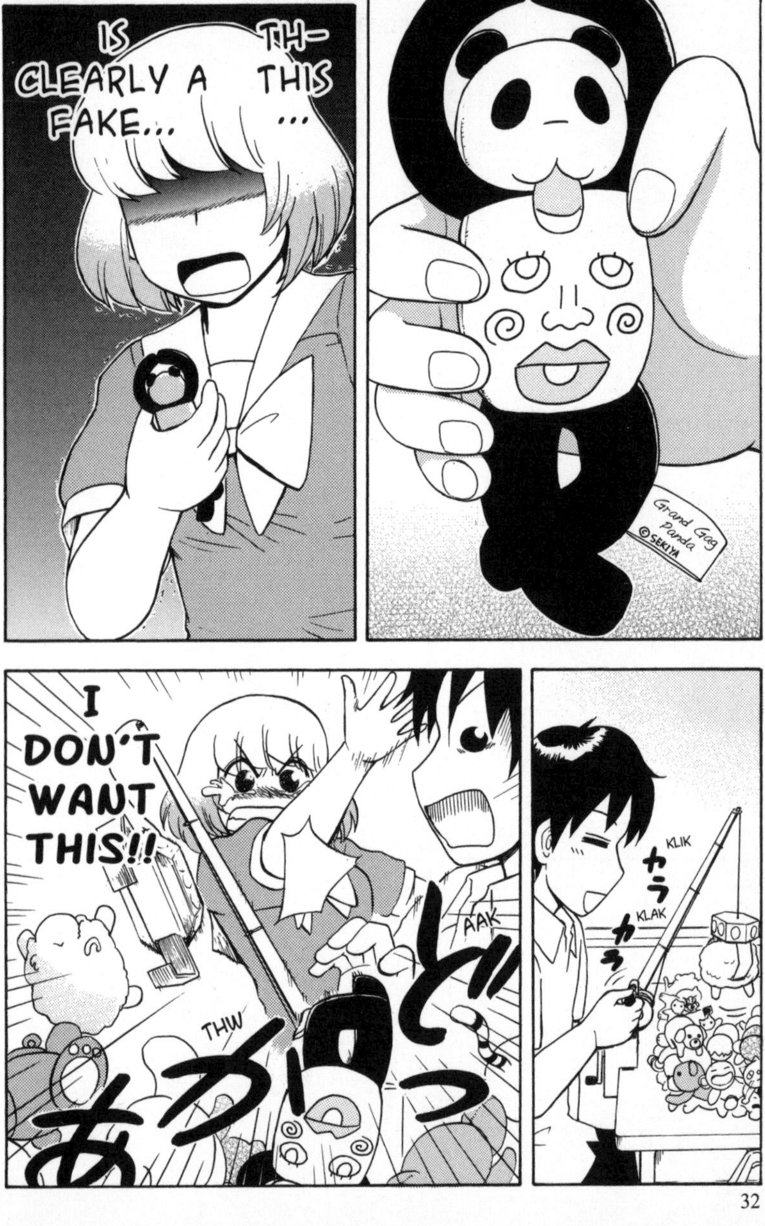
Grand Gag Panda ©SEKIYA
TH- THIS ...
IS CLEARLY A FAKE...
KLIK
カラ
KLAK
カラ
I DON'T WANT THIS!!
AAK
THW

My Neighbor Seki

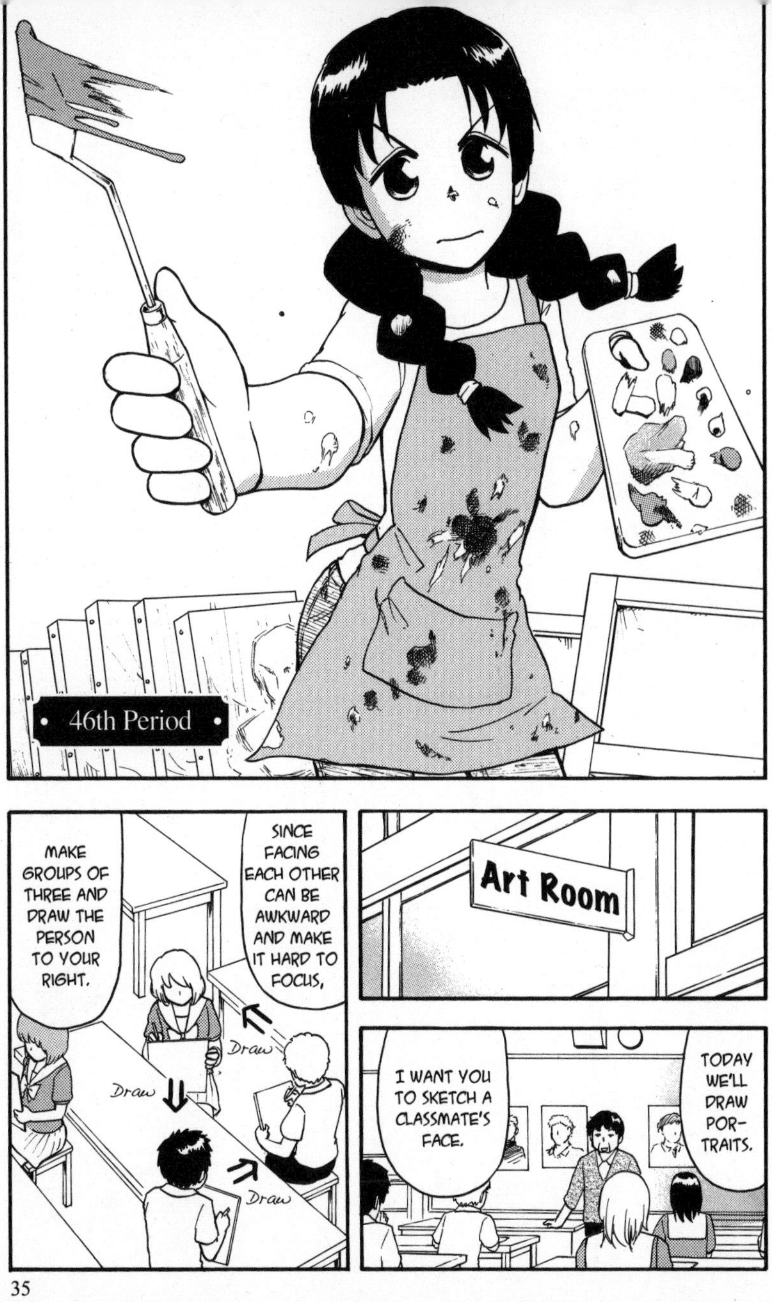

46th Period
Art Room
TODAY WE'LL DRAW POR-TRAITS.
I WANT YOU TO SKETCH A CLASSMATE'S FACE.
SINCE FACING EACH OTHER CAN BE AWKWARD AND MAKE IT HARD TO FOCUS,
MAKE GROUPS OF THREE AND DRAW THE PERSON TO YOUR RIGHT.
Draw
Draw
Draw

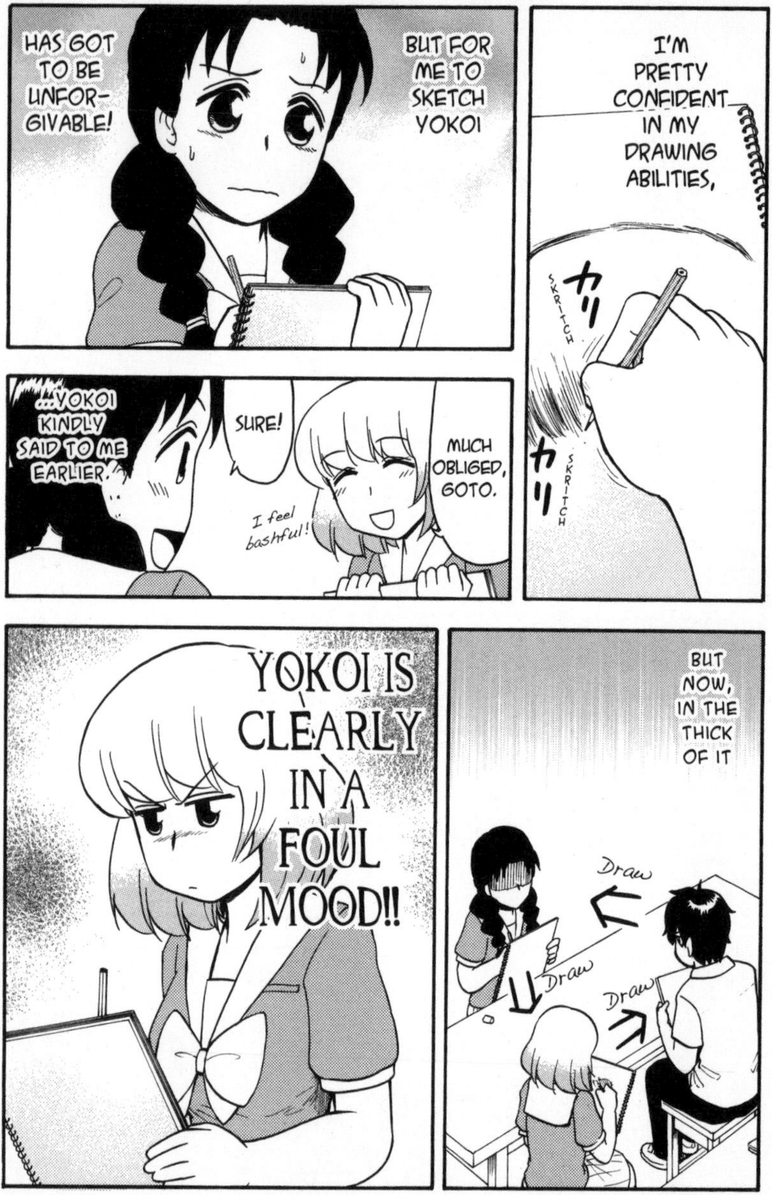

I'M PRETTY CONFIDENT IN MY DRAWING ABILITIES,
カリ
SKRITCH
カリ
SKRITCH
BUT FOR ME TO SKETCH YOKOI
HAS GOT TO BE UNFOR-GIVABLE!
MUCH OBLIGED, GOTO.
I feel bashful!
SURE!
...YOKOI KINDLY SAID TO ME EARLIER.
BUT NOW, IN THE THICK OF IT
Draw
Draw
Draw
YOKOI IS CLEARLY IN A FOUL MOOD!!

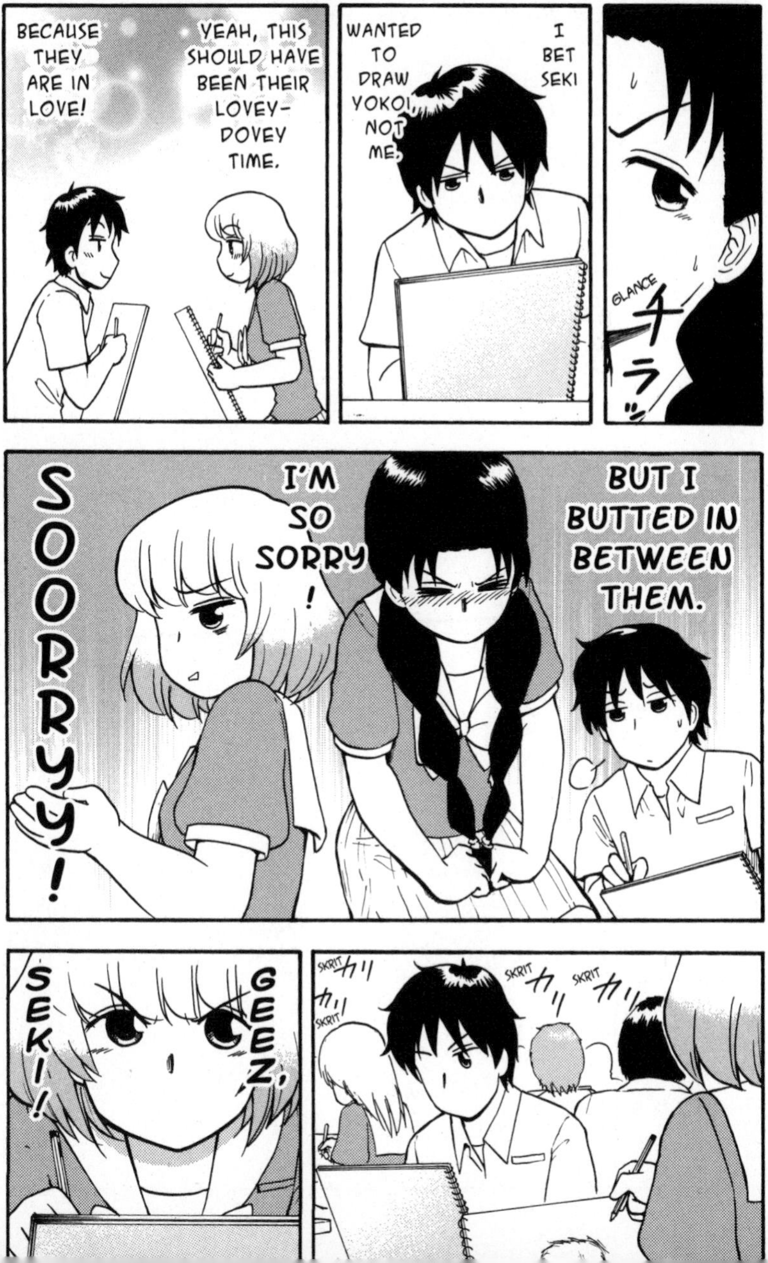
GLANCE
チラッ
I BET SEKI
WANTED TO DRAW YOKOI, NOT ME.
YEAH, THIS SHOULD HAVE BEEN THEIR LOVEY-DOVEY TIME.
BECAUSE THEY ARE IN LOVE!
BUT I BUTTED IN BETWEEN THEM.
I'M SO SORRY!
SOORRYY!
SKRIT
カリ
SKRIT
カリ
SKRIT
カリ
SKRIT
カリ
GEEZ,
SEKI!

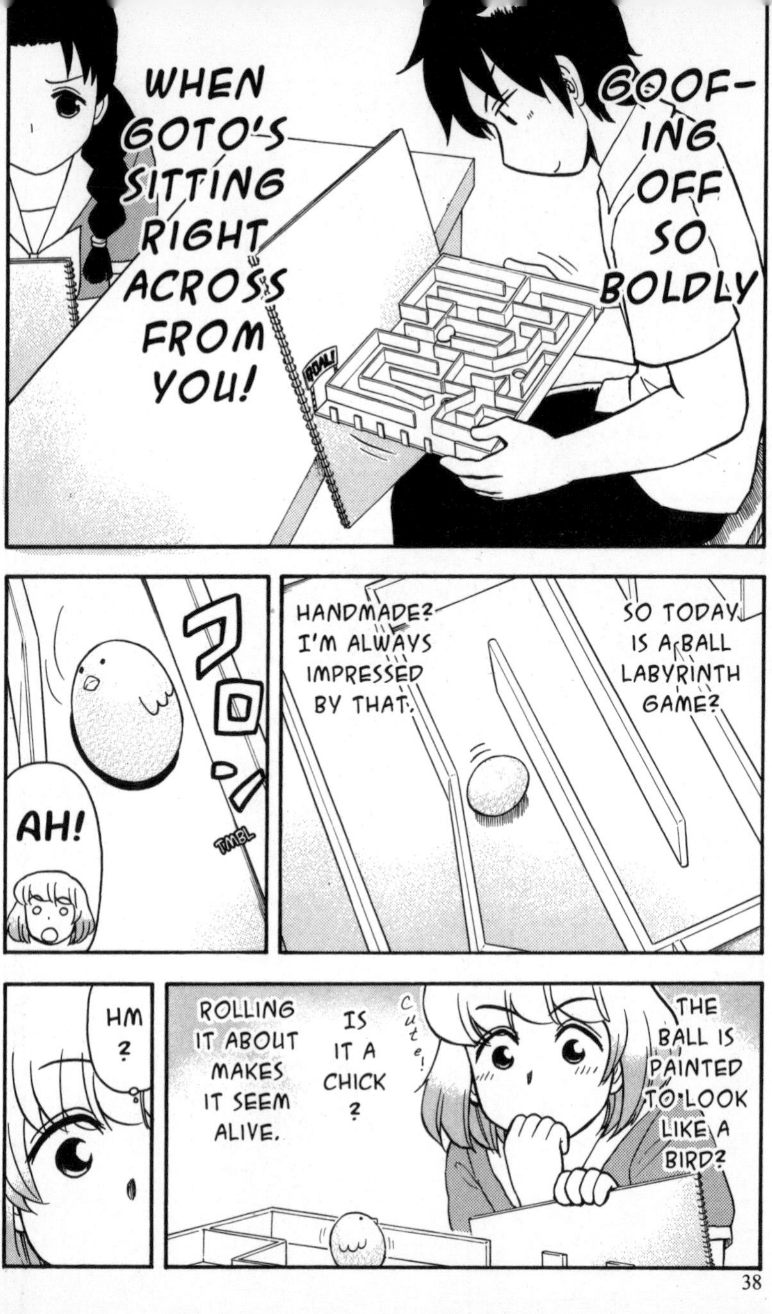
GOOFING OFF SO BOLDLY
WHEN GOTO'S SITTING RIGHT ACROSS FROM YOU!
SO TODAY IS A BALL LABYRINTH GAME?
HANDMADE? I'M ALWAYS IMPRESSED BY THAT.
TMBL
AH!
THE BALL IS PAINTED TO LOOK LIKE A BIRD?
Cute!
IS IT A CHICK?
ROLLING IT ABOUT MAKES IT SEEM ALIVE.
HM?

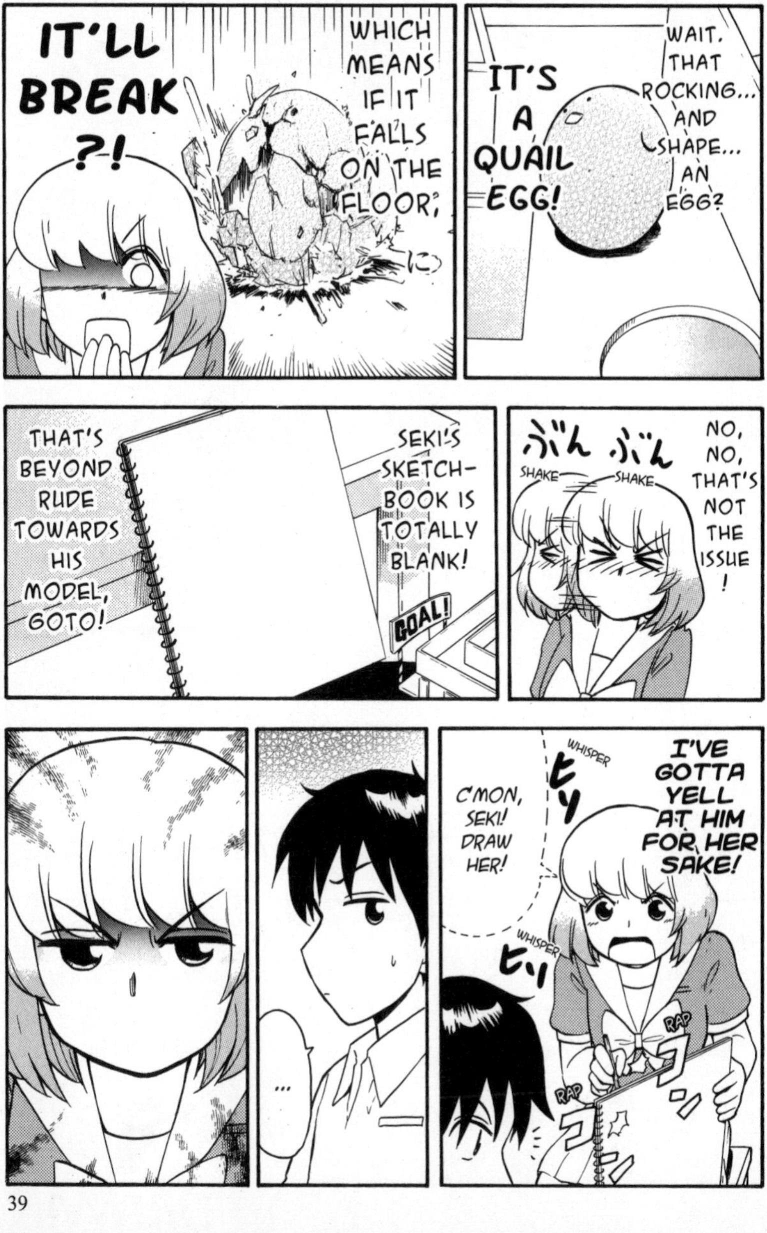
WAIT. THAT ROCKING... AND SHAPE... AN EGG?
IT'S A QUAIL EGG!
WHICH MEANS IF IT FALLS ON THE FLOOR,
に
IT'LL BREAK ?!
NO, NO, THAT'S NOT THE ISSUE!
ぶん ぶん
SHAKE SHAKE
SEKI'S SKETCH-BOOK IS TOTALLY BLANK!
THAT'S BEYOND RUDE TOWARDS HIS MODEL, GOTO!
GOAL!
I'VE GOTTA YELL AT HIM FOR HER SAKE!
ヒソ
WHISPER
C'MON, SEKI! DRAW HER!
ヒソ
WHISPER
RAP
RAP
...

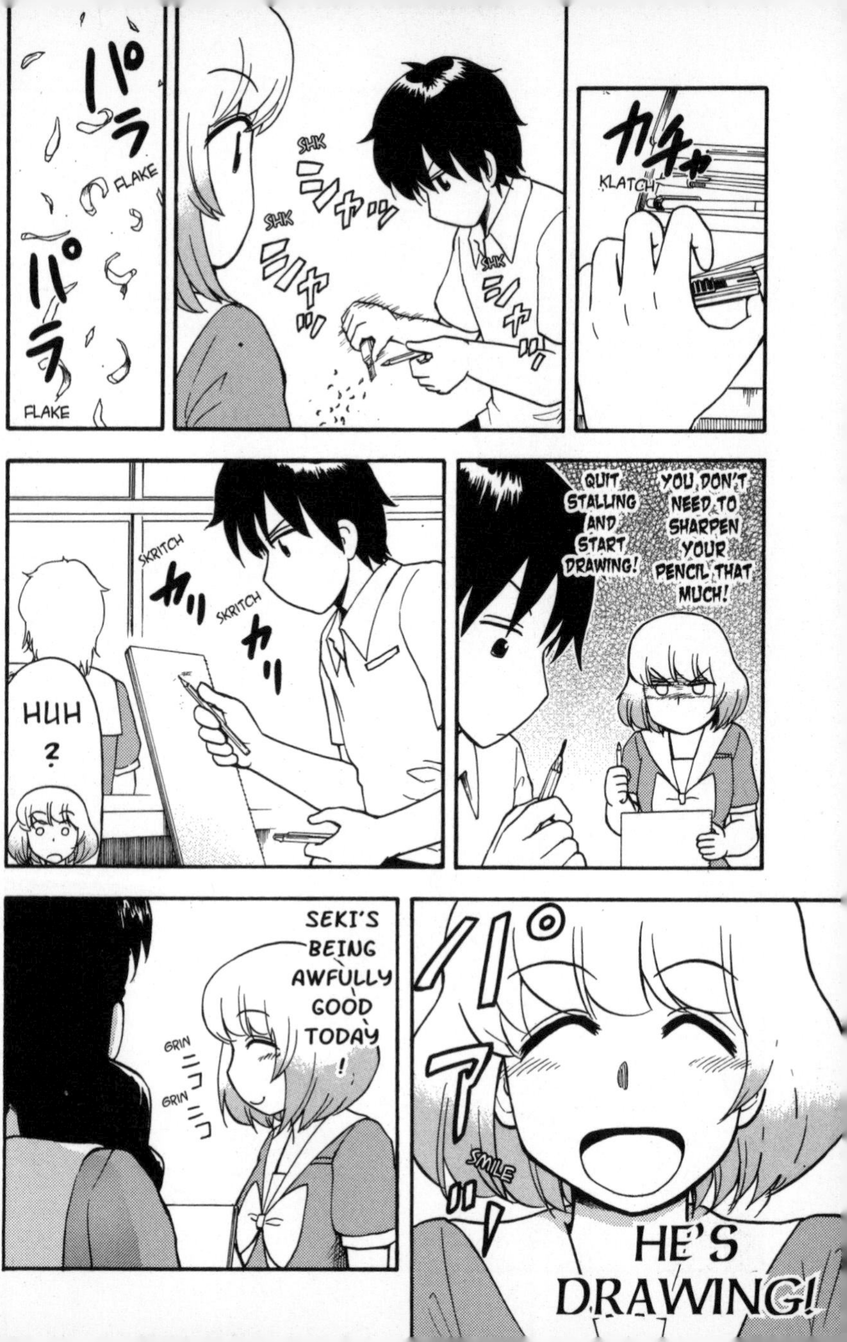
カチャ
KLATCH
SHK
シャッ
SHK
シャッ
SHK
シャッ
パラ
FLAKE
パラ
FLAKE
YOU DON'T NEED TO SHARPEN YOUR PENCIL THAT MUCH!
QUIT STALLING AND START DRAWING!
SKRITCH
カリ
SKRITCH
カリ
HUH?
パア
SMILE
HE'S DRAWING!
SEKI'S BEING AWFULLY GOOD TODAY!
GRIN
ニコ
GRIN
ニコ

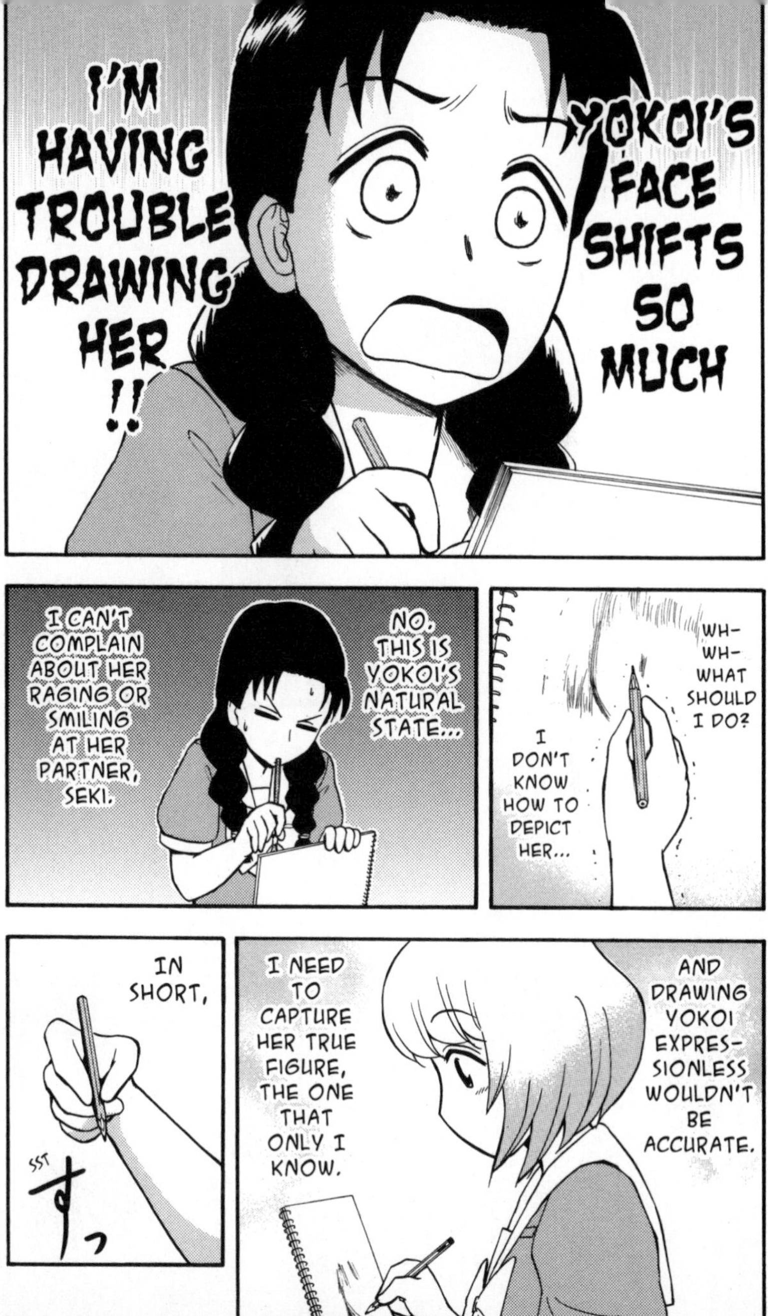
YOKOI'S FACE SHIFTS SO MUCH
I'M HAVING TROUBLE DRAWING HER!!
WH-WH-WHAT SHOULD I DO?
I DON'T KNOW HOW TO DEPICT HER...
NO. THIS IS YOKOI'S NATURAL STATE...
I CAN'T COMPLAIN ABOUT HER RAGING OR SMILING AT HER PARTNER, SEKI.
AND DRAWING YOKOI EXPRES-SIONLESS WOULDN'T BE ACCURATE.
I NEED TO CAPTURE HER TRUE FIGURE, THE ONE THAT ONLY I KNOW.
IN SHORT,
SST
すっ

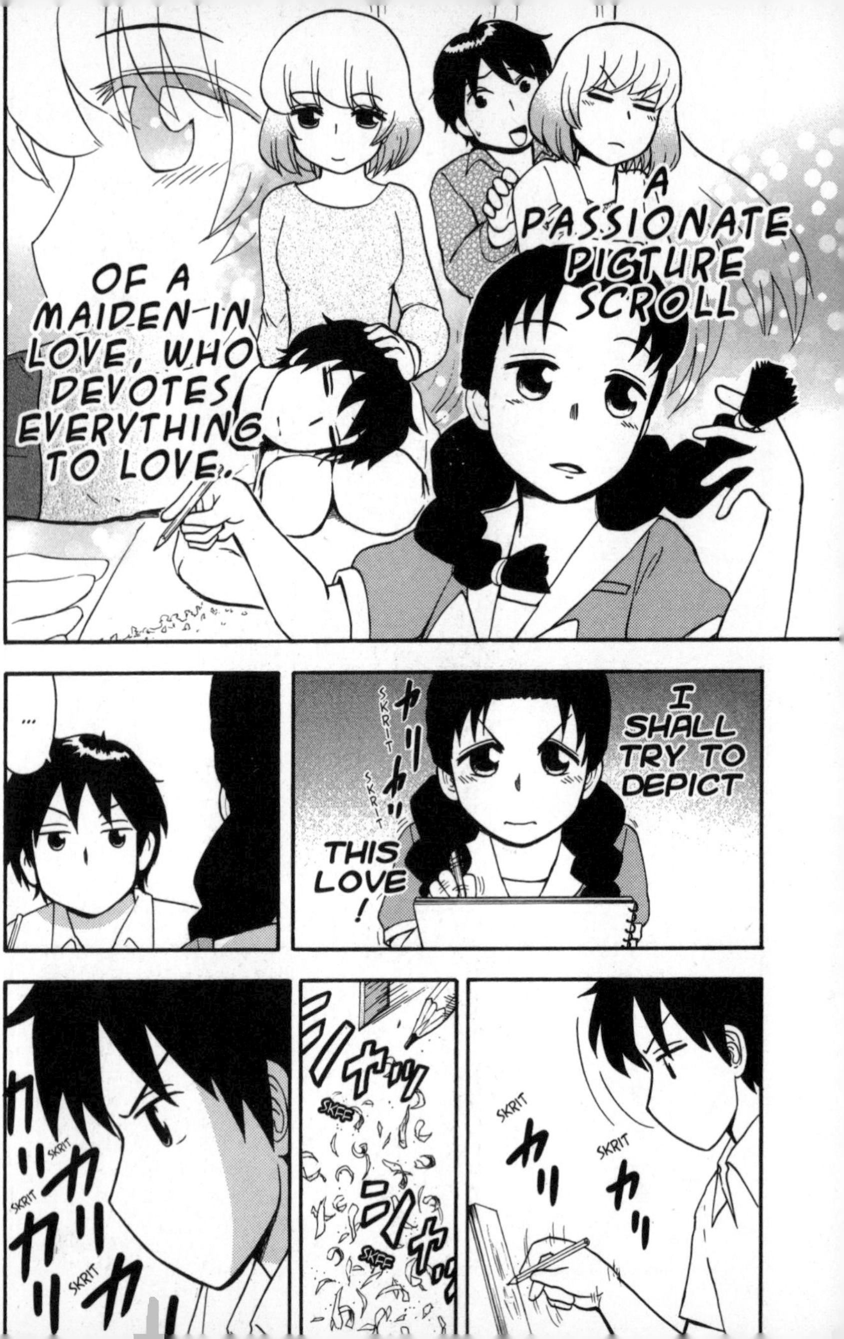
A PASSIONATE PICTURE SCROLL
OF A MAIDEN IN LOVE, WHO DEVOTES EVERYTHING TO LOVE.
I SHALL TRY TO DEPICT
SKRIT
SKRIT
THIS LOVE!
...
SKRIT
SKRIT
SKFF
SKFF
SKRIT
SKRIT
SKRIT

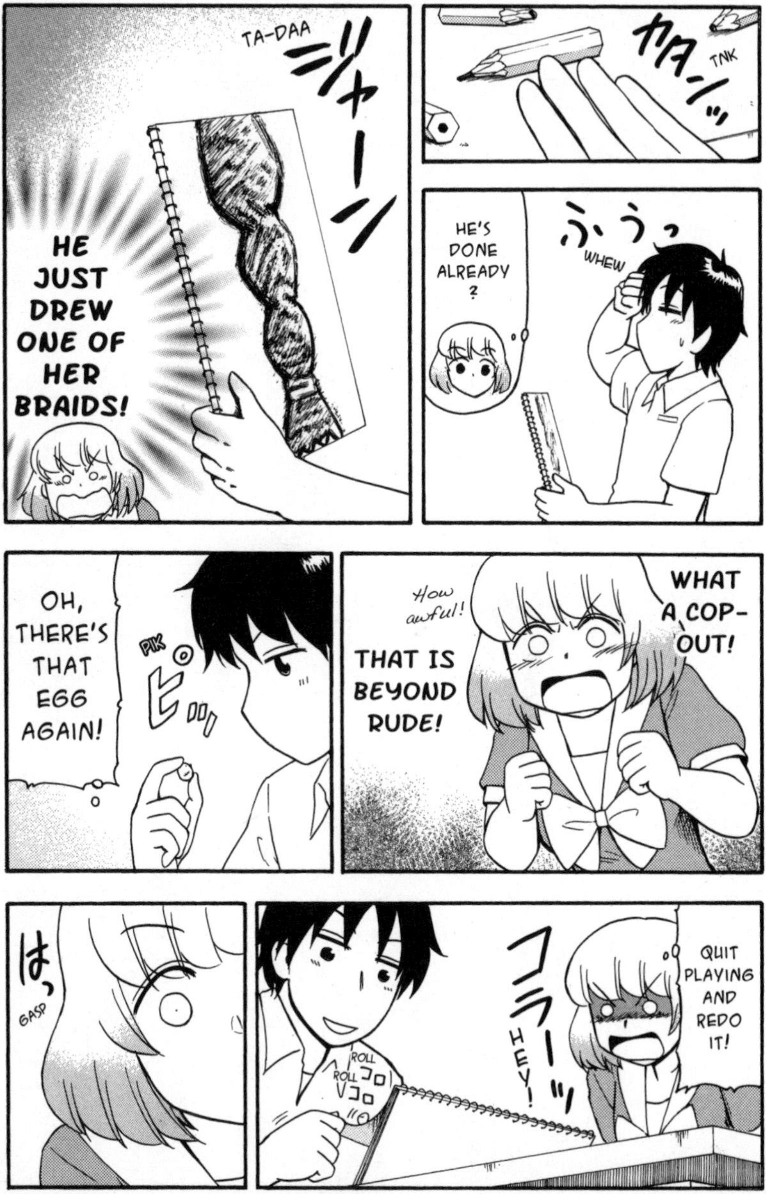

カタンッ
TNK
ふうっ
WHEW
HE'S DONE ALREADY?
ジャーン
TA-DAA
HE JUST DREW ONE OF HER BRAIDS!
WHAT A COP-OUT!
How awful!
THAT IS BEYOND RUDE!
OH, THERE'S THAT EGG AGAIN!
PIK
コラーッ
HEY!
QUIT PLAYING AND REDO IT!
ROLL
ROLL
コロコロ
は
GASP

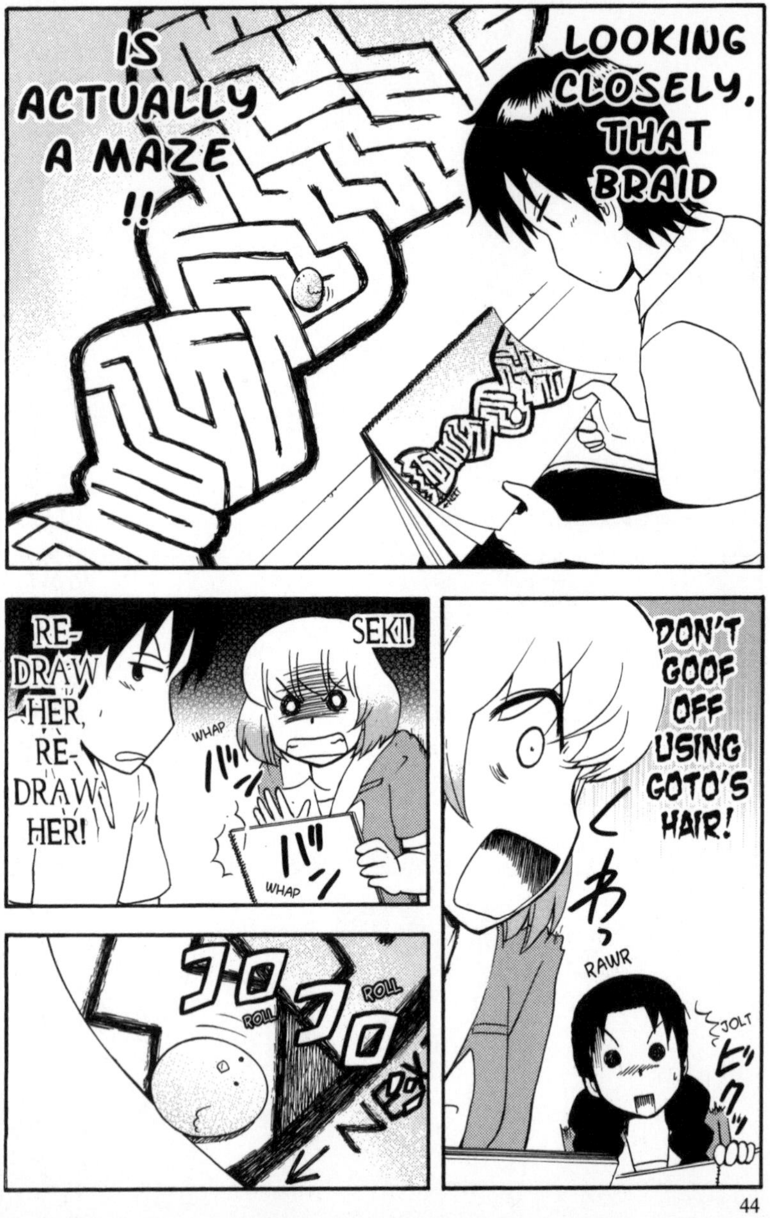

LOOKING CLOSELY, THAT BRAID
IS ACTUALLY A MAZE!!
DON'T GOOF OFF USING GOTO'S HAIR!
くわっ
RAWR
ビクッ
JOLT
SEKI!
バン
WHAP
バン
WHAP
RE-DRAW HER, RE-DRAW HER!
コロ
ROLL
コロ
ROLL

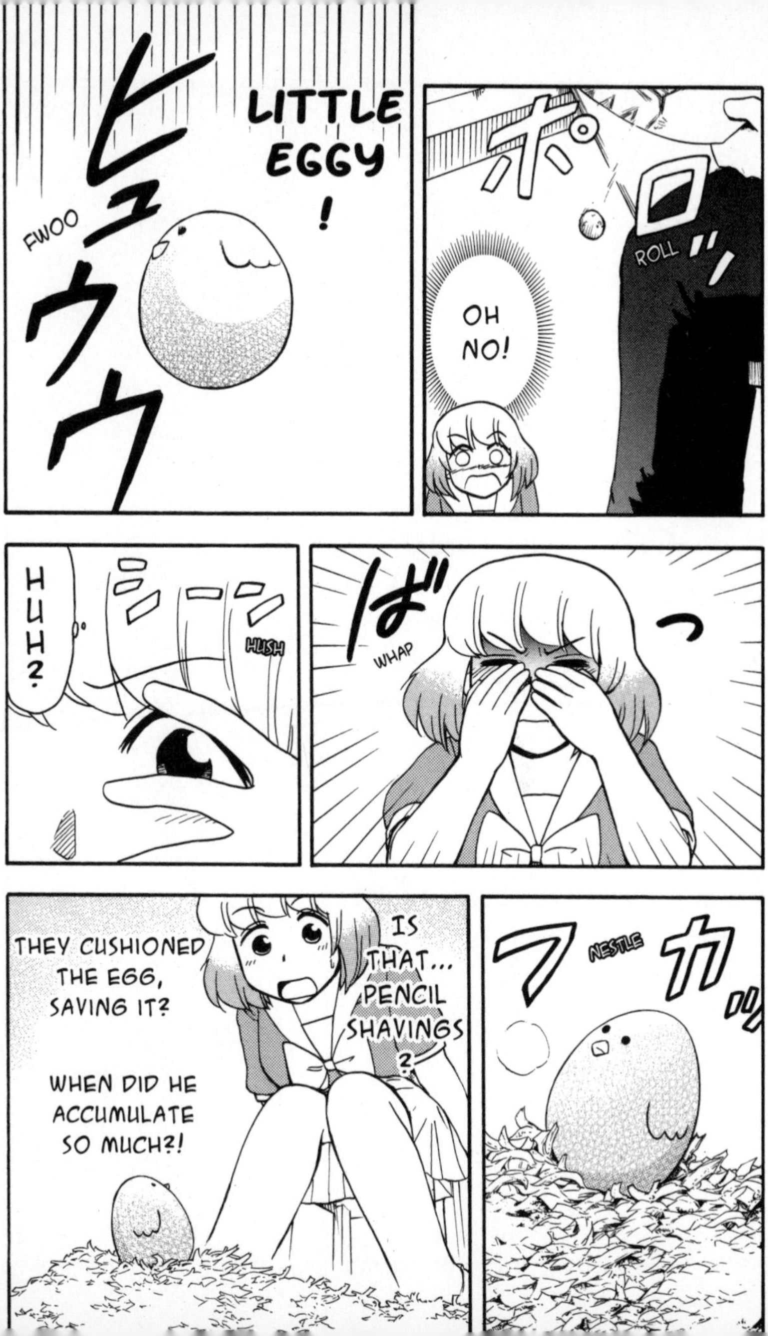

ポロッ
ROLL
OH NO!
ヒュウウウ
FWOO
LITTLE EGGY!
ばっ
WHAP
シーン
HUSH
HUH?
フカッ
NESTLE
IS THAT... PENCIL SHAVINGS?
THEY CUSHIONED THE EGG, SAVING IT?
WHEN DID HE ACCUMULATE SO MUCH?!

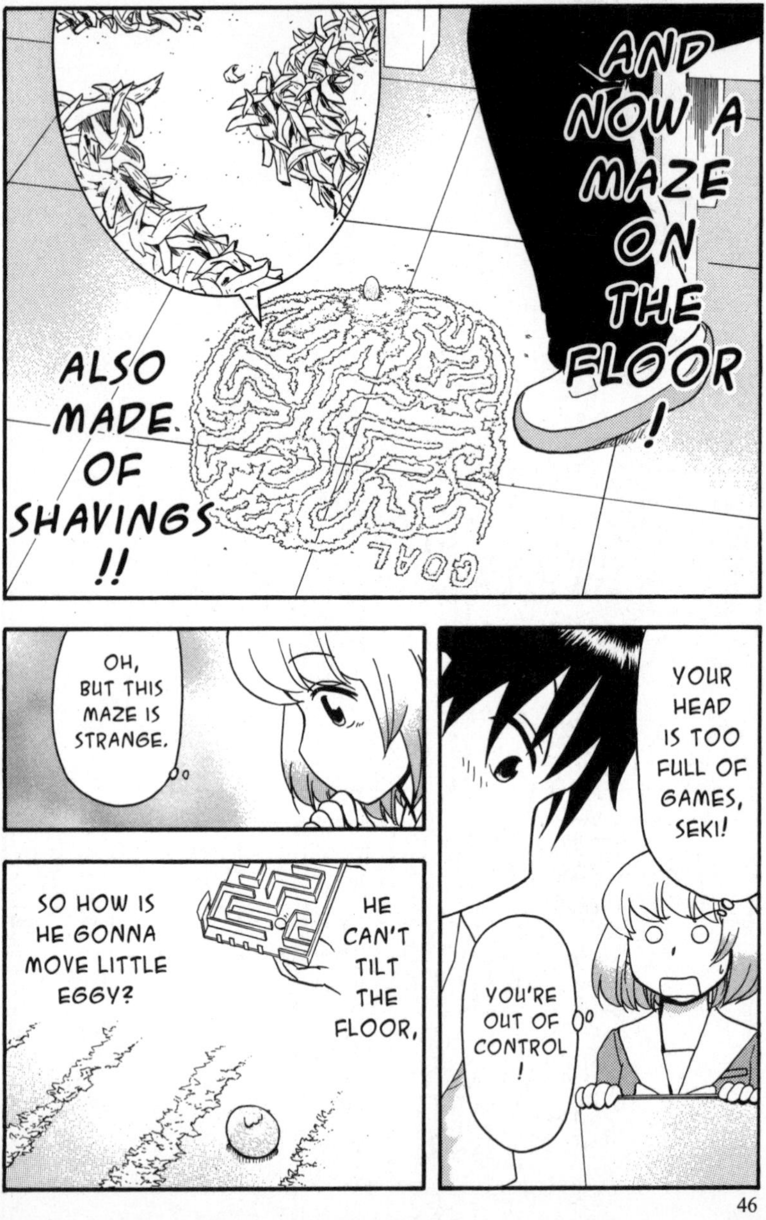
AND NOW A MAZE ON THE FLOOR!
ALSO MADE OF SHAVINGS!!
GOAL
YOUR HEAD IS TOO FULL OF GAMES, SEKI!
YOU'RE OUT OF CONTROL!
OH, BUT THIS MAZE IS STRANGE.
HE CAN'T TILT THE FLOOR,
SO HOW IS HE GONNA MOVE LITTLE EGGY?

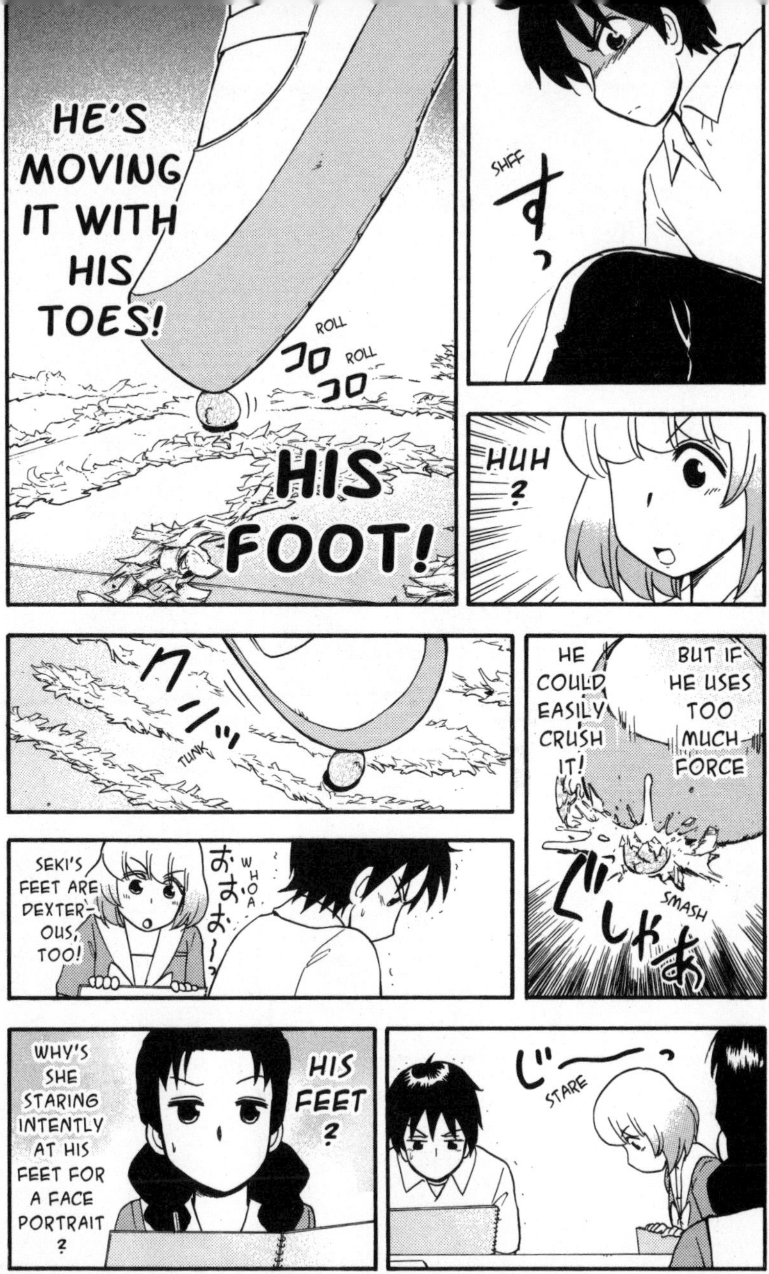
すっ
SHFF
HUH ?
HE'S MOVING IT WITH HIS TOES!
コロ
ROLL
コロ
ROLL
HIS FOOT!
BUT IF HE USES TOO MUCH FORCE
HE COULD EASILY CRUSH IT!
ぐしゃあ
SMASH
クンッ
TUNK
おおお～っ
WHOA
SEKI'S FEET ARE DEXTER-OUS, TOO!
じーっ
STARE
HIS FEET ?
WHY'S SHE STARING INTENTLY AT HIS FEET FOR A FACE PORTRAIT ?

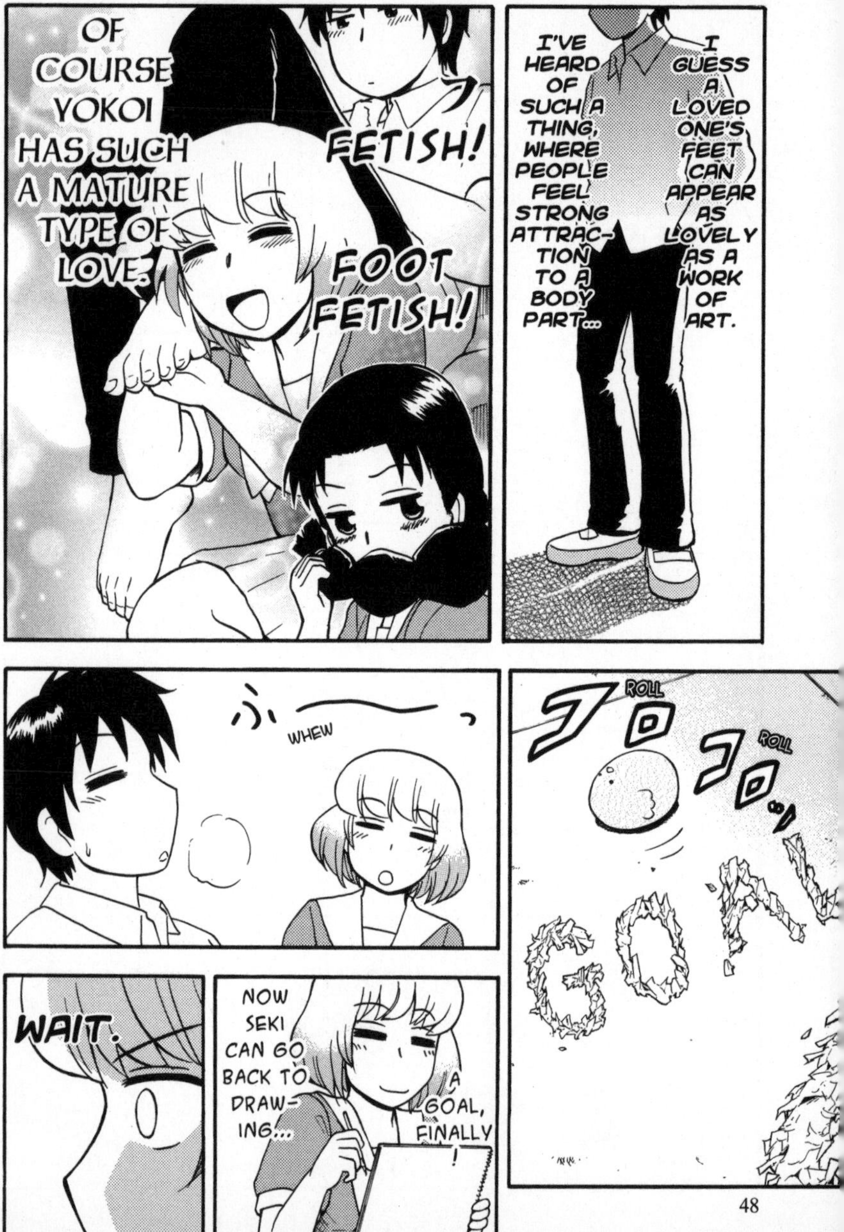
I GUESS A LOVED ONE'S FEET CAN APPEAR AS LOVELY AS A WORK OF ART.
I'VE HEARD OF SUCH A THING, WHERE PEOPLE FEEL STRONG ATTRAC-TION TO A BODY PART...
FETISH!
FOOT FETISH!
OF COURSE YOKOI HAS SUCH A MATURE TYPE OF LOVE.
ROLL
ROLL
GON
ふー
WHEW
A GOAL, FINALLY!
NOW SEKI CAN GO BACK TO DRAW-ING...
WAIT.

NOT WHEN IT COMES TO SEKI.

NO WAY.

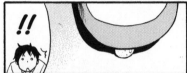

!!

...

ZWOOOM

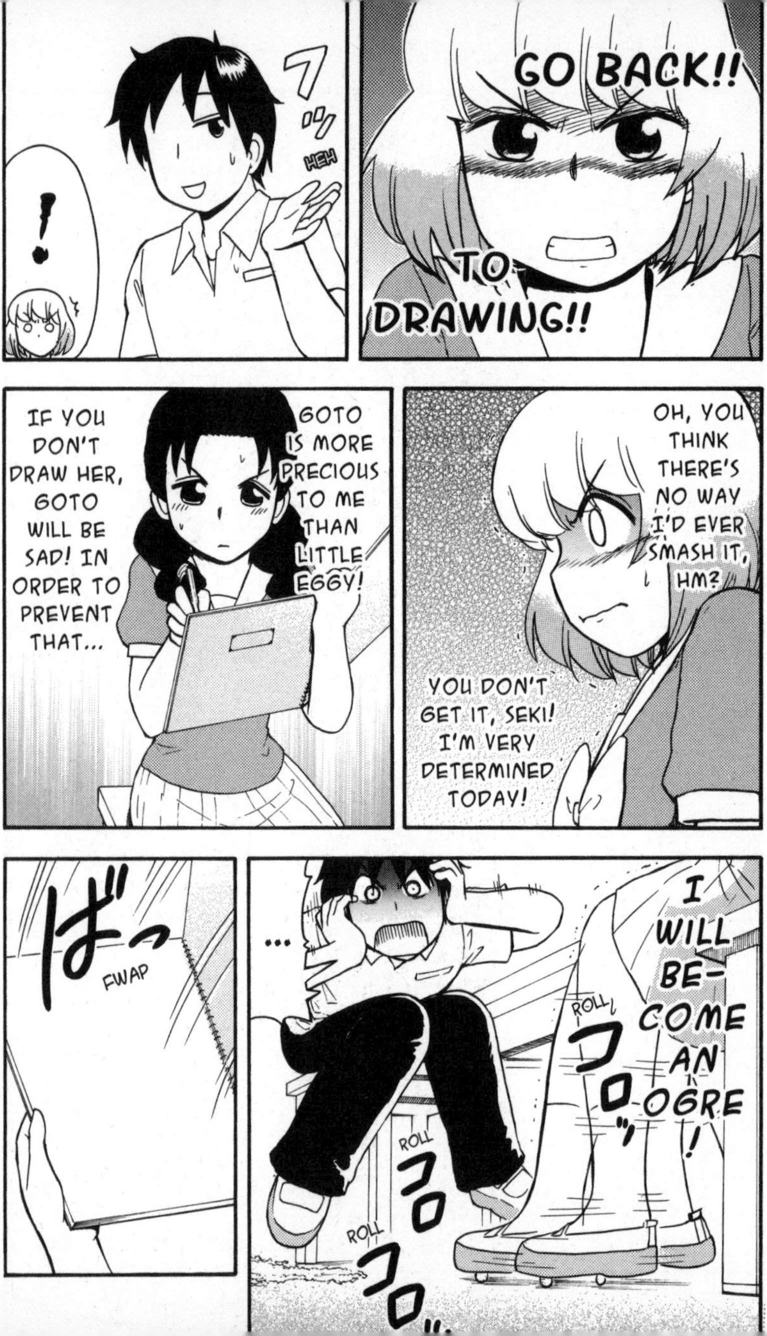
GO BACK!!
TO DRAWING!!
フッ
HEH
!
OH, YOU THINK THERE'S NO WAY I'D EVER SMASH IT, HM?
YOU DON'T GET IT, SEKI! I'M VERY DETERMINED TODAY!
GOTO IS MORE PRECIOUS TO ME THAN LITTLE EGGY!
IF YOU DON'T DRAW HER, GOTO WILL BE SAD! IN ORDER TO PREVENT THAT...
I WILL BE-COME AN OGRE!
ROLL
コロッ
...
ROLL
コロ
ROLL
コロッ
ばっ
FWAP

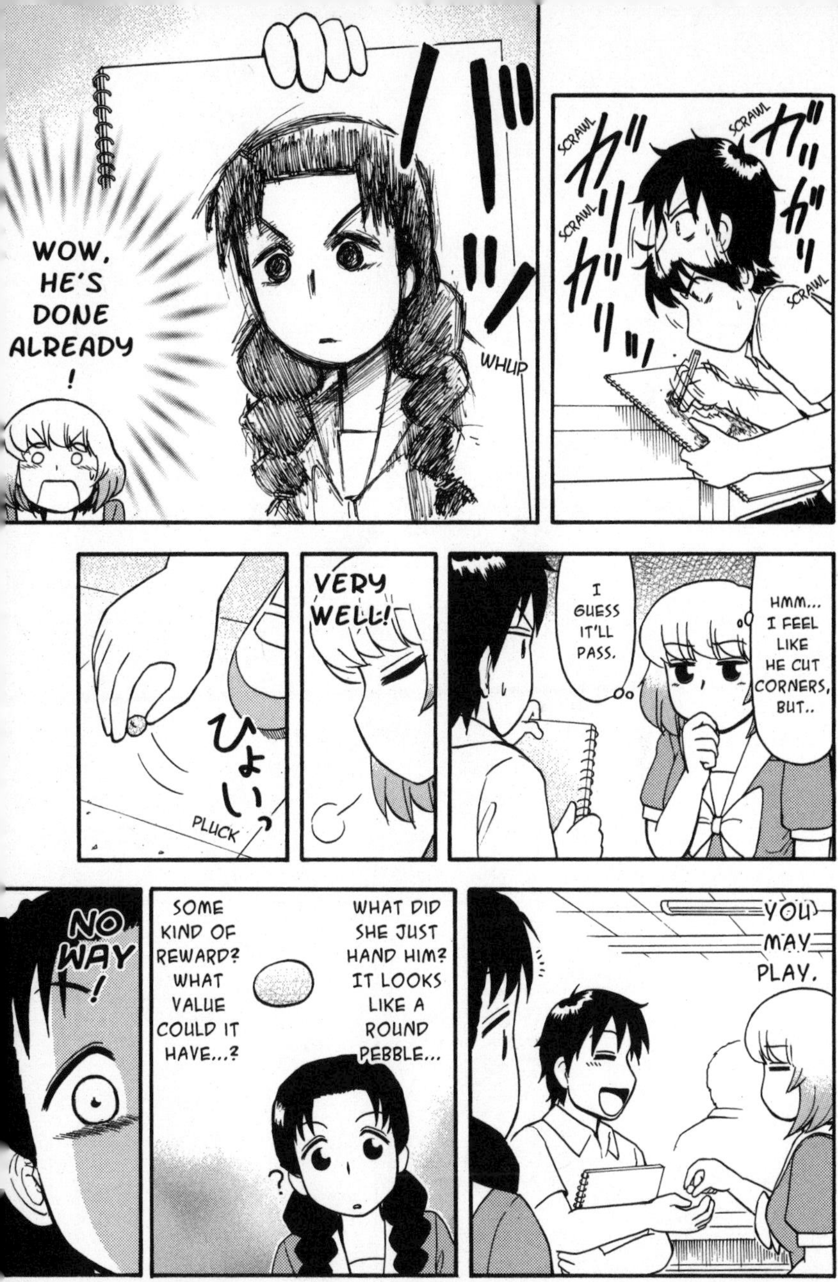
ガリガリ
ガリガリッ
SCRAWL
SCRAWL
SCRAWL
SCRAWL
WHUP
WOW, HE'S DONE ALREADY!
HMM... I FEEL LIKE HE CUT CORNERS, BUT..
I GUESS IT'LL PASS.
VERY WELL!
ひょいっ
PLUCK
YOU MAY PLAY.
WHAT DID SHE JUST HAND HIM? IT LOOKS LIKE A ROUND PEBBLE...
SOME KIND OF REWARD? WHAT VALUE COULD IT HAVE...?
NO WAY!

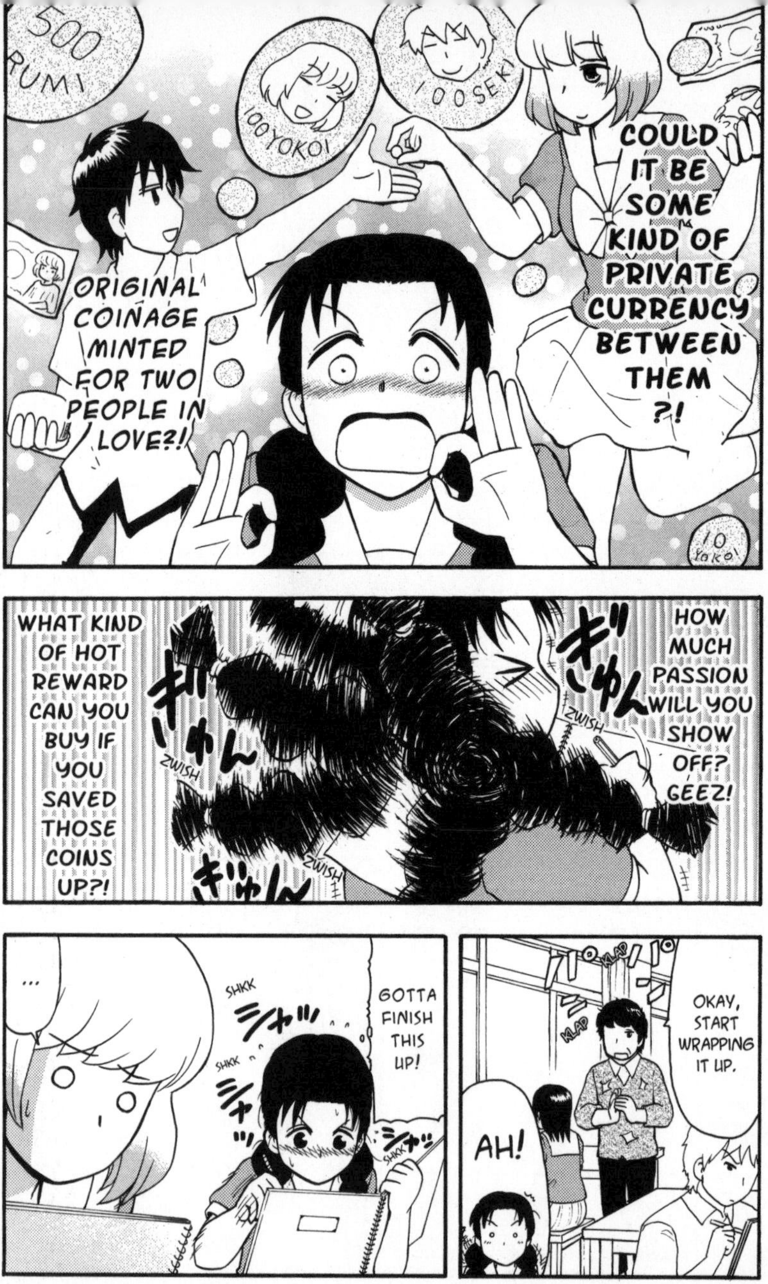
500 RUMI
100 SEKI
100 YOKOI
COULD IT BE SOME KIND OF PRIVATE CURRENCY BETWEEN THEM ?!
ORIGINAL COINAGE MINTED FOR TWO PEOPLE IN LOVE?!
10 YOKOI
HOW MUCH PASSION WILL YOU SHOW OFF? GEEZ!
ZWISH
ZWISH
WHAT KIND OF HOT REWARD CAN YOU BUY IF YOU SAVED THOSE COINS UP?!
ZWISH
KLAP
KLAP
OKAY, START WRAPPING IT UP.
AH!
GOTTA FINISH THIS UP!
SHKK
SHKK
SHKK
...

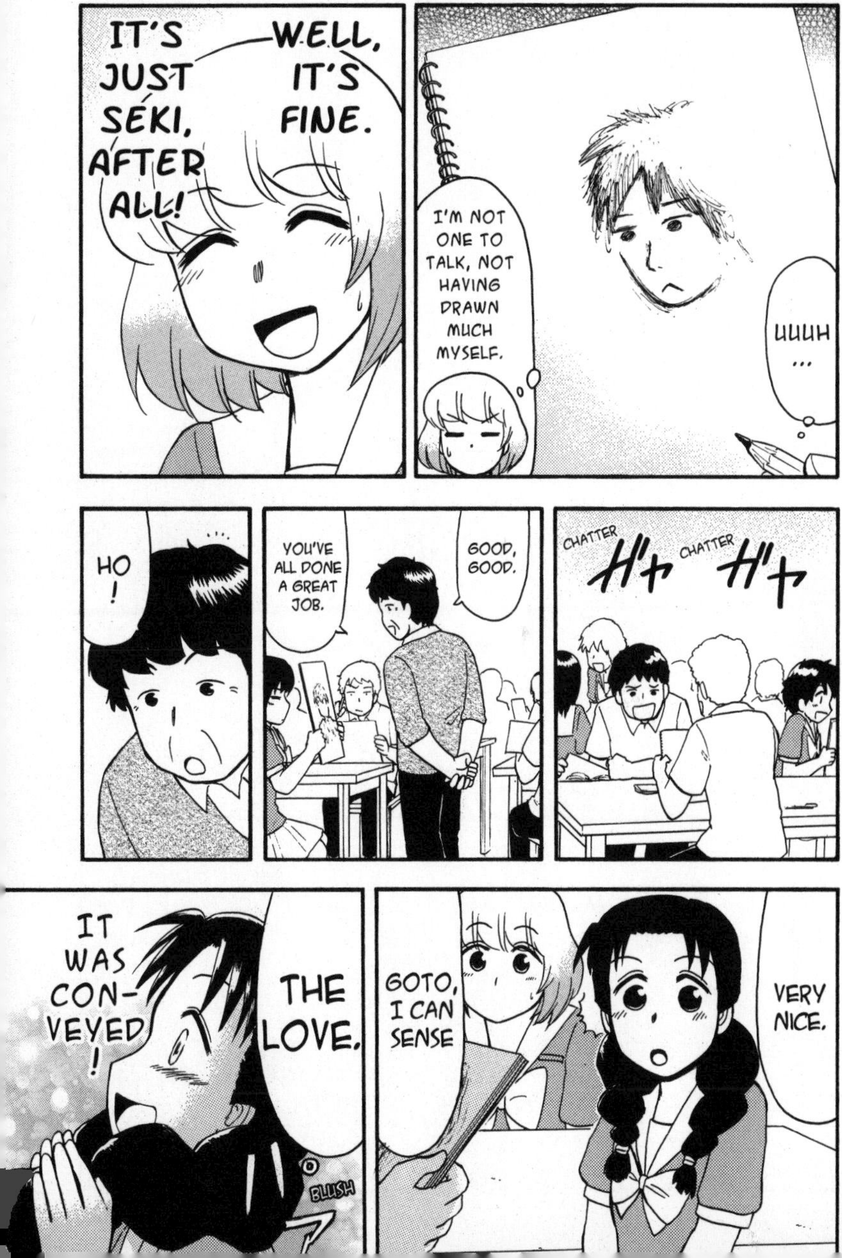
UUUH...
I'M NOT ONE TO TALK, NOT HAVING DRAWN MUCH MYSELF.
WELL, IT'S FINE.
IT'S JUST SEKI, AFTER ALL!
CHATTER
ガヤ
CHATTER
ガヤ
GOOD, GOOD.
YOU'VE ALL DONE A GREAT JOB.
...
HO!
VERY NICE.
GOTO, I CAN SENSE
THE LOVE.
IT WAS CON-VEYED!
BLUSH

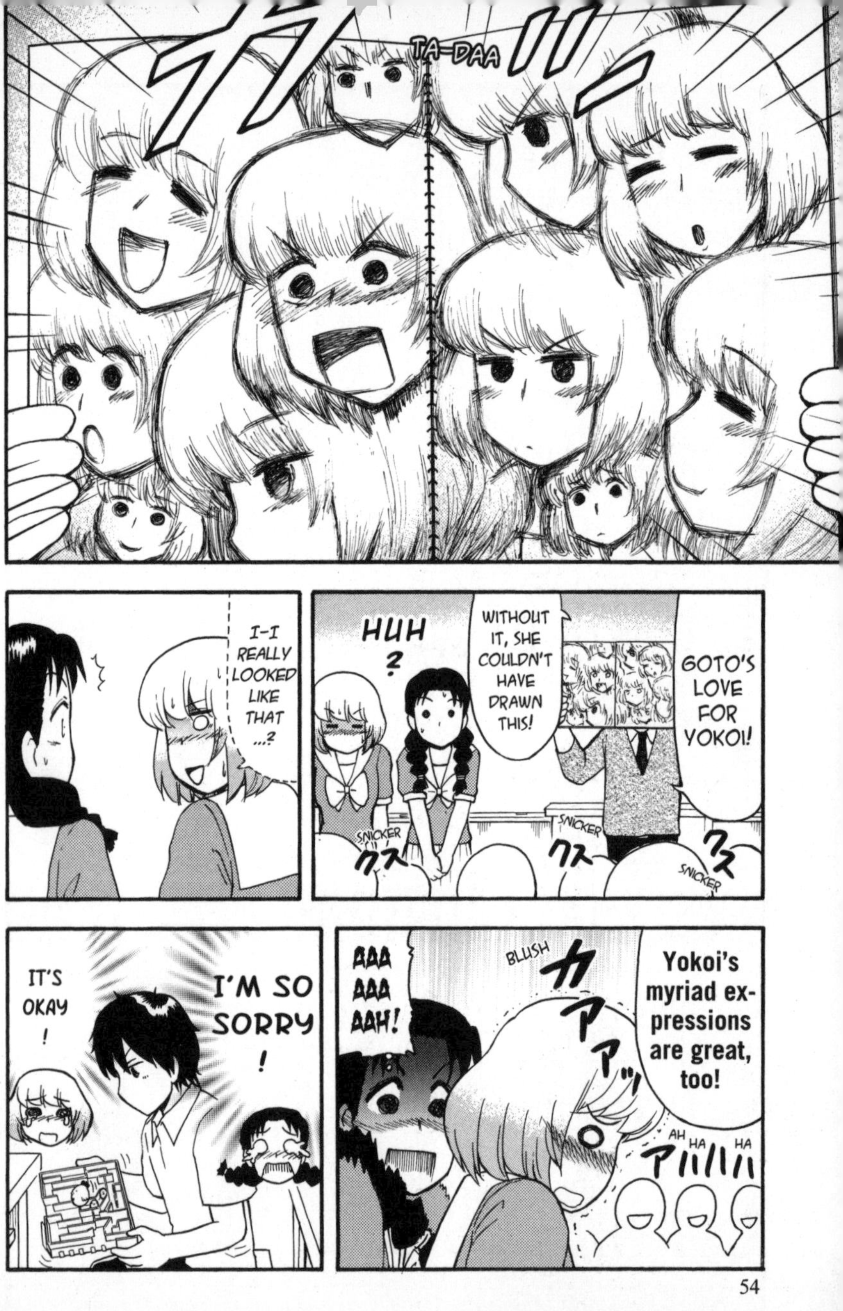
TA-DAA
GOTO'S LOVE FOR YOKOI!
WITHOUT IT, SHE COULDN'T HAVE DRAWN THIS!
HUH?
SNICKER
SNICKER
SNICKER
I-I REALLY LOOKED LIKE THAT...?
Yokoi's myriad expressions are great, too!
BLUSH
AH HA HA
AAA AAA AAH!
I'M SO SORRY!
IT'S OKAY!

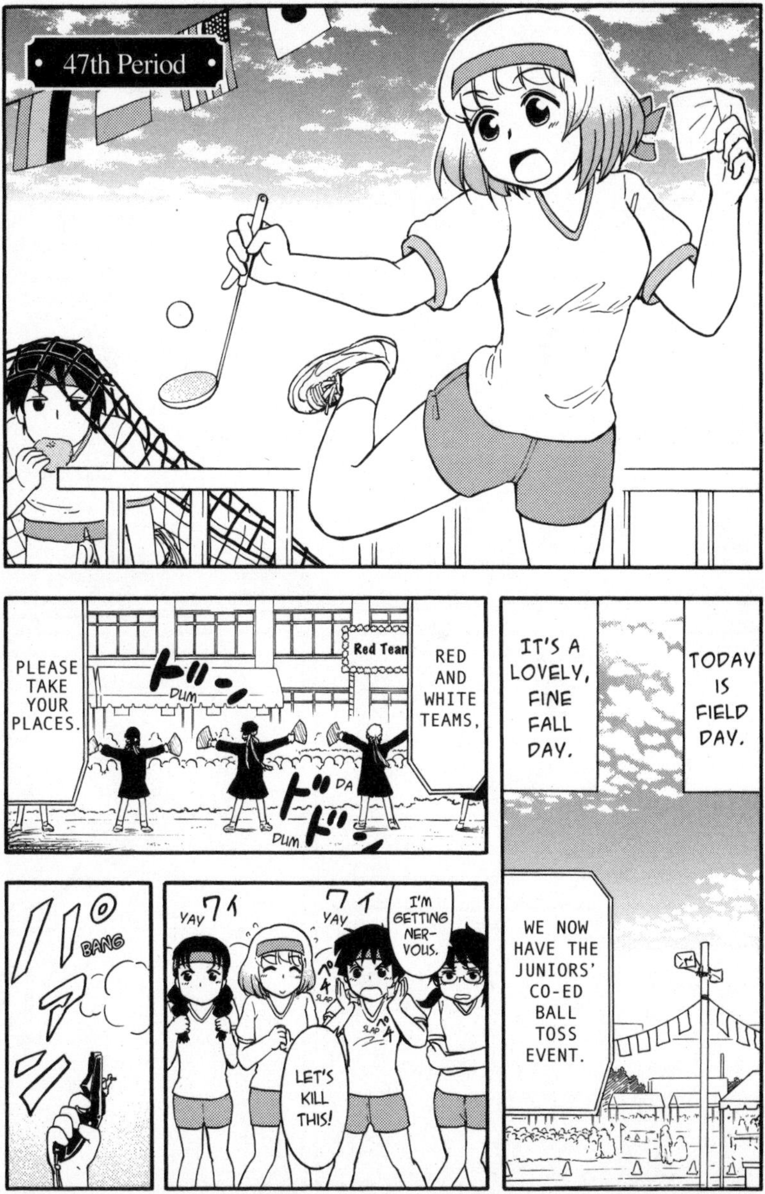
• 47th Period •
TODAY IS FIELD DAY.
IT'S A LOVELY, FINE FALL DAY.
WE NOW HAVE THE JUNIORS' CO-ED BALL TOSS EVENT.
RED AND WHITE TEAMS,
Red Team
DUM
PLEASE TAKE YOUR PLACES.
DA
DUM
YAY
YAY
I'M GETTING NER-VOUS.
SLAP
SLAP
LET'S KILL THIS!
BANG

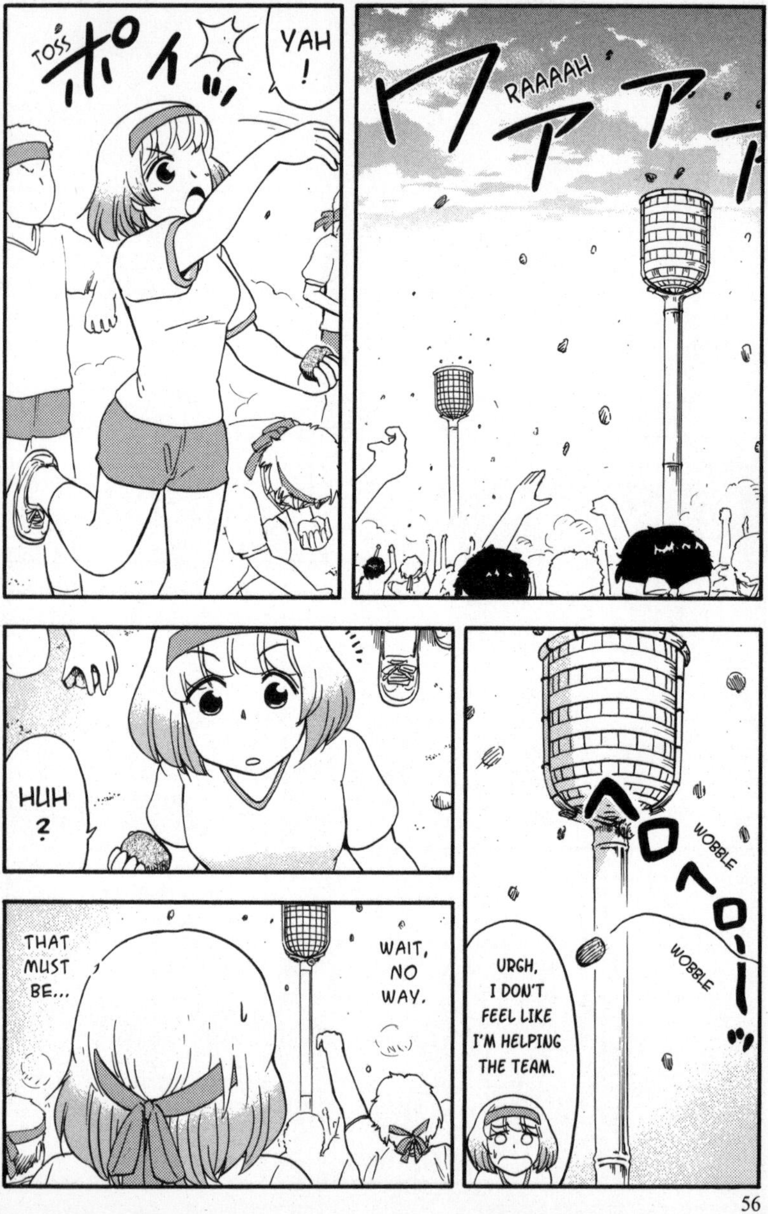
RAAAAH
YAH!
TOSS
WOBBLE
WOBBLE
URGH, I DON'T FEEL LIKE I'M HELPING THE TEAM.
HUH?
WAIT, NO WAY.
THAT MUST BE...

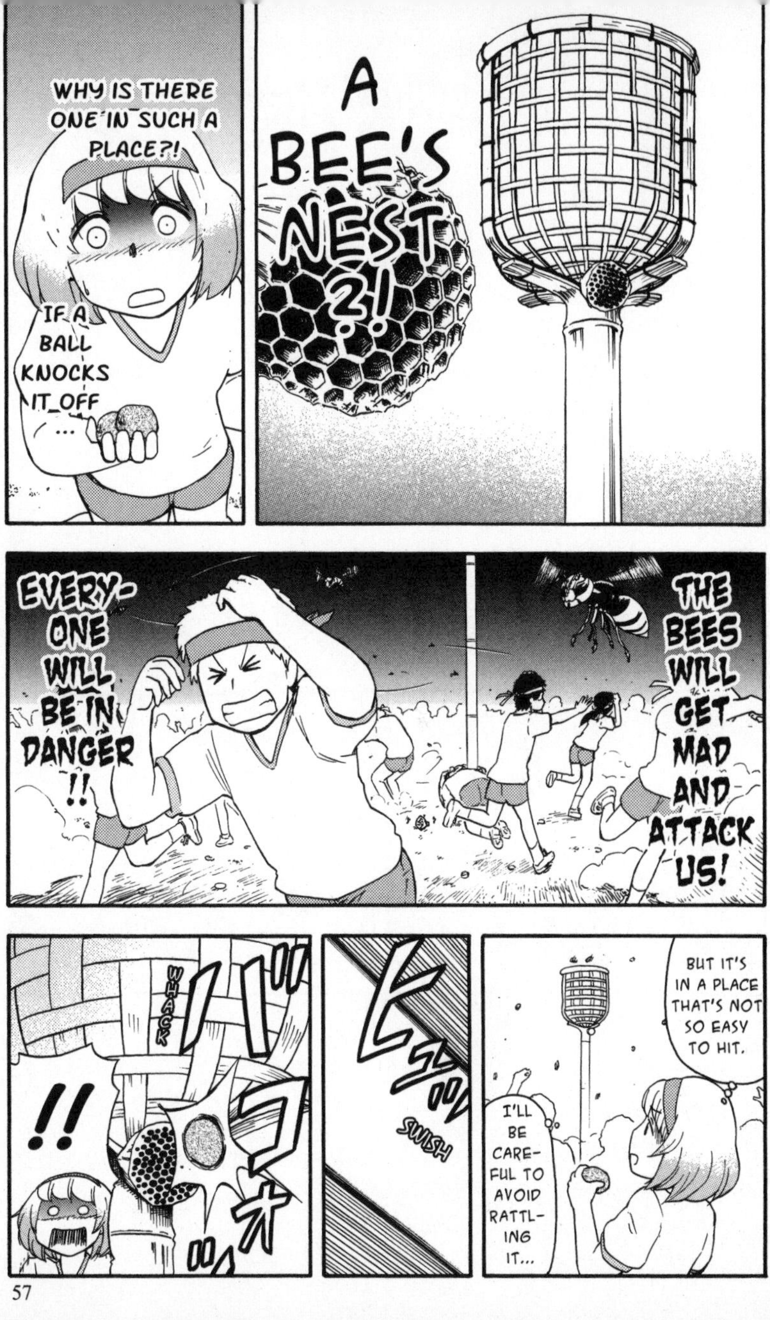
A BEE'S NEST?!
WHY IS THERE ONE IN SUCH A PLACE?!
IF A BALL KNOCKS IT OFF...
THE BEES WILL GET MAD AND ATTACK US!
EVERY-ONE WILL BE IN DANGER!!
BUT IT'S IN A PLACE THAT'S NOT SO EASY TO HIT.
I'LL BE CARE-FUL TO AVOID RATTL-ING IT...
SWISH
WHACK
!!

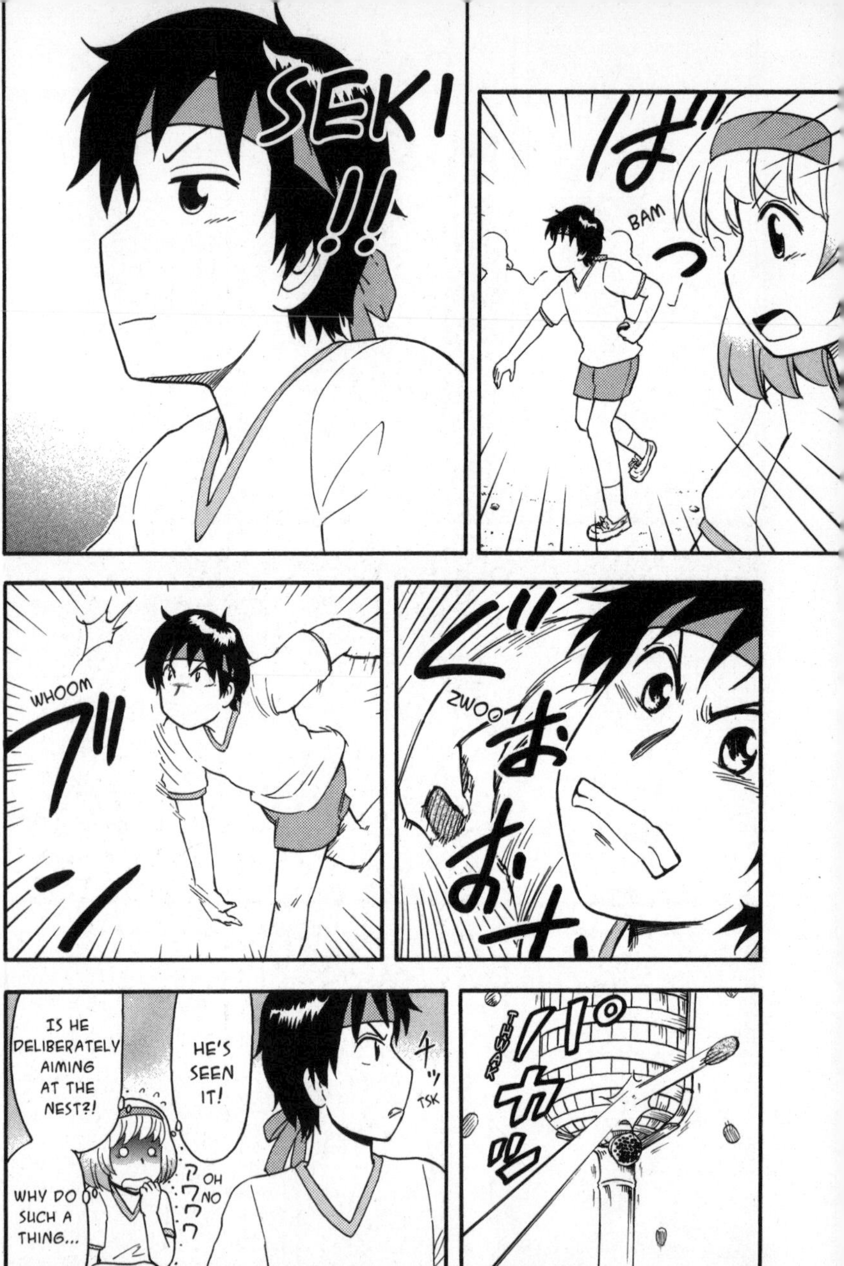
ばっ
BAM
SEKI!!
ぐおお
ZWOO
ブン
WHOOM
パカッ
THWAK
HE'S SEEN IT!
チッ
TSK
IS HE DELIBERATELY AIMING AT THE NEST?!
アワワワ
OH NO
WHY DO SUCH A THING...

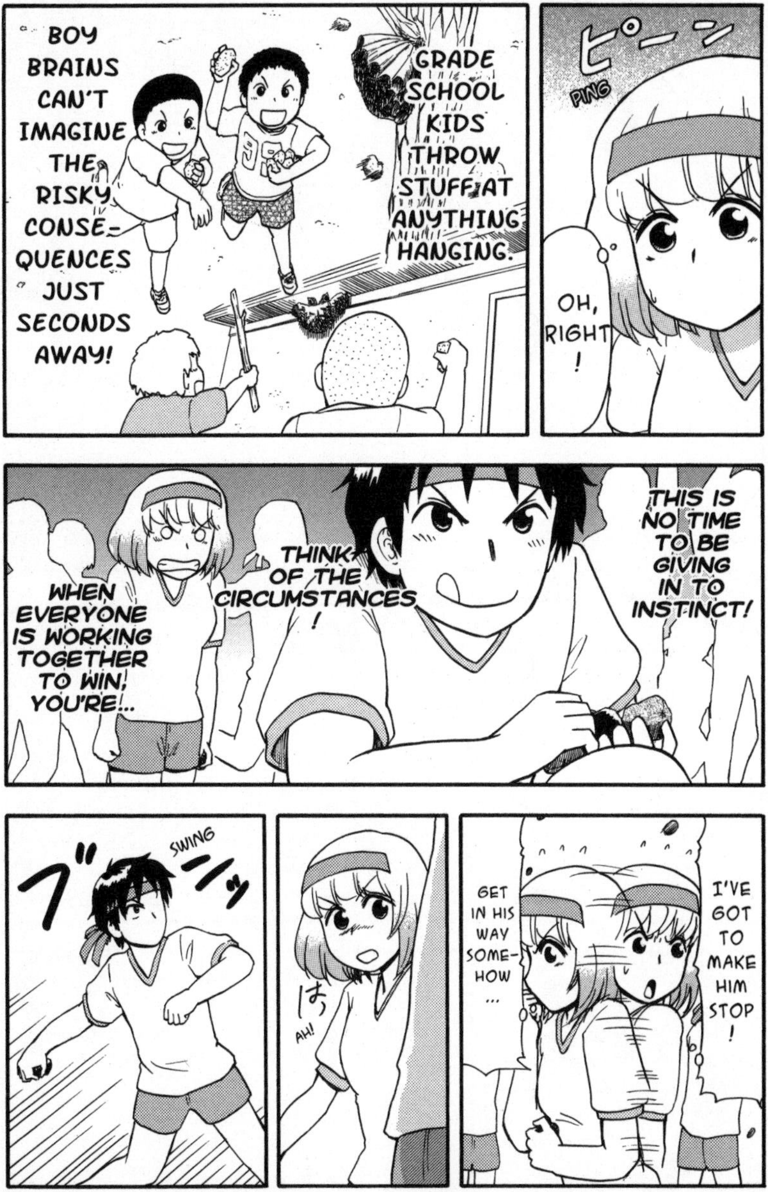
ピーン
PING
OH, RIGHT!
GRADE SCHOOL KIDS THROW STUFF AT ANYTHING HANGING.
BOY BRAINS CAN'T IMAGINE THE RISKY CONSE-QUENCES JUST SECONDS AWAY!
THIS IS NO TIME TO BE GIVING IN TO INSTINCT!
THINK OF THE CIRCUMSTANCES!
WHEN EVERYONE IS WORKING TOGETHER TO WIN, YOU'RE...
I'VE GOT TO MAKE HIM STOP!
GET IN HIS WAY SOME-HOW...
は、
AH!
ブンッ
SWING

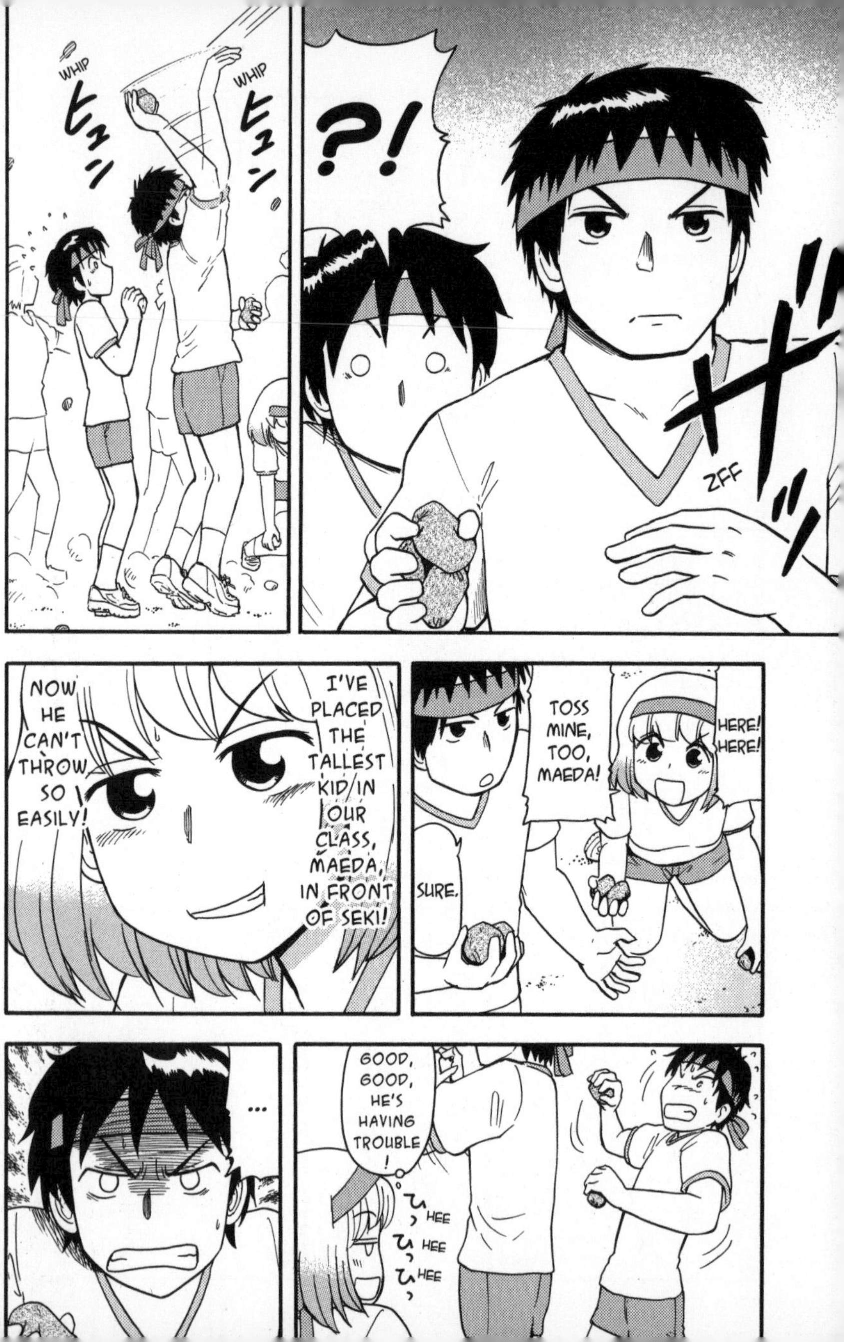
?!
ZFF
WHIP
ヒュン
WHIP
ヒュン
HERE! HERE!
TOSS MINE, TOO, MAEDA!
SURE.
I'VE PLACED THE TALLEST KID IN OUR CLASS, MAEDA, IN FRONT OF SEKI!
NOW HE CAN'T THROW SO EASILY!
GOOD, GOOD, HE'S HAVING TROUBLE!
ひっ HEE
ひっ HEE
ひっ HEE
...

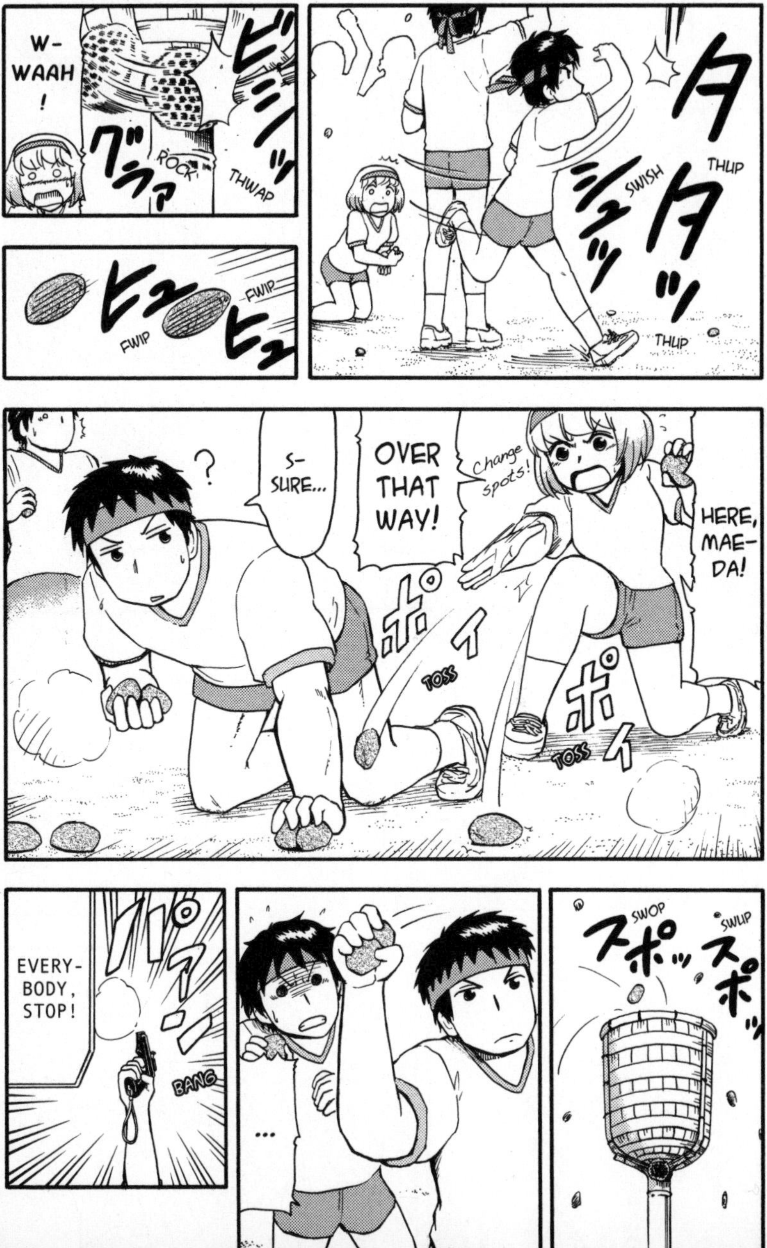

タタッ
THUP
THUP
シュッ
SWISH
W-WAAH!
ビシッ
THWAP
グラァ
ROCK
ヒュ
FWIP
ヒュ
FWIP
HERE, MAEDA!
Change spots!
OVER THAT WAY!
S-SURE...
?
ポイ
TOSS
ポイ
TOSS
スポッ
SWOP
スポッ
SWUP
...
パァーン
BANG
EVERY-BODY, STOP!

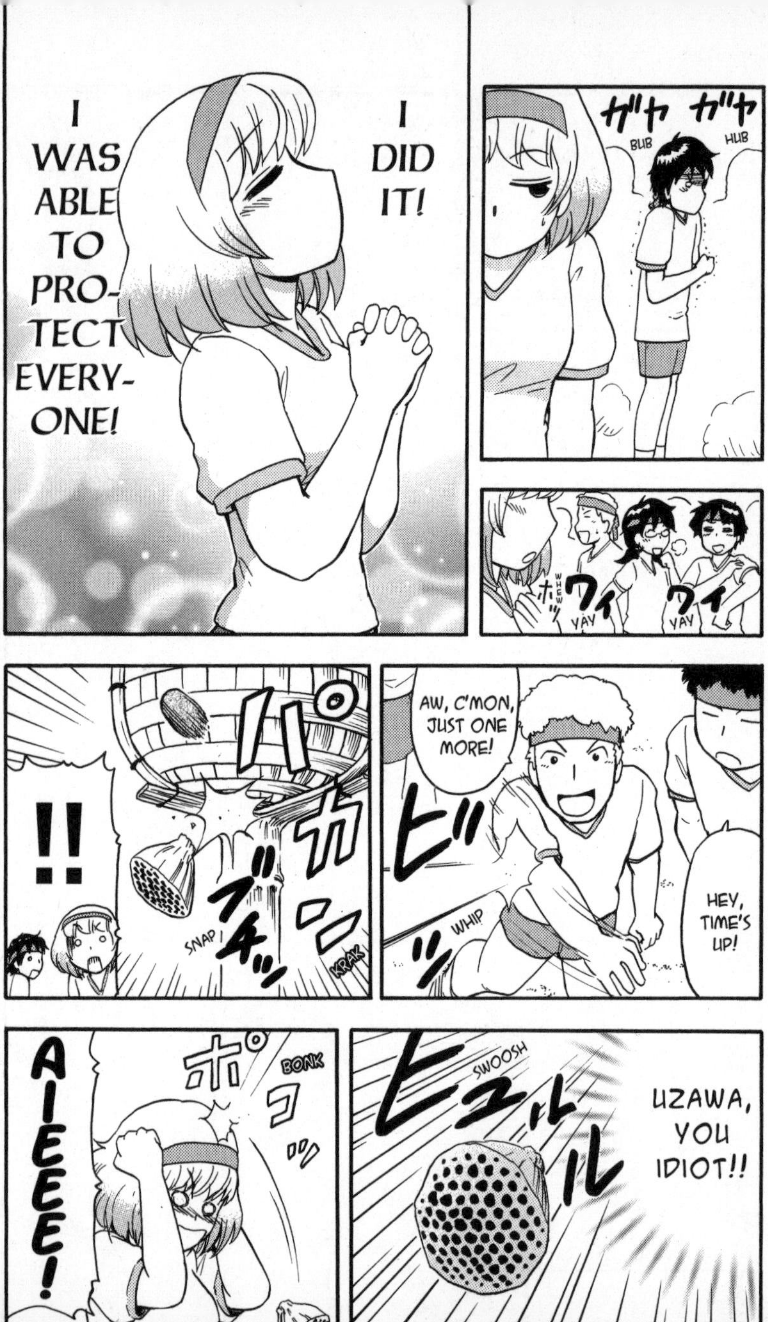

ガヤ ガヤ
BUB HUB
ホッ
WHEW
ワイ
YAY
ワイ
YAY
I DID IT!
I WAS ABLE TO PRO-TECT EVERY-ONE!
AW, C'MON, JUST ONE MORE!
ビッ
WHIP
HEY, TIME'S UP!
パカーン
KRAK
ブチッ
SNAP
!!
ヒュルル
SWOOSH
UZAWA, YOU IDIOT!!
ポコッ
BONK
AIEEEE!

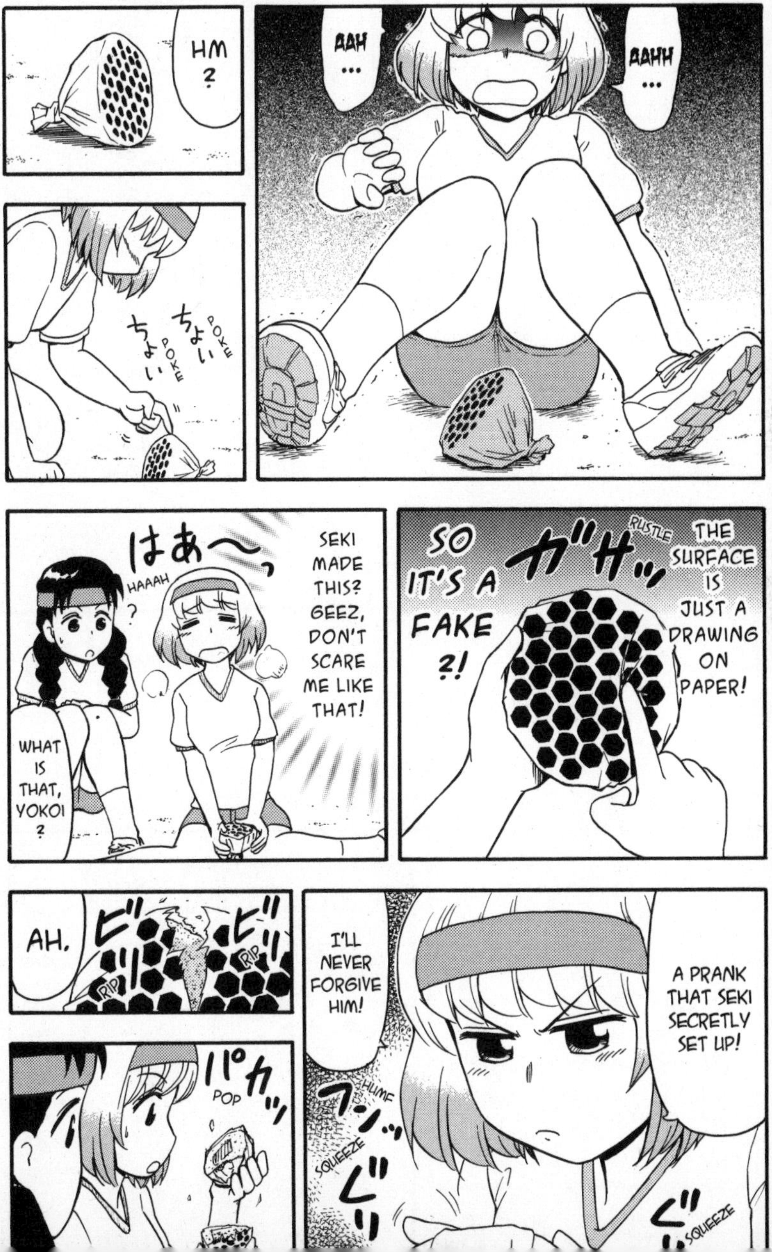
AAHH ...
AAH ...
HM?
ちょい POKE
ちょい POKE
THE SURFACE IS JUST A DRAWING ON PAPER!
ガサッ
RUSTLE
SO IT'S A FAKE?!
SEKI MADE THIS? GEEZ, DON'T SCARE ME LIKE THAT!
はあ〜っ
HAAAH
?
WHAT IS THAT, YOKOI?
A PRANK THAT SEKI SECRETLY SET UP!
I'LL NEVER FORGIVE HIM!
フンッ
HUMF
ぐっ
SQUEEZE
ぐり
SQUEEZE
AH.
ビリ
RIP
ビリ
RIP
パカッ
POP

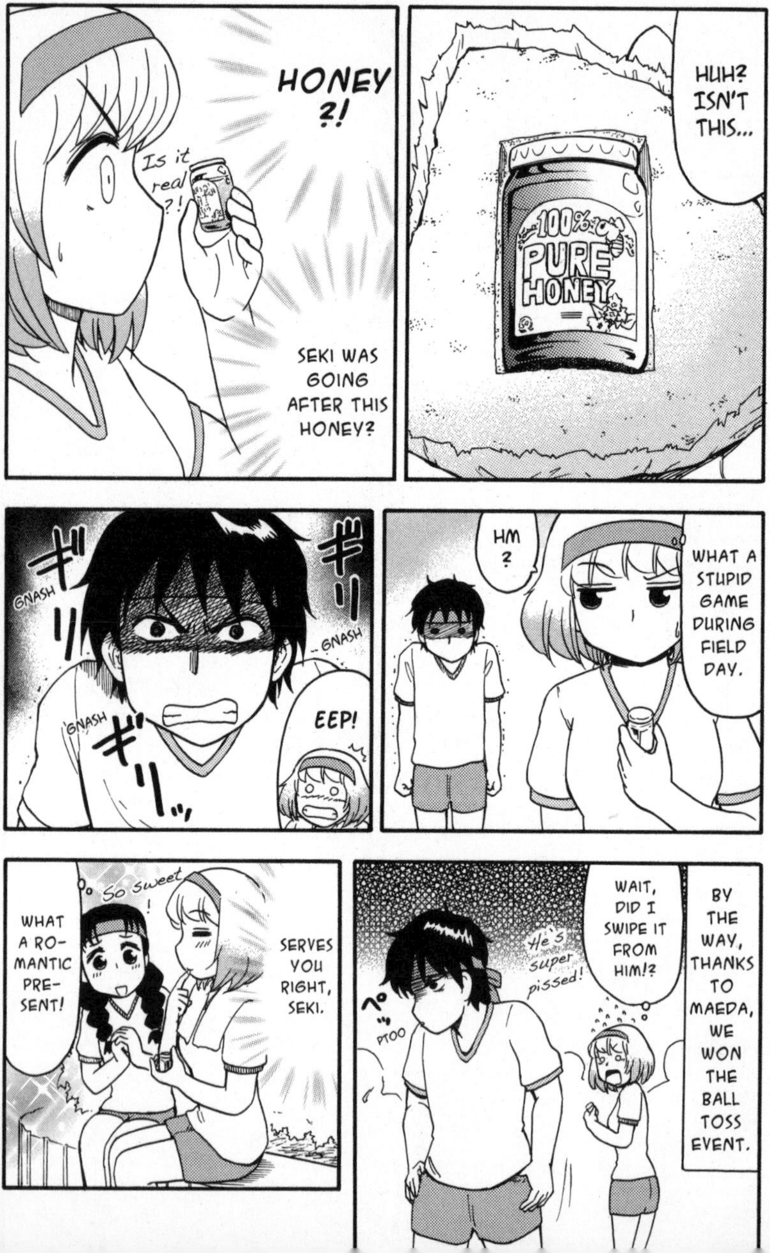
HUH? ISN'T THIS...
100% PURE HONEY
HONEY ?!
Is it real ?!
SEKI WAS GOING AFTER THIS HONEY?
HM ?
WHAT A STUPID GAME DURING FIELD DAY.
ギリ
GNASH
ギリ
GNASH
ギリッ
GNASH
EEP!
BY THE WAY, THANKS TO MAEDA, WE WON THE BALL TOSS EVENT.
WAIT, DID I SWIPE IT FROM HIM!?
He's super pissed!
PTOO
SERVES YOU RIGHT, SEKI.
So sweet!
WHAT A RO-MANTIC PRE-SENT!

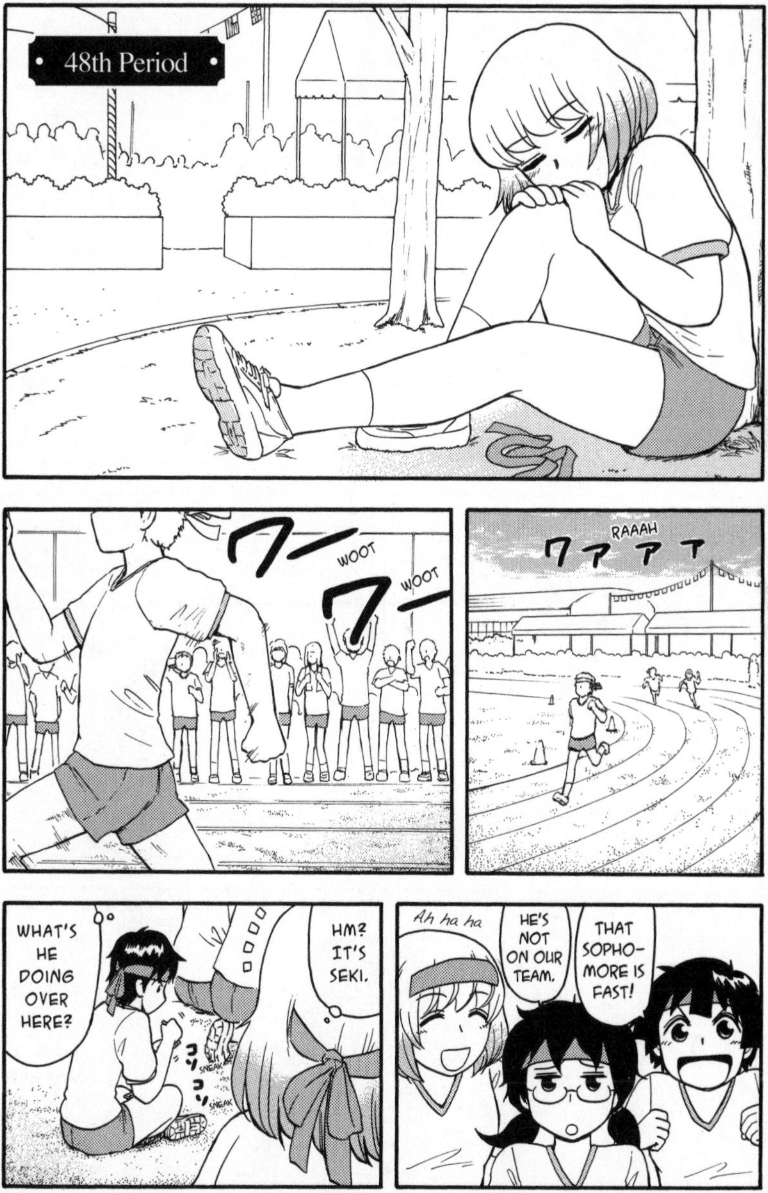
• 48th Period •
ワァアア
RAAAH
ワー
WOOT
ワー
WOOT
THAT SOPHOMORE IS FAST!
HE'S NOT ON OUR TEAM.
Ah ha ha
HM? IT'S SEKI.
WHAT'S HE DOING OVER HERE?
コソ
SNEAK
コソ
SNEAK

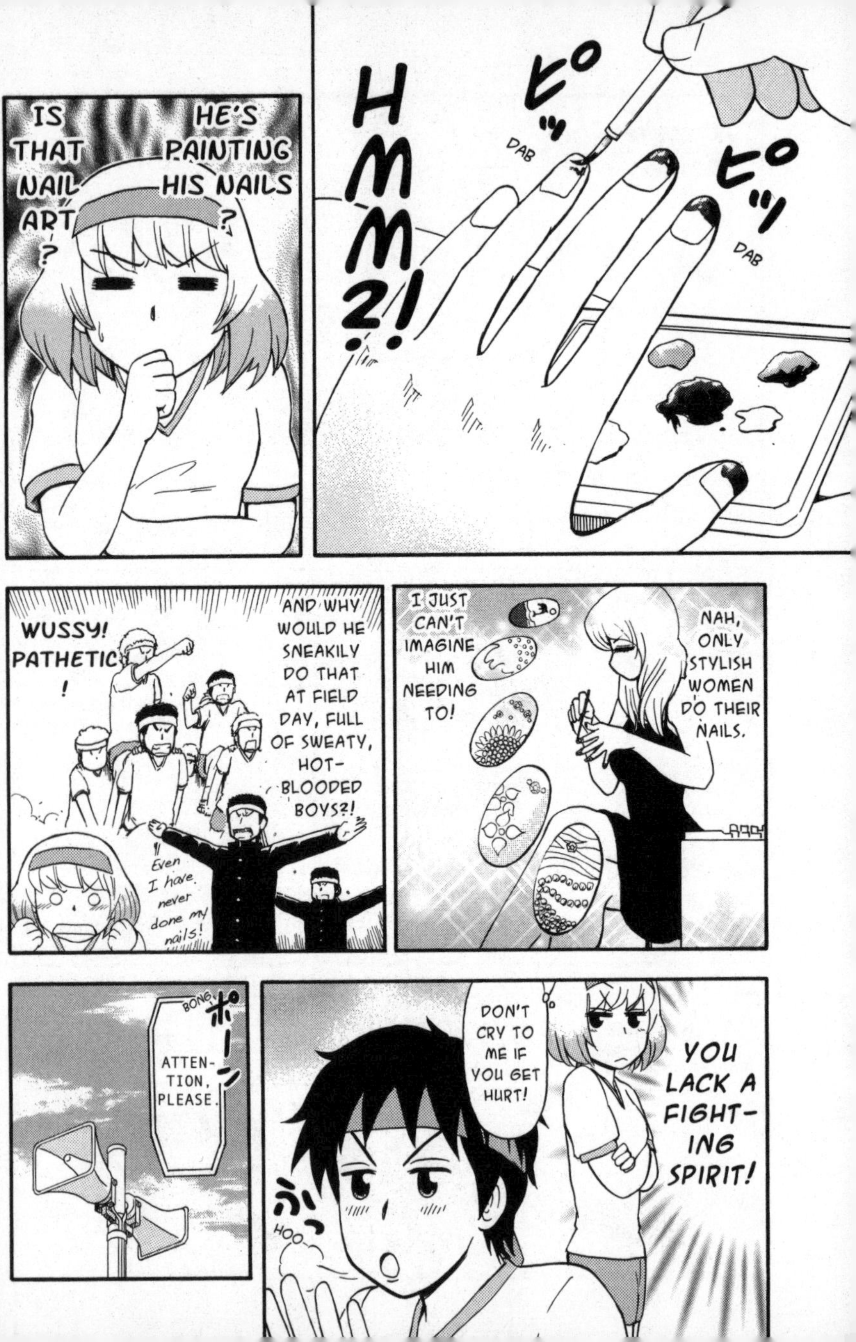
HMM?!
DAB
DAB
HE'S PAINTING HIS NAILS?
IS THAT NAIL ART?
NAH, ONLY STYLISH WOMEN DO THEIR NAILS.
I JUST CAN'T IMAGINE HIM NEEDING TO!
AND WHY WOULD HE SNEAKILY DO THAT AT FIELD DAY, FULL OF SWEATY, HOT-BLOODED BOYS?!
WUSSY! PATHETIC!
Even I have never done my nails!
YOU LACK A FIGHTING SPIRIT!
DON'T CRY TO ME IF YOU GET HURT!
HOO—
BONG
ATTENTION, PLEASE.

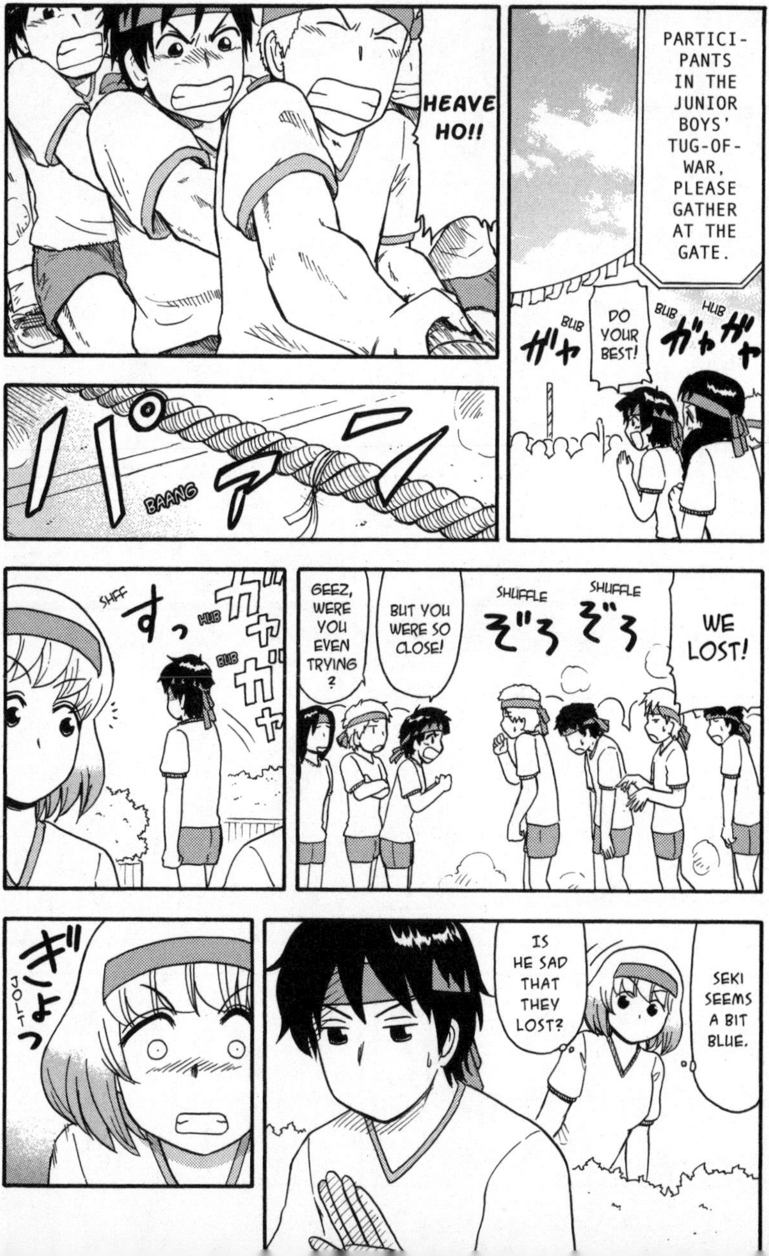
PARTICIPANTS IN THE JUNIOR BOYS' TUG-OF-WAR, PLEASE GATHER AT THE GATE.
HUB BUB
ガヤガヤ
DO YOUR BEST!
BUB
ガヤ
HEAVE HO!!
パァーン
BAANG
WE LOST!
SHUFFLE SHUFFLE
ぞろぞろ
BUT YOU WERE SO CLOSE!
GEEZ, WERE YOU EVEN TRYING?
HUB BUB
ガヤガヤ
SHFF
すっ
SEKI SEEMS A BIT BLUE.
IS HE SAD THAT THEY LOST?
ぎょっ
JOLT

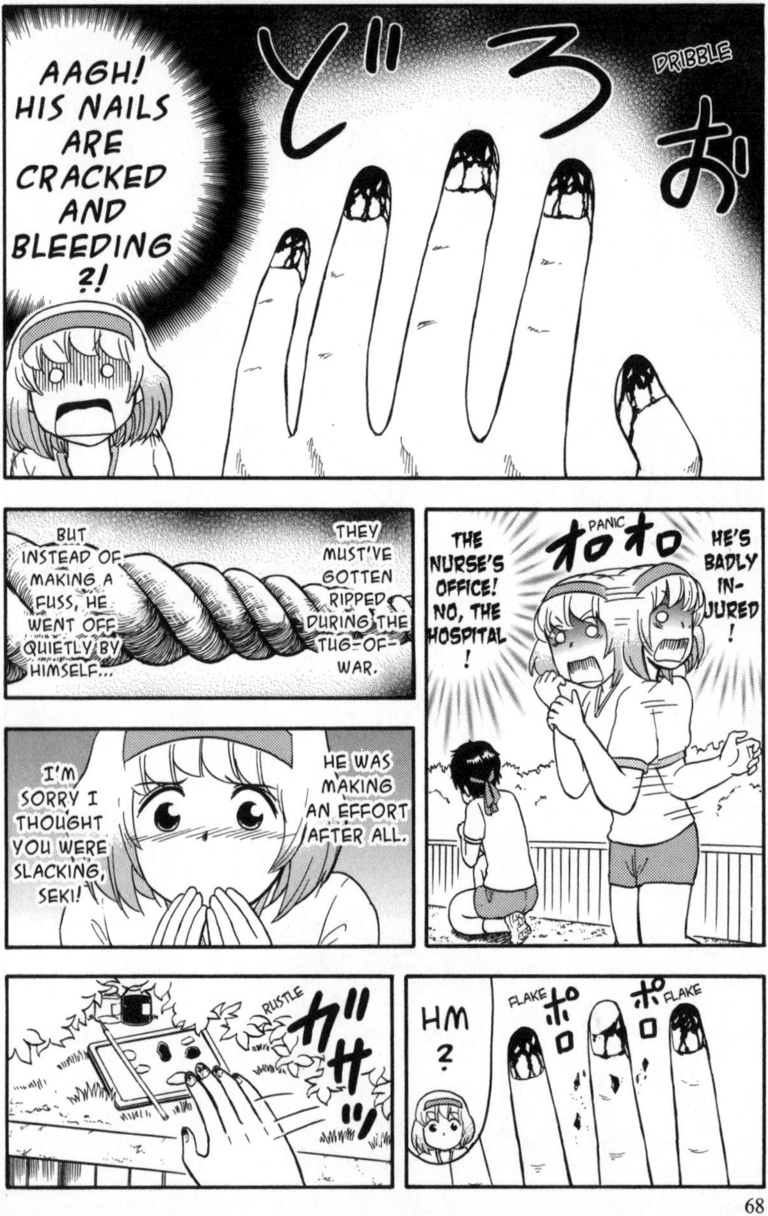
どろぉ
DRIBBLE
AAGH! HIS NAILS ARE CRACKED AND BLEEDING ?!
オロオロ
PANIC
HE'S BADLY IN-JURED!
THE NURSE'S OFFICE! NO, THE HOSPITAL!
THEY MUST'VE GOTTEN RIPPED DURING THE TUG-OF-WAR.
BUT INSTEAD OF MAKING A FUSS, HE WENT OFF QUIETLY BY HIMSELF...
HE WAS MAKING AN EFFORT AFTER ALL.
I'M SORRY I THOUGHT YOU WERE SLACKING, SEKI!
ポロ
FLAKE
ポロ
FLAKE
HM ?
ガサッ
RUSTLE

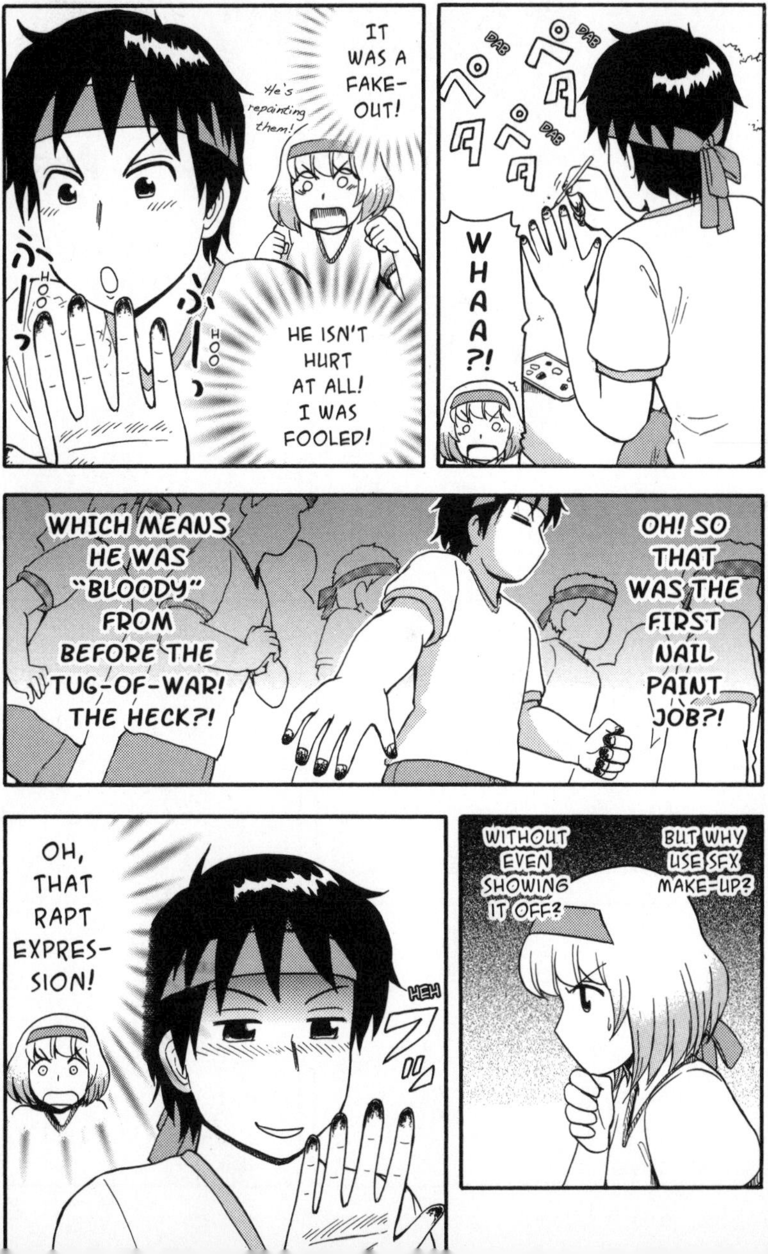
DAB
DAB
DAB
WHAAA?!
IT WAS A FAKE-OUT!
He's repainting them!
HOO
HOO
HE ISN'T HURT AT ALL! I WAS FOOLED!
OH! SO THAT WAS THE FIRST NAIL PAINT JOB?!
WHICH MEANS HE WAS "BLOODY" FROM BEFORE THE TUG-OF-WAR! THE HECK?!
BUT WHY USE SFX MAKE-UP?
WITHOUT EVEN SHOWING IT OFF?
OH, THAT RAPT EXPRESSION!
HEH

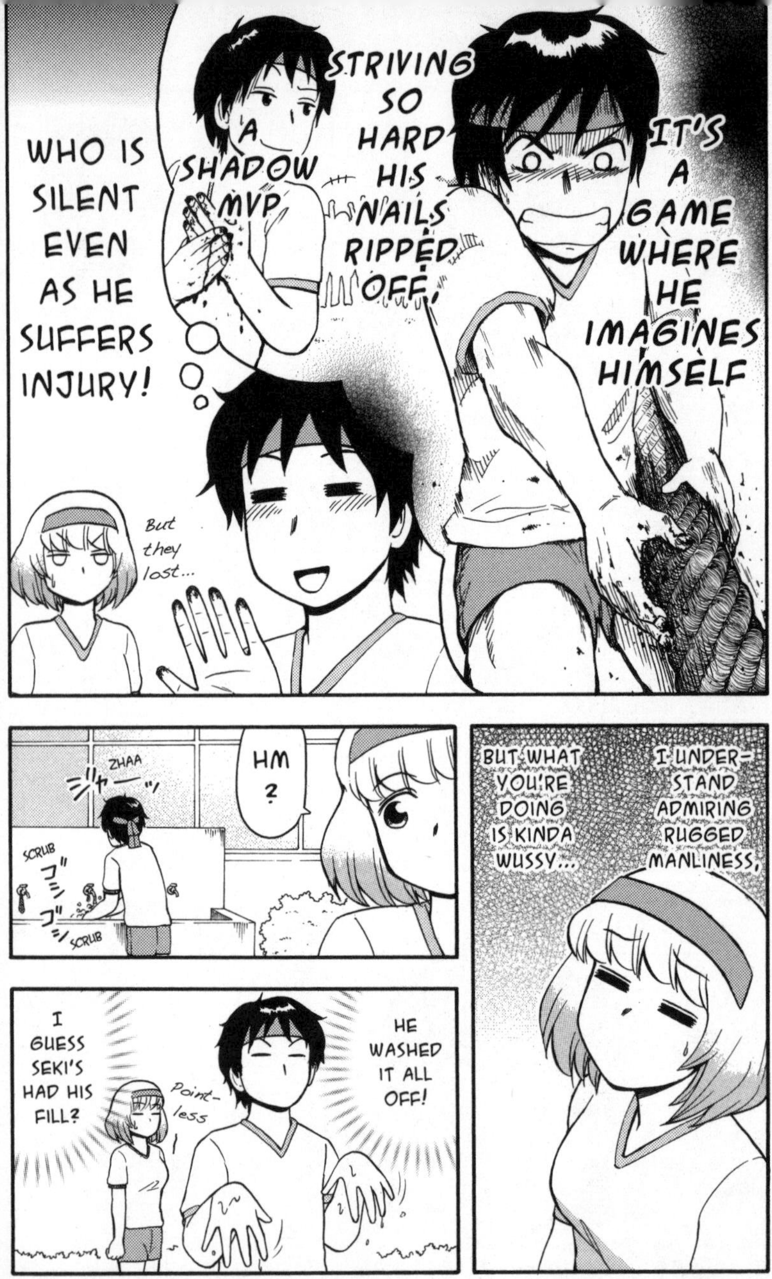
IT'S A GAME WHERE HE IMAGINES HIMSELF
STRIVING SO HARD HIS NAILS RIPPED OFF,
A SHADOW MVP
WHO IS SILENT EVEN AS HE SUFFERS INJURY!
But they lost...
I UNDER-STAND ADMIRING RUGGED MANLINESS,
BUT WHAT YOU'RE DOING IS KINDA WUSSY...
HM?
ZHAA
ジャーッ
SCRUB
ゴシゴシ
SCRUB
HE WASHED IT ALL OFF!
Point-less
I GUESS SEKI'S HAD HIS FILL?

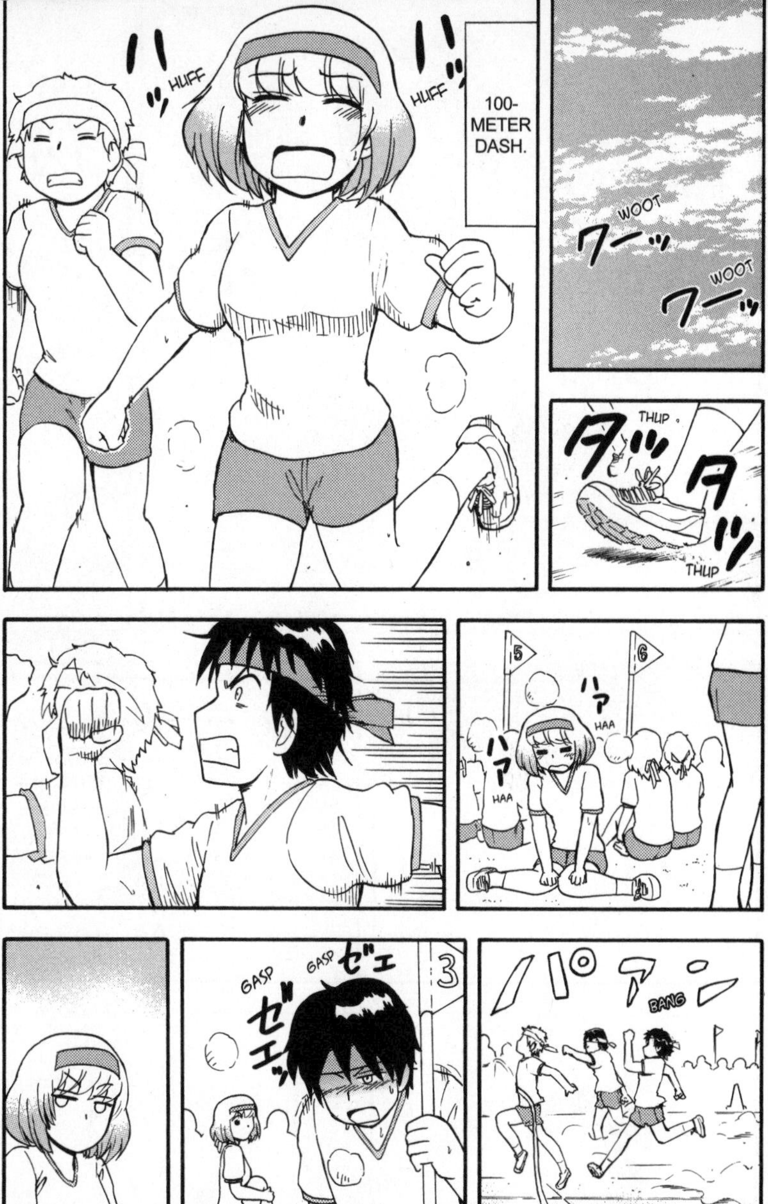
WOOT
ワーッ
WOOT
ワーッ
タッ
THUP
タッ
THUP
100-METER DASH.
ハッ
HUFF
ハッ
HUFF
ハァ
HAA
ハァ
HAA
5
6
パァン
BANG
ゼェ
GASP
ゼェッ
GASP
3

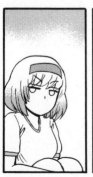

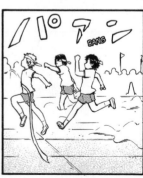

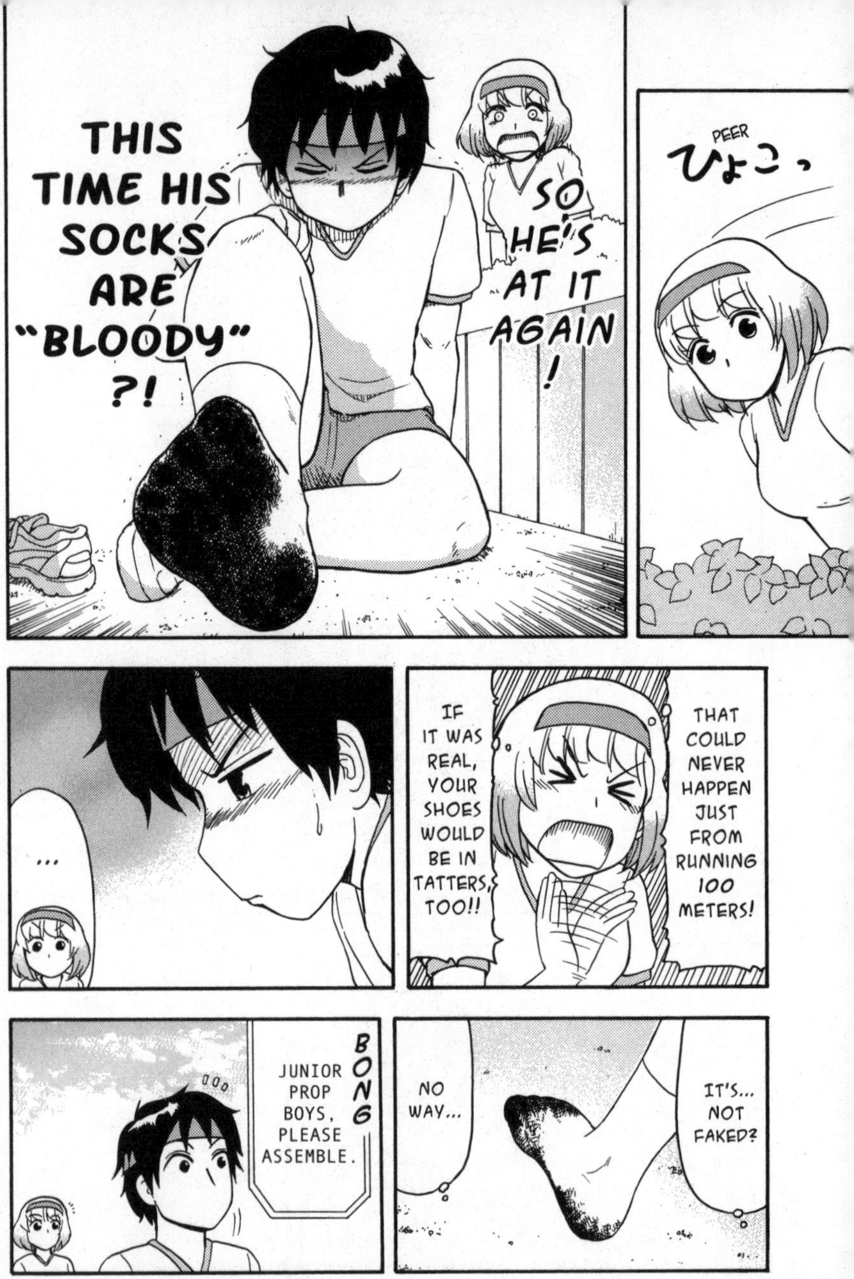
PEER
ひょこっ
SO HE'S AT IT AGAIN!
THIS TIME HIS SOCKS ARE "BLOODY"?!
THAT COULD NEVER HAPPEN JUST FROM RUNNING 100 METERS!
IF IT WAS REAL, YOUR SHOES WOULD BE IN TATTERS, TOO!!
...
IT'S... NOT FAKED?
NO WAY...
BONG
JUNIOR PROP BOYS, PLEASE ASSEMBLE.

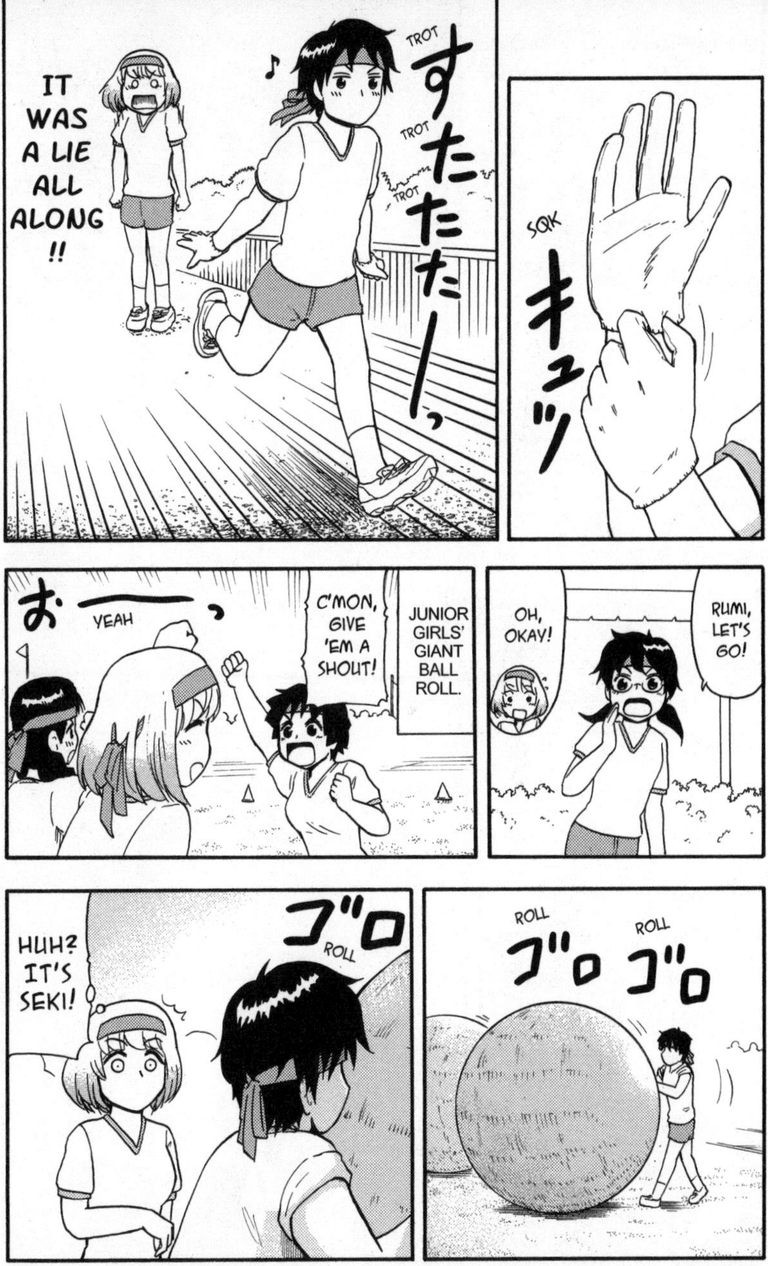
SQK
キュッ
TROT
TROT
TROT
すたたたーっ
IT WAS A LIE ALL ALONG!!
RUMI, LET'S GO!
OH, OKAY!
JUNIOR GIRLS' GIANT BALL ROLL.
C'MON, GIVE 'EM A SHOUT!
おーーっ
YEAH
ROLL
ROLL
ゴロゴロ
ゴロ
ROLL
HUH? IT'S SEKI!

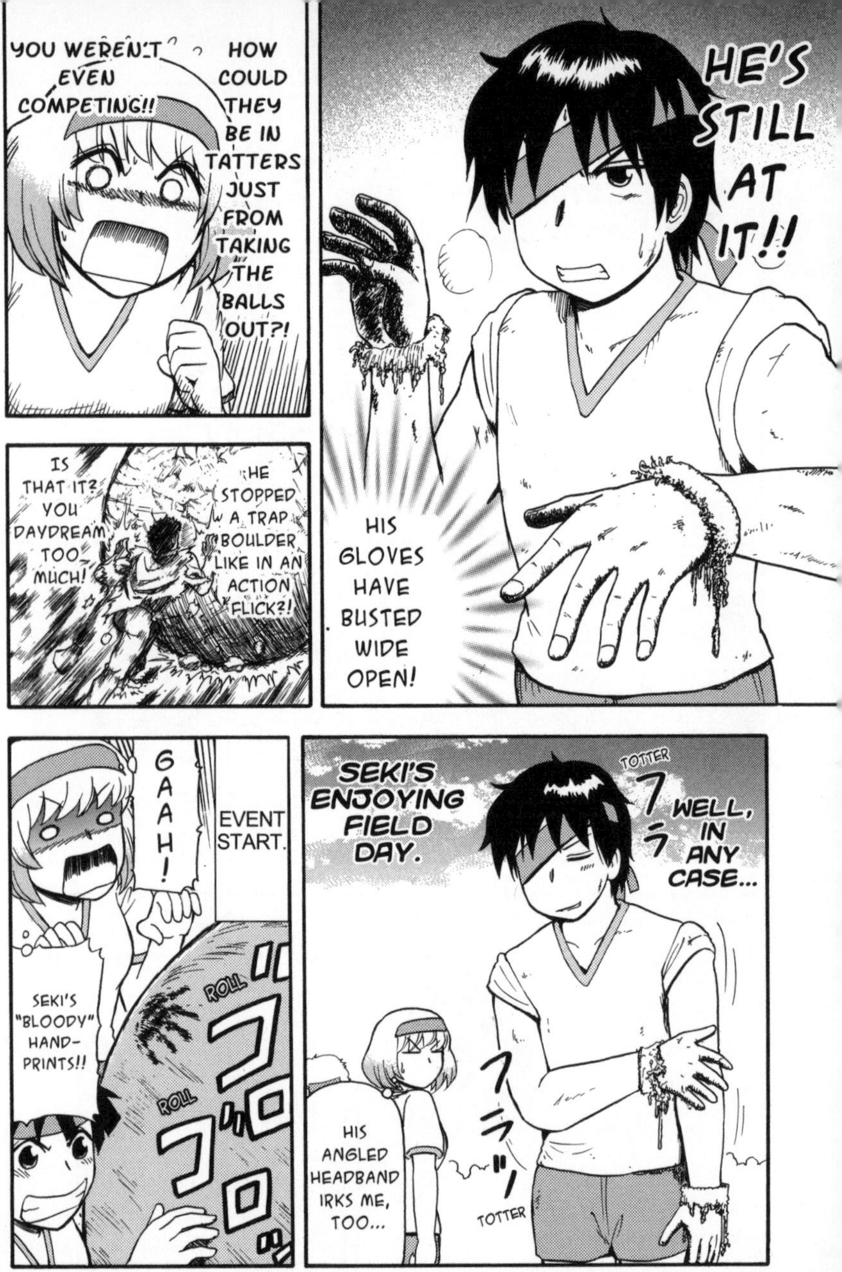
HE'S STILL AT IT!!
HIS GLOVES HAVE BUSTED WIDE OPEN!
HOW COULD THEY BE IN TATTERS JUST FROM TAKING THE BALLS OUT?!
YOU WEREN'T EVEN COMPETING!!
HE STOPPED A TRAP BOULDER LIKE IN AN ACTION FLICK?!
IS THAT IT? YOU DAYDREAM TOO MUCH!
TOTTER
WELL, IN ANY CASE...
SEKI'S ENJOYING FIELD DAY.
HIS ANGLED HEADBAND IRKS ME, TOO...
TOTTER
GAAAH!
EVENT START.
SEKI'S "BLOODY" HAND-PRINTS!!
ROLL
ROLL

My Neighbor Seki

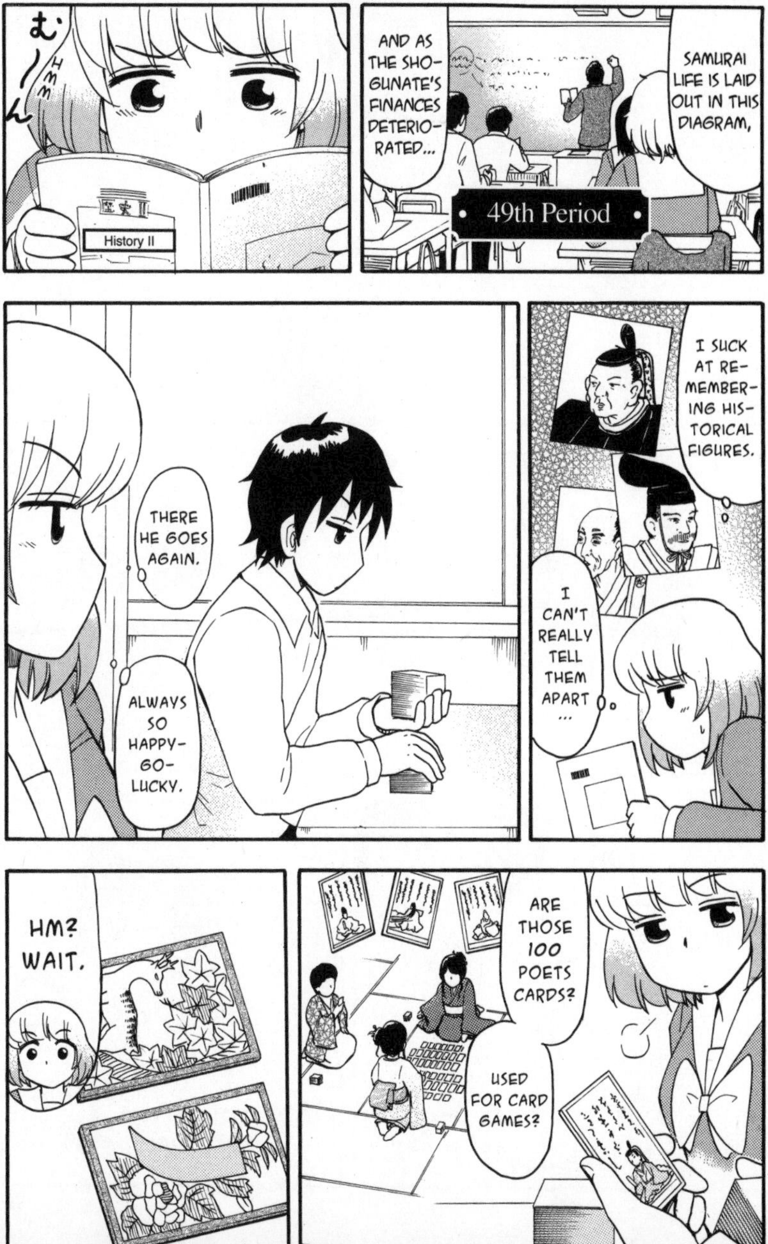

SAMURAI LIFE IS LAID OUT IN THIS DIAGRAM,
AND AS THE SHOGUNATE'S FINANCES DETERIORATED...
49th Period
むーん
HMM
History II
I SUCK AT REMEMBERING HISTORICAL FIGURES.
I CAN'T REALLY TELL THEM APART...
THERE HE GOES AGAIN.
ALWAYS SO HAPPY-GO-LUCKY.
ARE THOSE 100 POETS CARDS?
USED FOR CARD GAMES?
HM? WAIT.

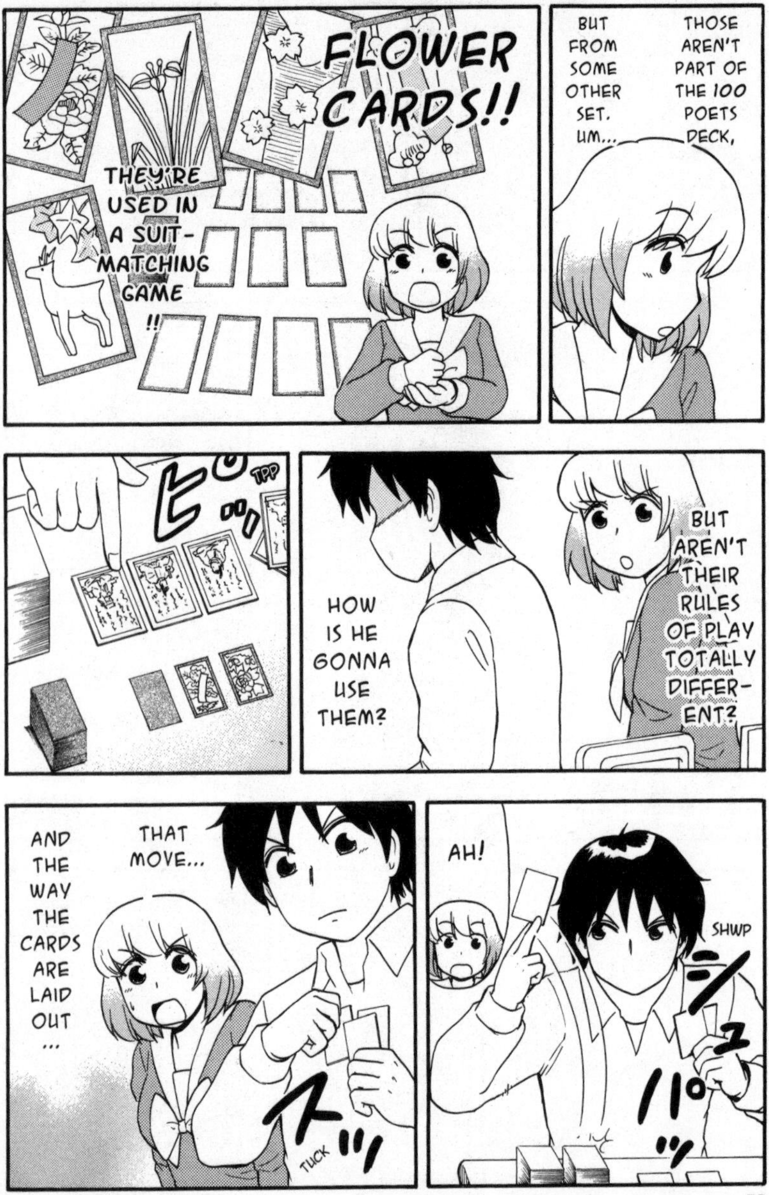
THOSE AREN'T PART OF THE 100 POETS DECK,
BUT FROM SOME OTHER SET. UM...
FLOWER CARDS!!
THEY'RE USED IN A SUIT-MATCHING GAME !!
BUT AREN'T THEIR RULES OF PLAY TOTALLY DIFFER-ENT?
HOW IS HE GONNA USE THEM?
TPP
AH!
SHWP
THAT MOVE...
AND THE WAY THE CARDS ARE LAID OUT ...
TUCK

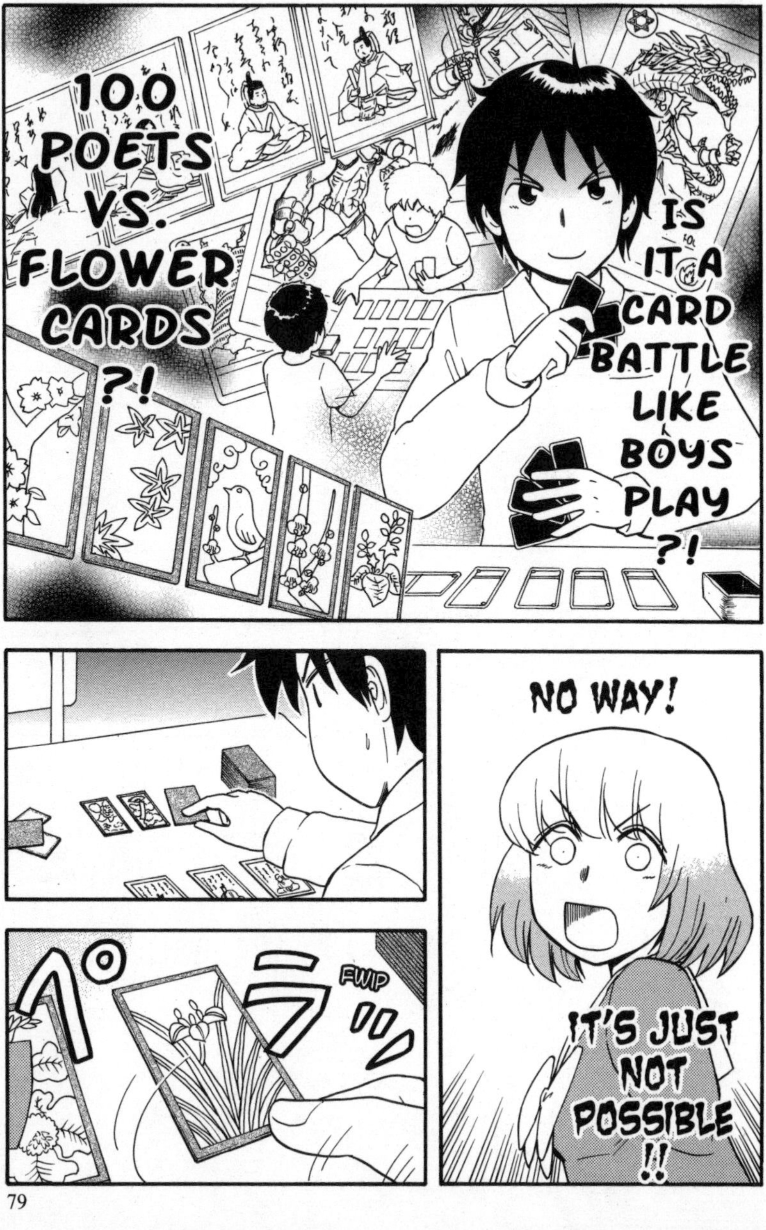
100 POETS VS. FLOWER CARDS ?!
IS IT A CARD BATTLE LIKE BOYS PLAY ?!
NO WAY!
IT'S JUST NOT POSSIBLE !!
ペラッ
FWIP

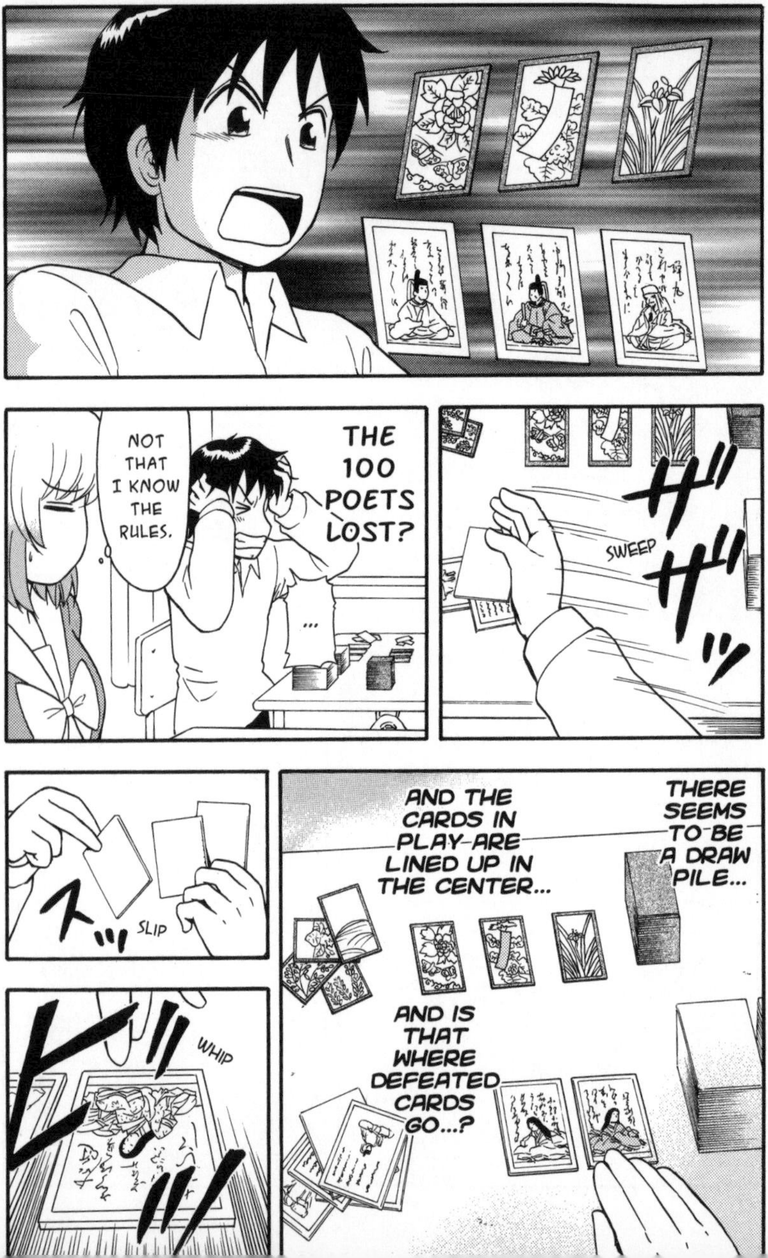
ザザッ
SWEEP
THE 100 POETS LOST?
NOT THAT I KNOW THE RULES.
...
THERE SEEMS TO BE A DRAW PILE...
AND THE CARDS IN PLAY ARE LINED UP IN THE CENTER...
AND IS THAT WHERE DEFEATED CARDS GO...?
スッ
SLIP
WHIP

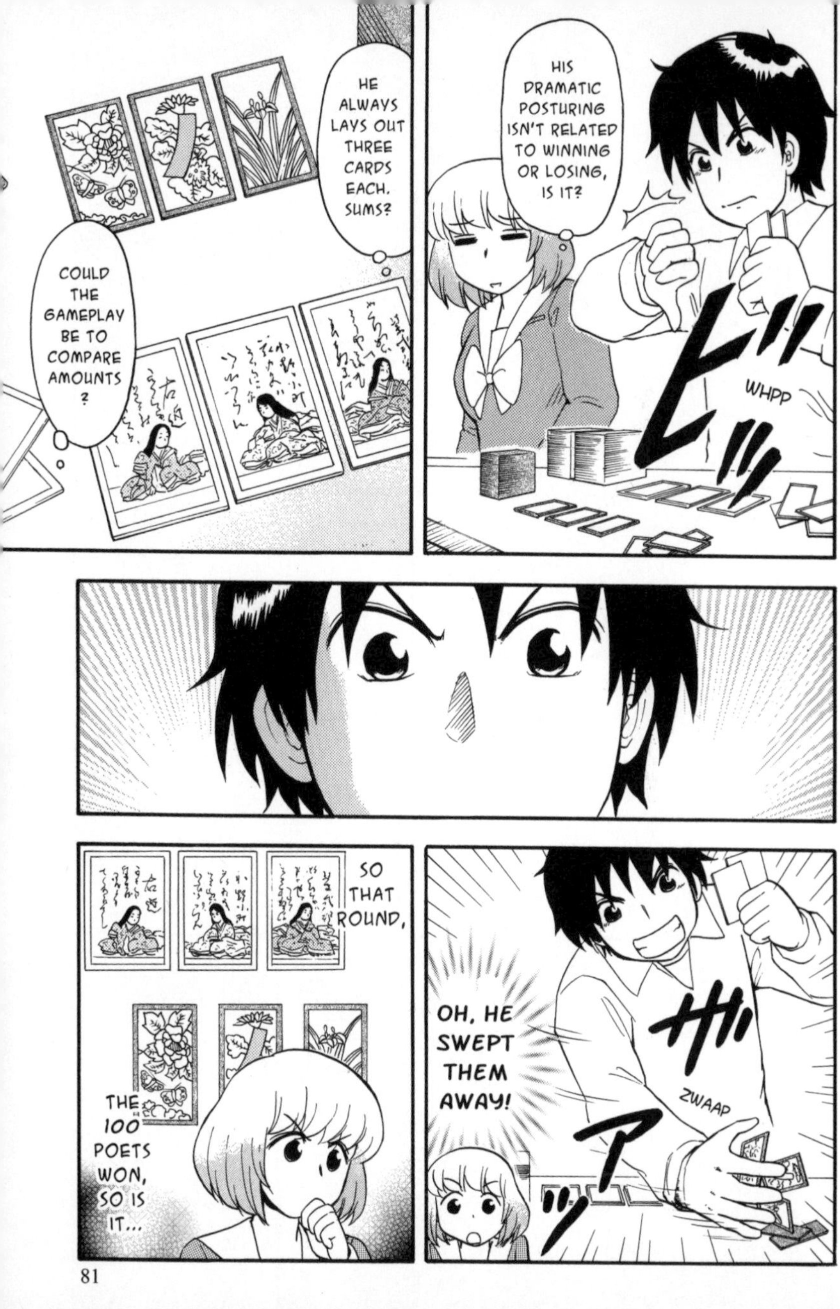
HIS DRAMATIC POSTURING ISN'T RELATED TO WINNING OR LOSING, IS IT?
WHPP
HE ALWAYS LAYS OUT THREE CARDS EACH. SUMS?
COULD THE GAMEPLAY BE TO COMPARE AMOUNTS ?
OH, HE SWEPT THEM AWAY!
ZWAAP
SO THAT ROUND,
THE 100 POETS WON, SO IS IT...

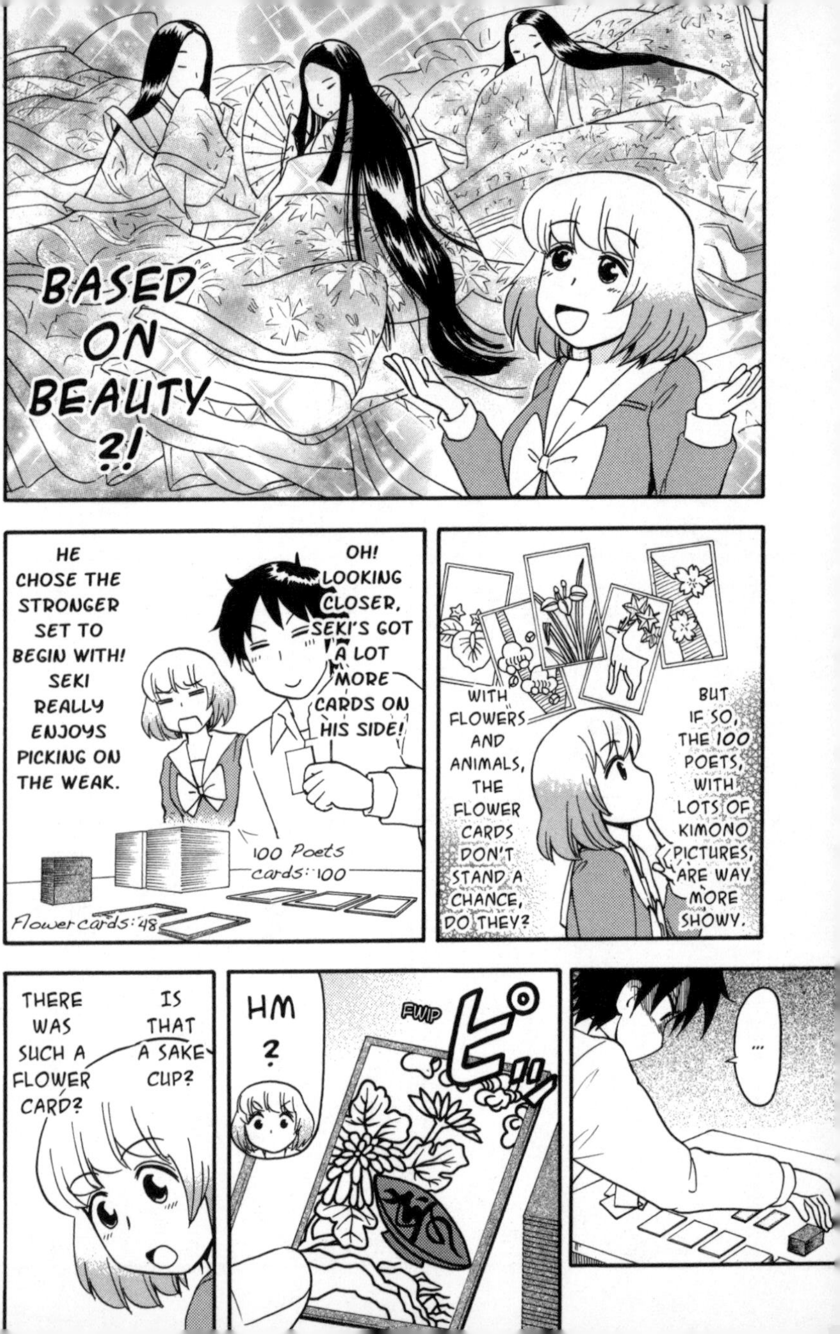
BASED ON BEAUTY ?!
BUT IF SO, THE 100 POETS, WITH LOTS OF KIMONO PICTURES, ARE WAY MORE SHOWY.
WITH FLOWERS AND ANIMALS, THE FLOWER CARDS DON'T STAND A CHANCE, DO THEY?
OH! LOOKING CLOSER, SEKI'S GOT A LOT MORE CARDS ON HIS SIDE!
HE CHOSE THE STRONGER SET TO BEGIN WITH! SEKI REALLY ENJOYS PICKING ON THE WEAK.
100 Poets cards: 100
Flower cards: 48
...
HM ?
FWIP
IS THAT A SAKE CUP?
THERE WAS SUCH A FLOWER CARD?

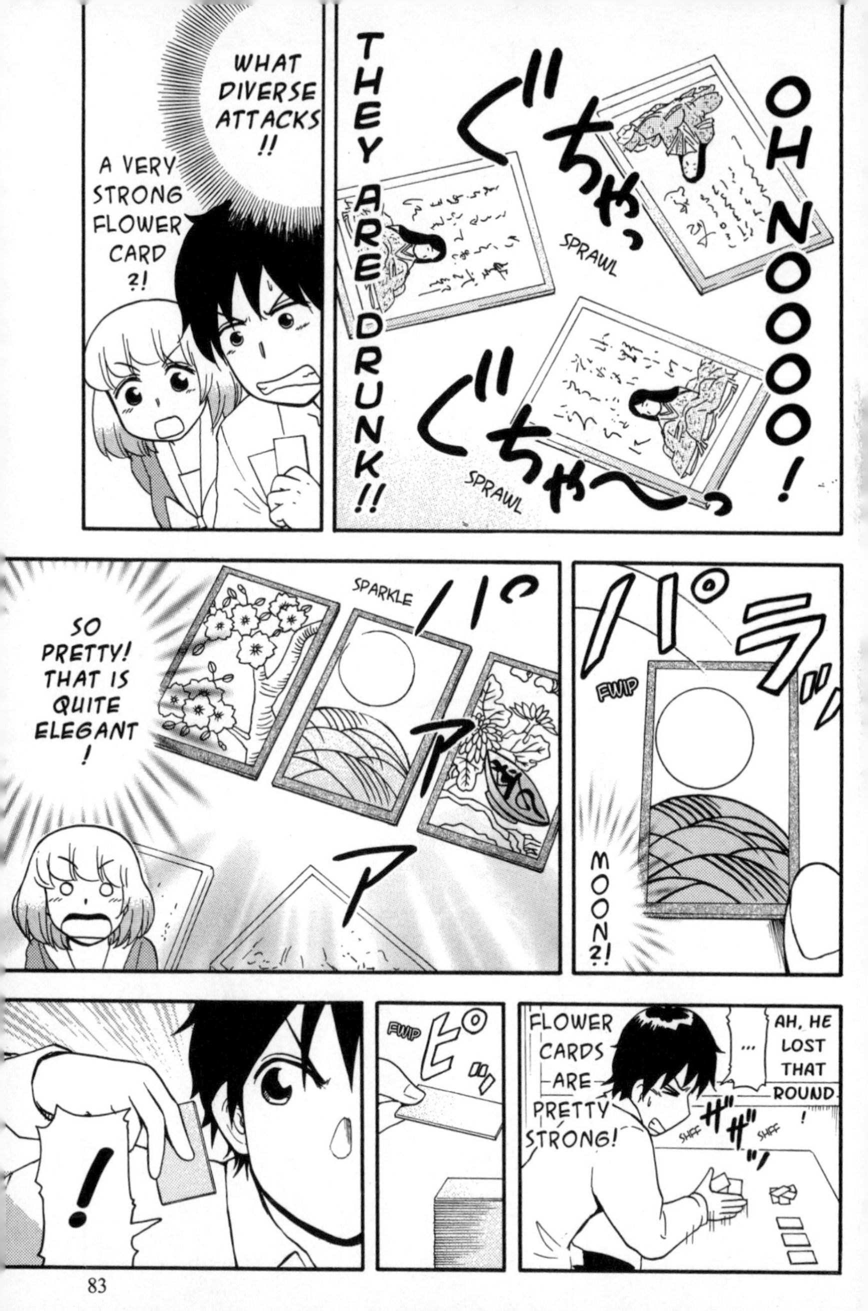
OH NOOOOO!
SPRAWL
SPRAWL
THEY ARE DRUNK!!
WHAT DIVERSE ATTACKS!!
A VERY STRONG FLOWER CARD?!
FWIP
MOON?!
SPARKLE
SO PRETTY! THAT IS QUITE ELEGANT!
AH, HE LOST THAT ROUND!
...
FLOWER CARDS ARE PRETTY STRONG!
SHFF
SHFF
FWIP
!

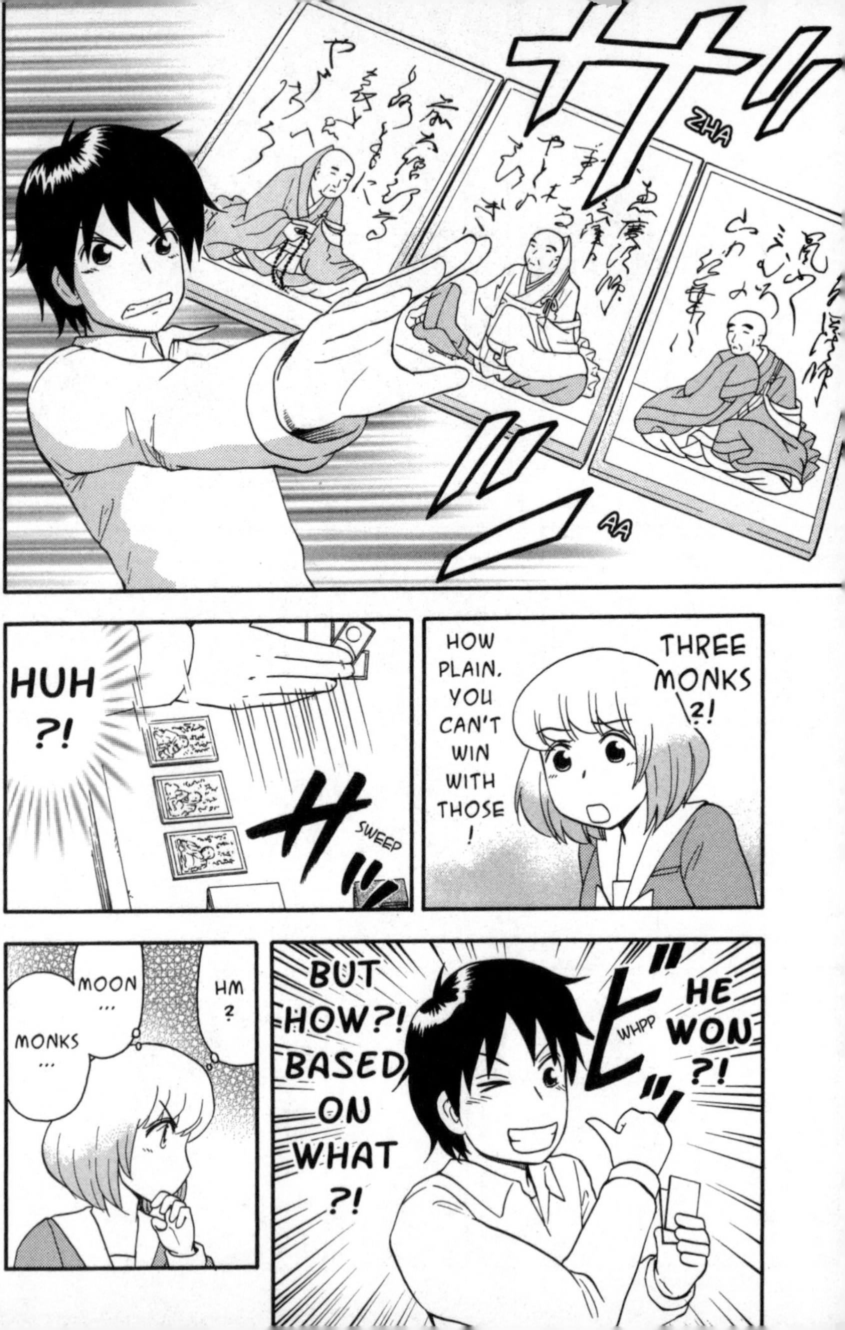
ZHA
AA
THREE MONKS ?!
HOW PLAIN. YOU CAN'T WIN WITH THOSE!
HUH ?!
SWEEP
HE WON ?!
WHPP
BUT HOW?! BASED ON WHAT ?!
HM ?
MOON ...
MONKS ...

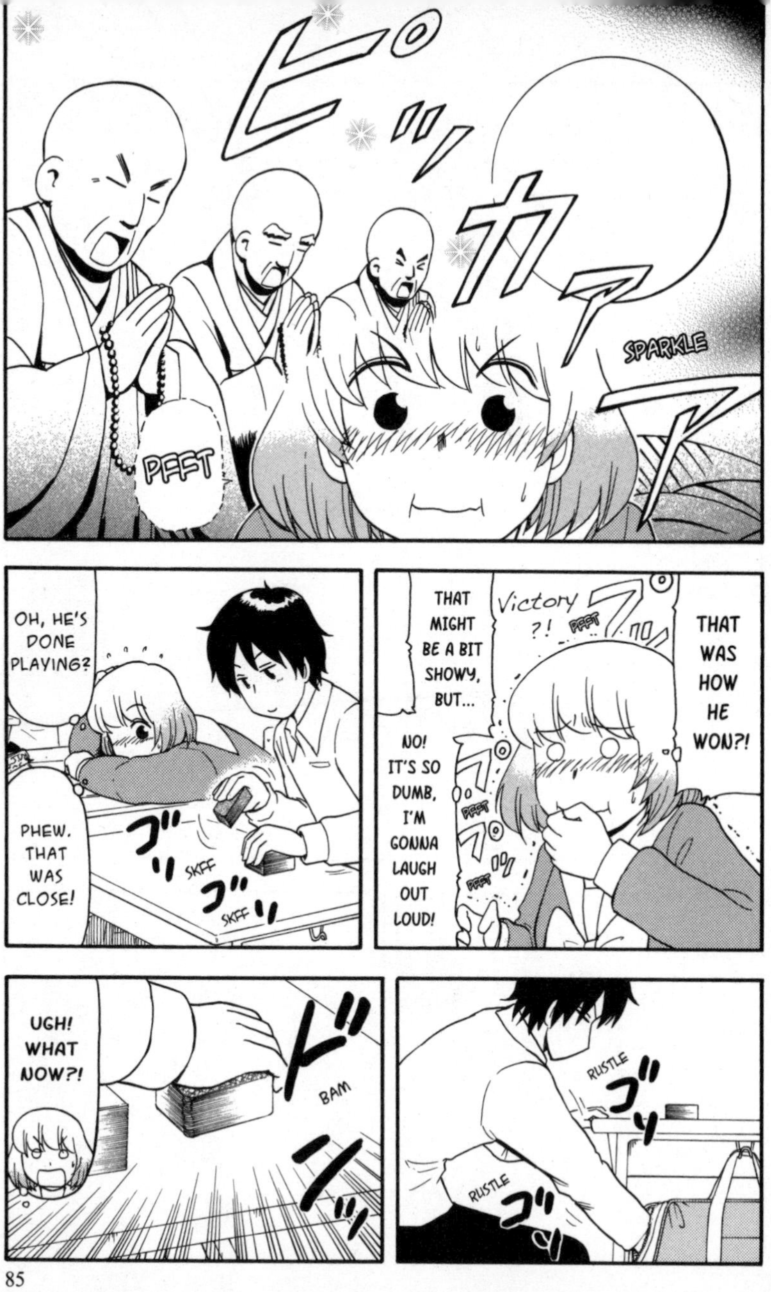
SPARKLE
PFFT
THAT WAS HOW HE WON?!
Victory ?!
PFFT
THAT MIGHT BE A BIT SHOWY, BUT...
NO! IT'S SO DUMB, I'M GONNA LAUGH OUT LOUD!
PFFT
PFFT
OH, HE'S DONE PLAYING?
PHEW. THAT WAS CLOSE!
SKFF
SKFF
RUSTLE
RUSTLE
BAM
UGH! WHAT NOW?!

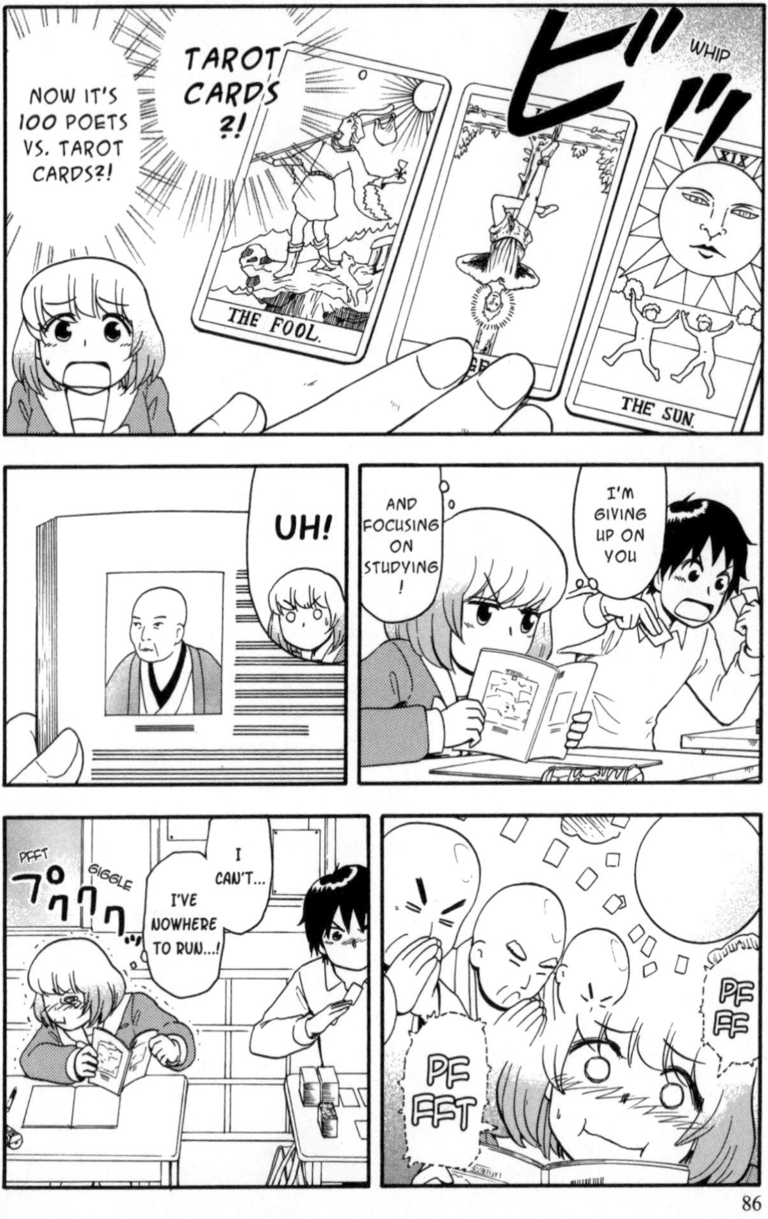
ビッ
WHIP
TAROT CARDS?!
NOW IT'S 100 POETS VS. TAROT CARDS?!
THE FOOL.
XIX
THE SUN.
I'M GIVING UP ON YOU
AND FOCUSING ON STUDYING!
UH!
PF FF
PF FFT
I CAN'T...
I'VE NOWHERE TO RUN...!
PFFT
GIGGLE
プククク

50th Period

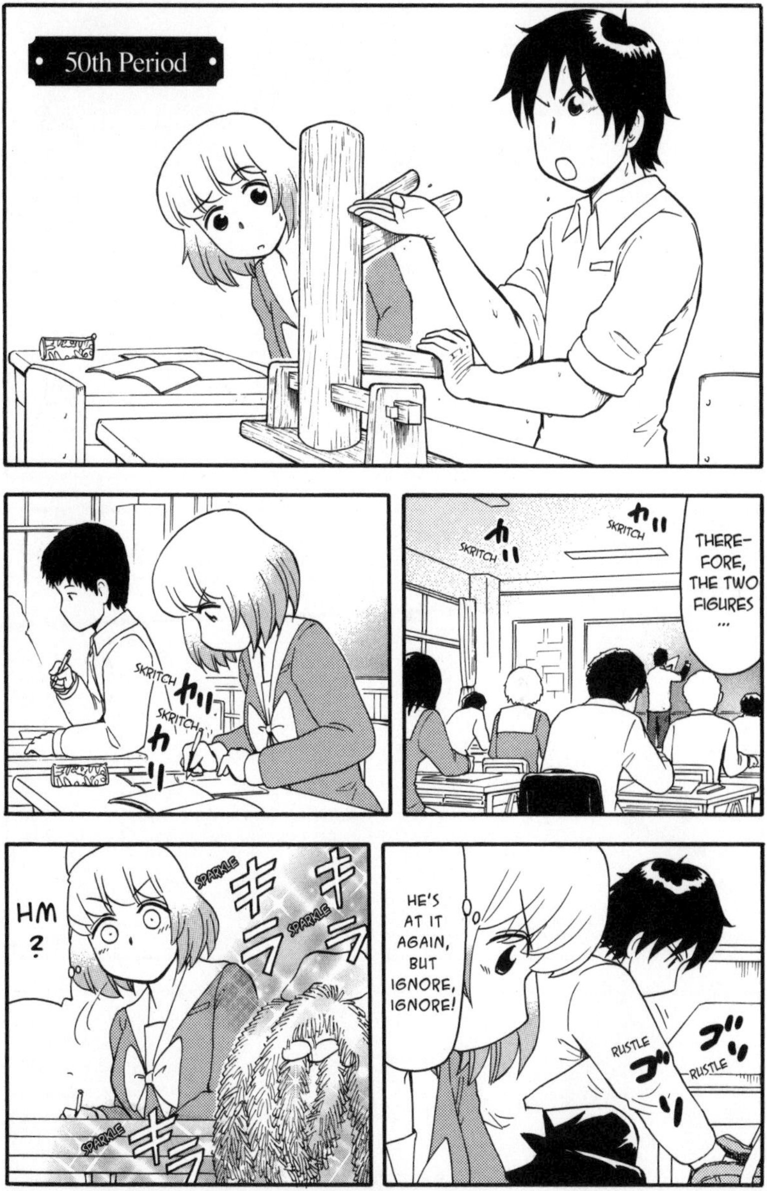

SKRITCH
SKRITCH
THERE-FORE, THE TWO FIGURES ...
SKRITCH
SKRITCH
HE'S AT IT AGAIN, BUT IGNORE, IGNORE!
RUSTLE
RUSTLE
HM ?
SPARKLE
SPARKLE
SPARKLE

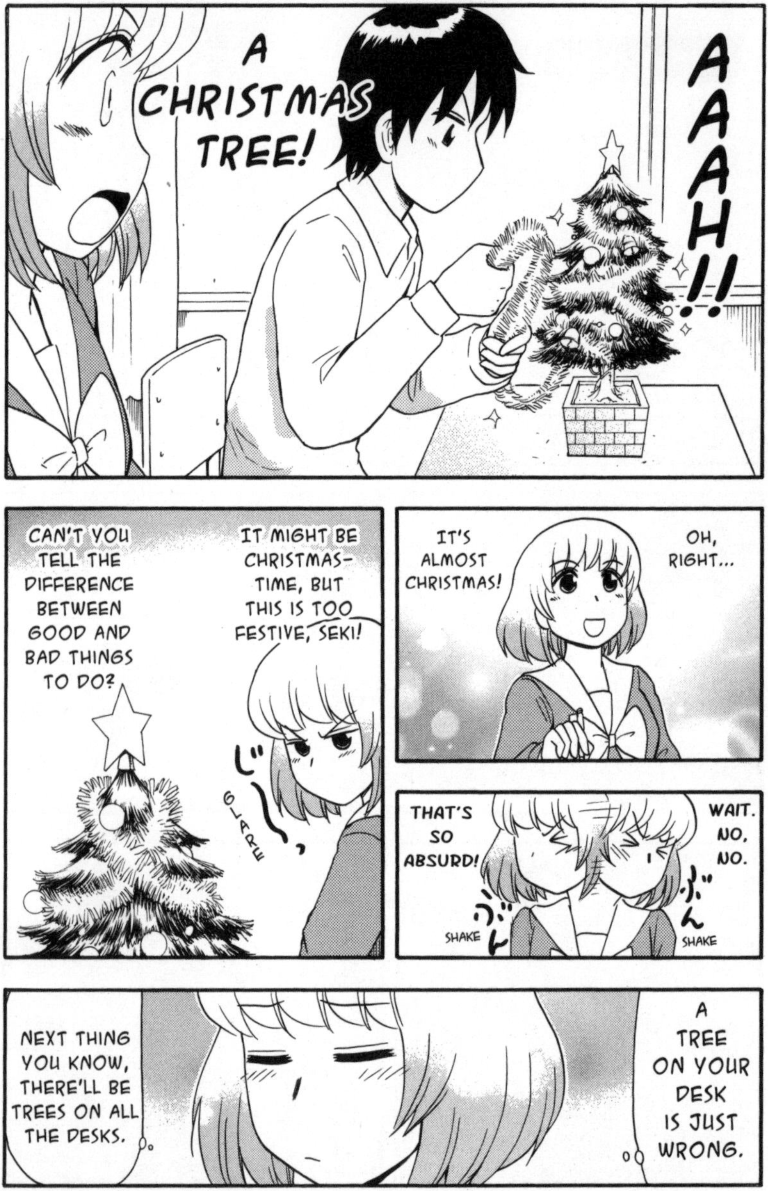
AAAAH!!
A CHRISTMAS TREE!
OH, RIGHT...
IT'S ALMOST CHRISTMAS!
WAIT. NO. NO.
SHAKE
THAT'S SO ABSURD!
SHAKE
IT MIGHT BE CHRISTMAS-TIME, BUT THIS IS TOO FESTIVE, SEKI!
CAN'T YOU TELL THE DIFFERENCE BETWEEN GOOD AND BAD THINGS TO DO?
GLARE
A TREE ON YOUR DESK IS JUST WRONG.
NEXT THING YOU KNOW, THERE'LL BE TREES ON ALL THE DESKS.

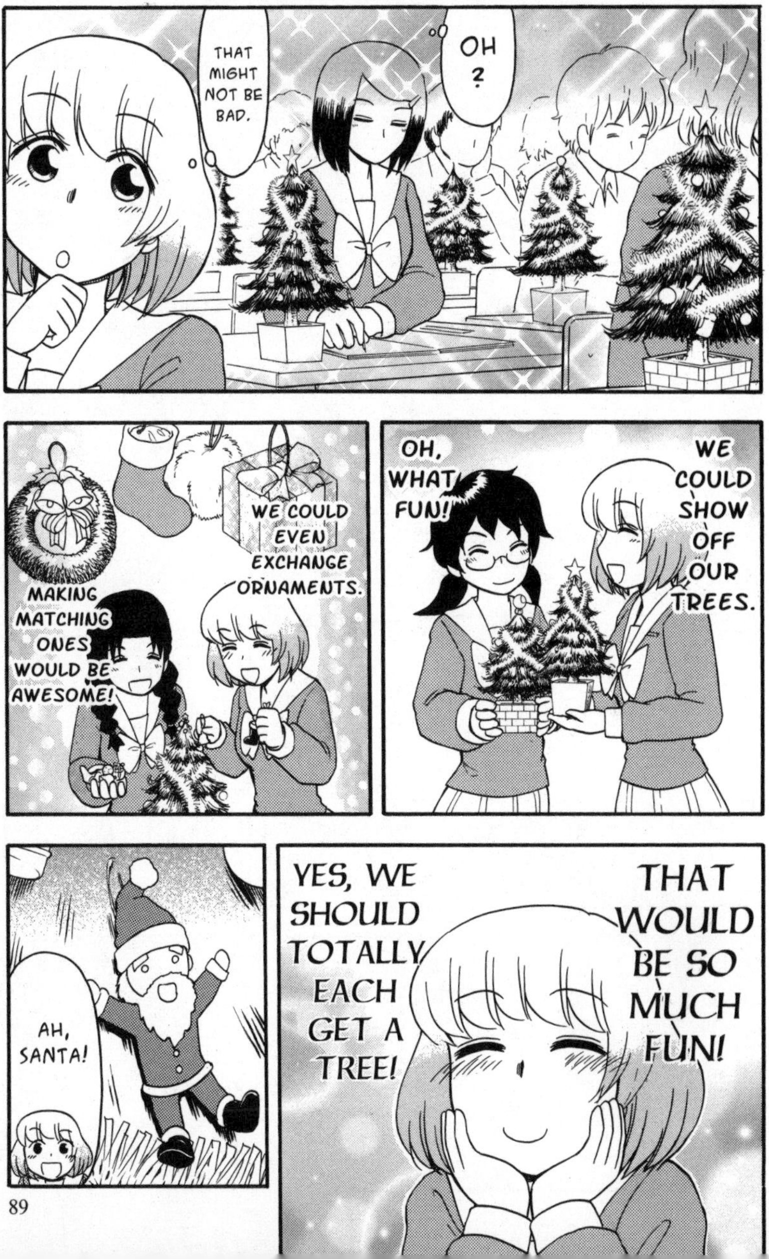
OH ?
THAT MIGHT NOT BE BAD.
WE COULD SHOW OFF OUR TREES.
OH, WHAT FUN!
WE COULD EVEN EXCHANGE ORNAMENTS.
MAKING MATCHING ONES WOULD BE AWESOME!
THAT WOULD BE SO MUCH FUN!
YES, WE SHOULD TOTALLY EACH GET A TREE!
AH, SANTA!

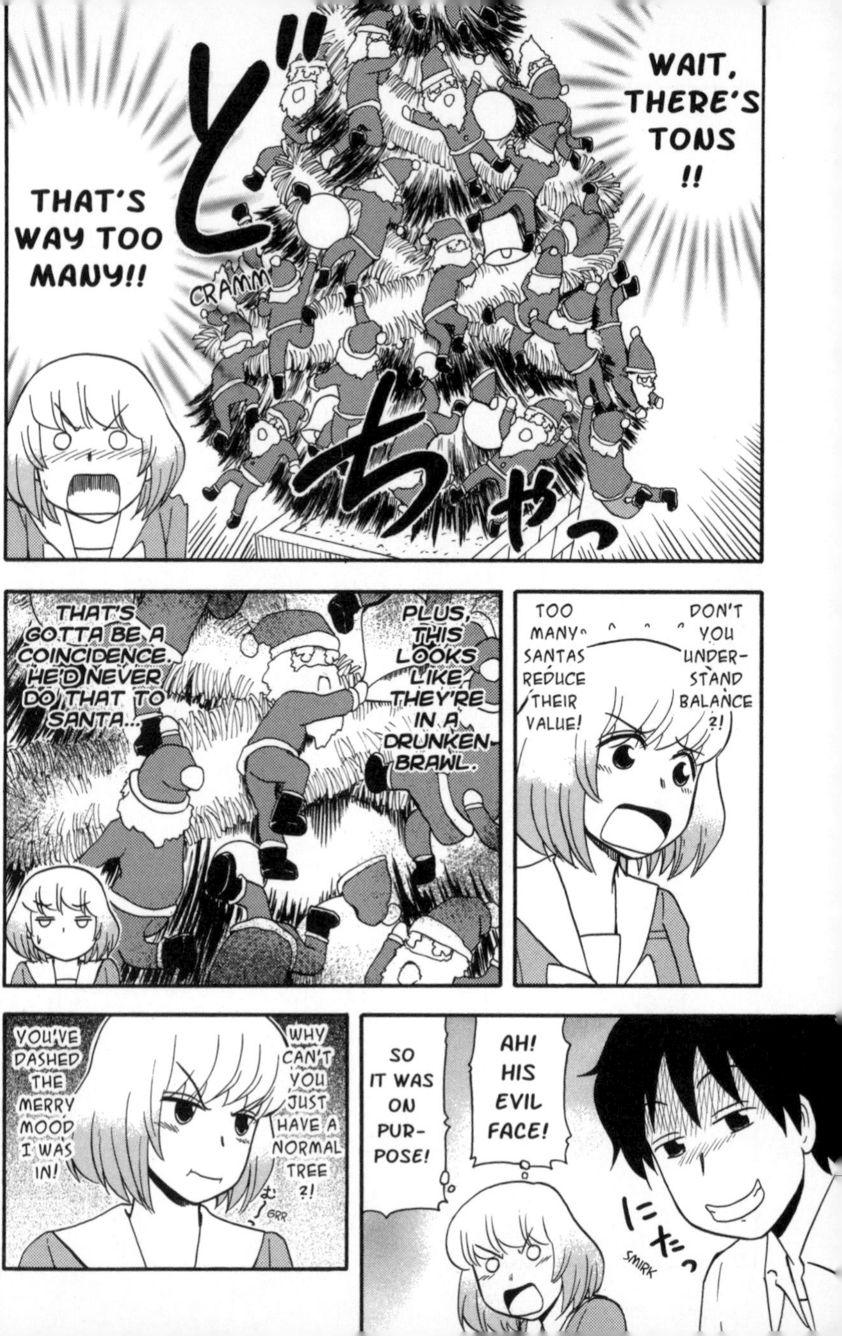
WAIT, THERE'S TONS !!
どちゃっ
CRAMM
THAT'S WAY TOO MANY!!
DON'T YOU UNDER-STAND BALANCE ?!
TOO MANY SANTAS REDUCE THEIR VALUE!
PLUS, THIS LOOKS LIKE THEY'RE IN A DRUNKEN BRAWL.
THAT'S GOTTA BE A COINCIDENCE. HE'D NEVER DO THAT TO SANTA...
AH! HIS EVIL FACE!
SO IT WAS ON PURPOSE!
にやっ
SMIRK
WHY CAN'T YOU JUST HAVE A NORMAL TREE ?!
YOU'VE DASHED THE MERRY MOOD I WAS IN!
む
GRR

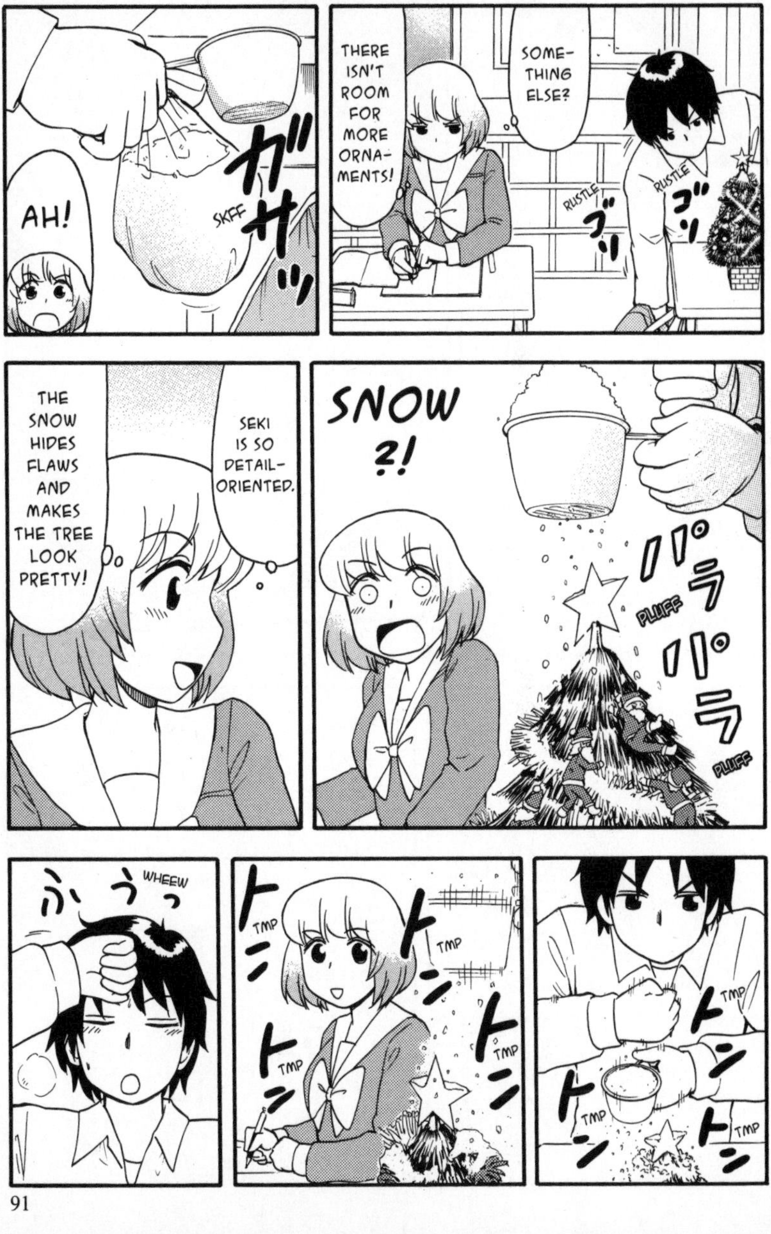
SOME-THING ELSE?
THERE ISN'T ROOM FOR MORE ORNA-MENTS!
ゴソ RUSTLE
ゴソ RUSTLE
ガザッ
SKFF
AH!
SNOW ?!
パラ PLUFF
パラ PLUFF
SEKI IS SO DETAIL-ORIENTED.
THE SNOW HIDES FLAWS AND MAKES THE TREE LOOK PRETTY!
トン TMP
トン TMP
トン TMP
トン TMP
トン TMP
トン TMP
トン TMP
トン TMP
ふうっ WHEEW

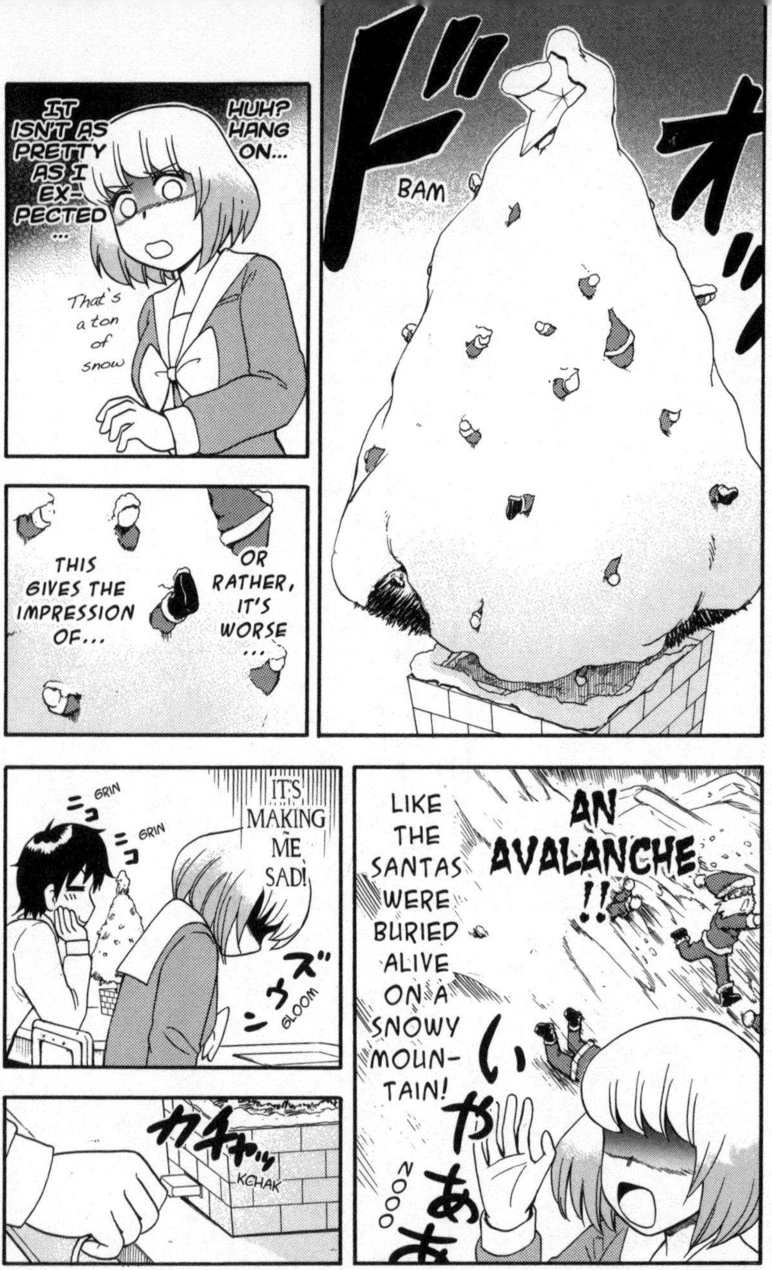
ドオッ
BAM
HUH? HANG ON...
IT ISN'T AS PRETTY AS I EX-PECTED...
That's a ton of snow
OR RATHER, IT'S WORSE...
THIS GIVES THE IMPRESSION OF...
AN AVALANCHE!!
LIKE THE SANTAS WERE BURIED ALIVE ON A SNOWY MOUN-TAIN!
いやあああ
NOOOO
IT'S MAKING ME SAD!
ニコ GRIN
ニコ GRIN
ズウン GLOOM
カチャッ
KCHAK

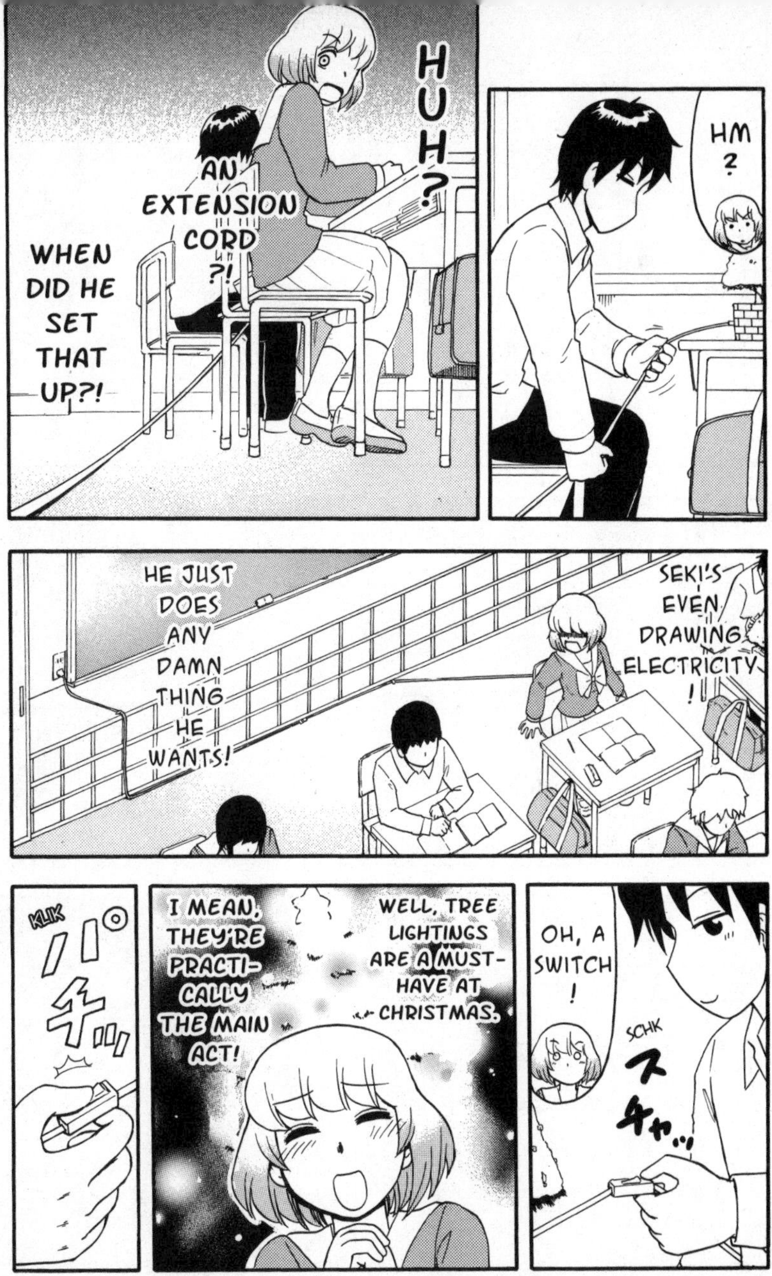
HM?
HUH?
AN EXTENSION CORD?!
WHEN DID HE SET THAT UP?!
SEKI'S EVEN DRAWING ELECTRICITY!
HE JUST DOES ANY DAMN THING HE WANTS!
OH, A SWITCH!
SCHK
スチャッ
WELL, TREE LIGHTINGS ARE A MUST-HAVE AT CHRISTMAS.
I MEAN, THEY'RE PRACTI-CALLY THE MAIN ACT!
KLIK
パチッ

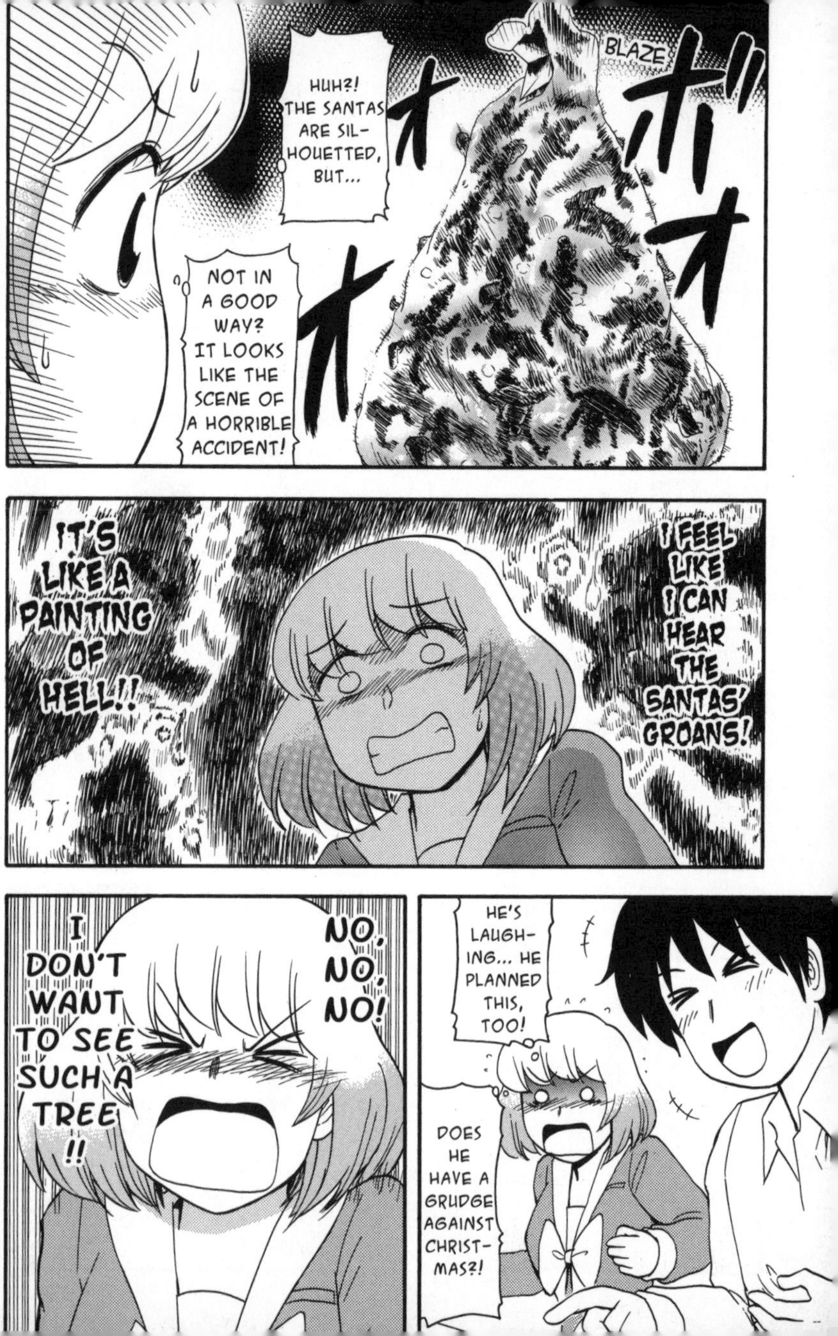
BLAZE
HUH?! THE SANTAS ARE SIL-HOUETTED, BUT...
NOT IN A GOOD WAY? IT LOOKS LIKE THE SCENE OF A HORRIBLE ACCIDENT!
I FEEL LIKE I CAN HEAR THE SANTAS' GROANS!
IT'S LIKE A PAINTING OF HELL!!
HE'S LAUGHING... HE PLANNED THIS, TOO!
DOES HE HAVE A GRUDGE AGAINST CHRIST-MAS?!
NO, NO, NO!
I DON'T WANT TO SEE SUCH A TREE!!

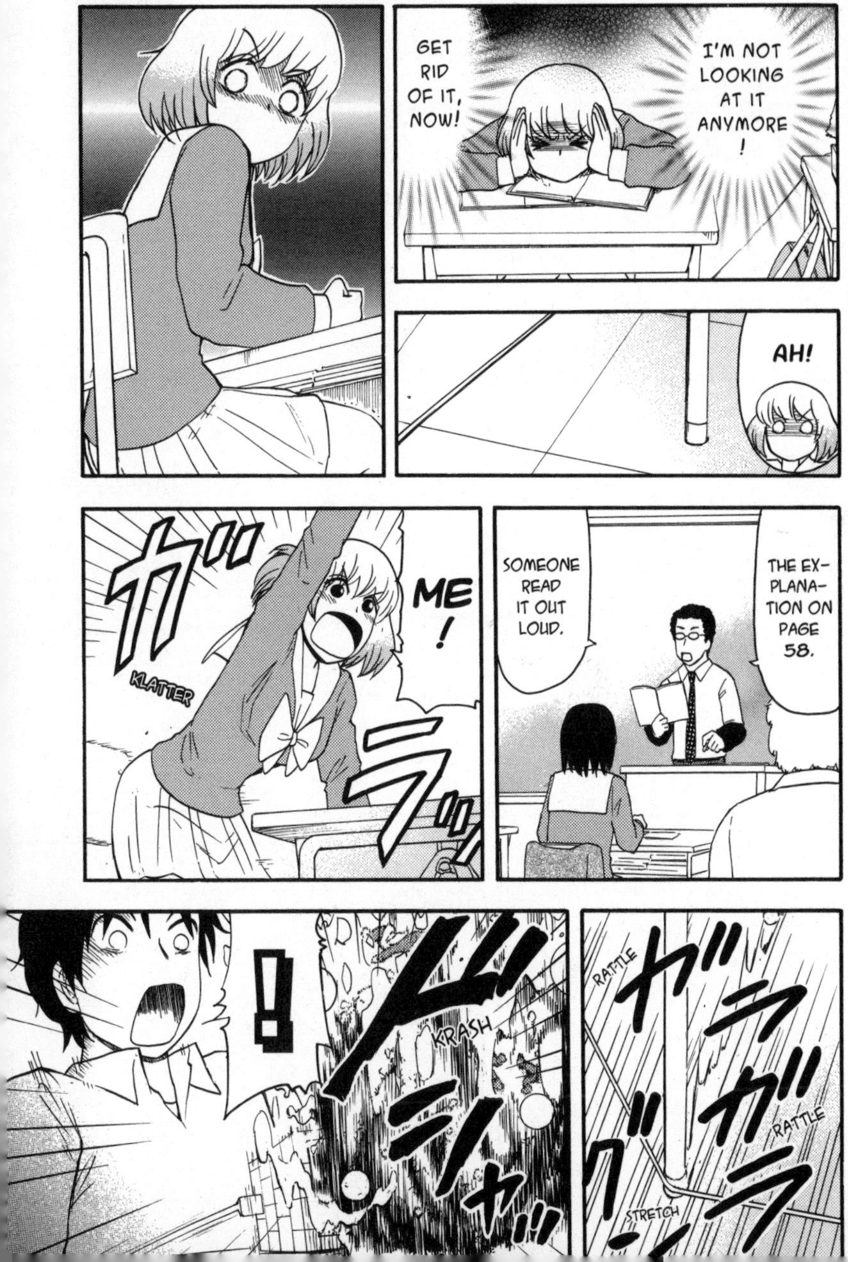
I'M NOT LOOKING AT IT ANYMORE!
GET RID OF IT, NOW!
AH!
THE EX-PLANA-TION ON PAGE 58.
SOMEONE READ IT OUT LOUD.
ME!
KLATTER
RATTLE
RATTLE
STRETCH
KRASH
!

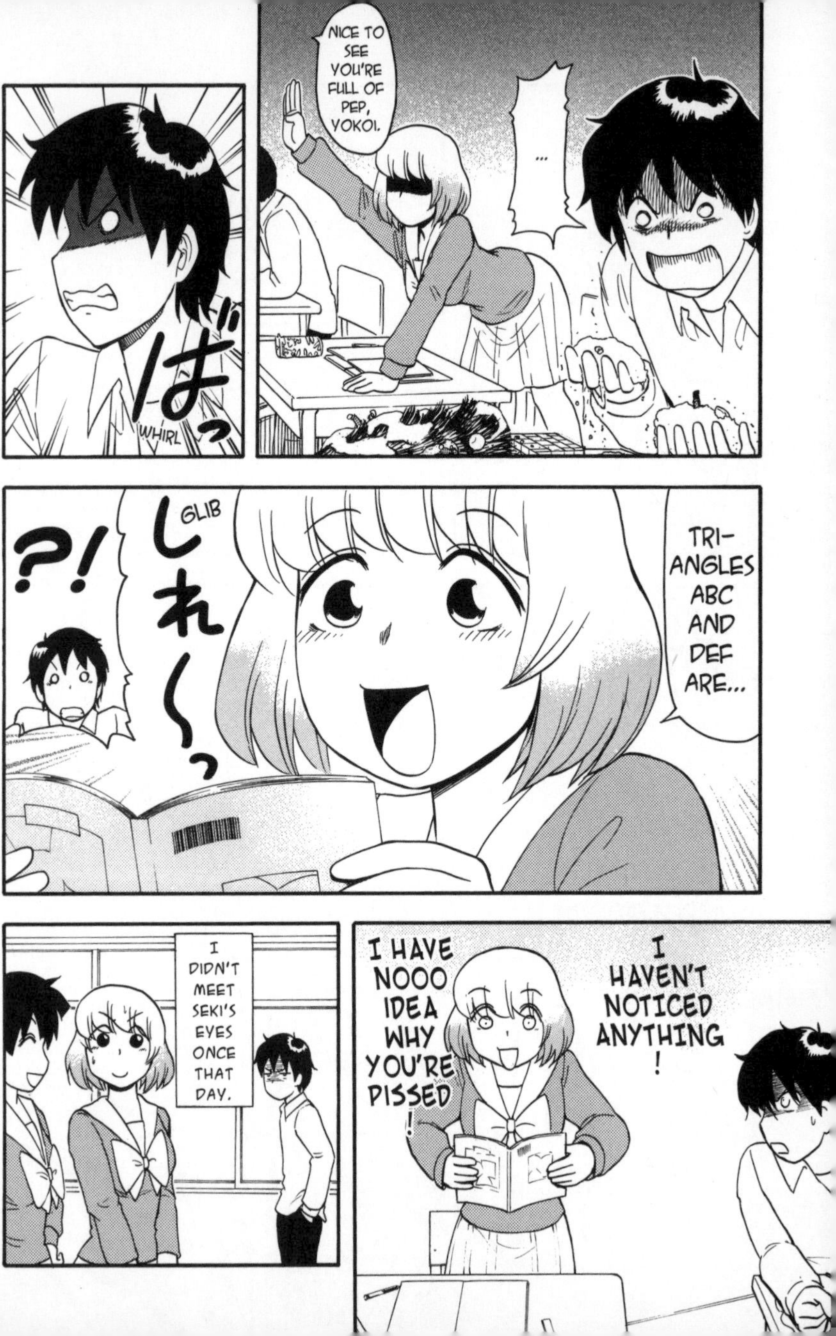
NICE TO SEE YOU'RE FULL OF PEP, YOKOI.
...
ばっ
WHIRL
TRI-ANGLES ABC AND DEF ARE...
しれ~っ
GLIB
?!
I HAVEN'T NOTICED ANYTHING!
I HAVE NOOO IDEA WHY YOU'RE PISSED!
I DIDN'T MEET SEKI'S EYES ONCE THAT DAY.

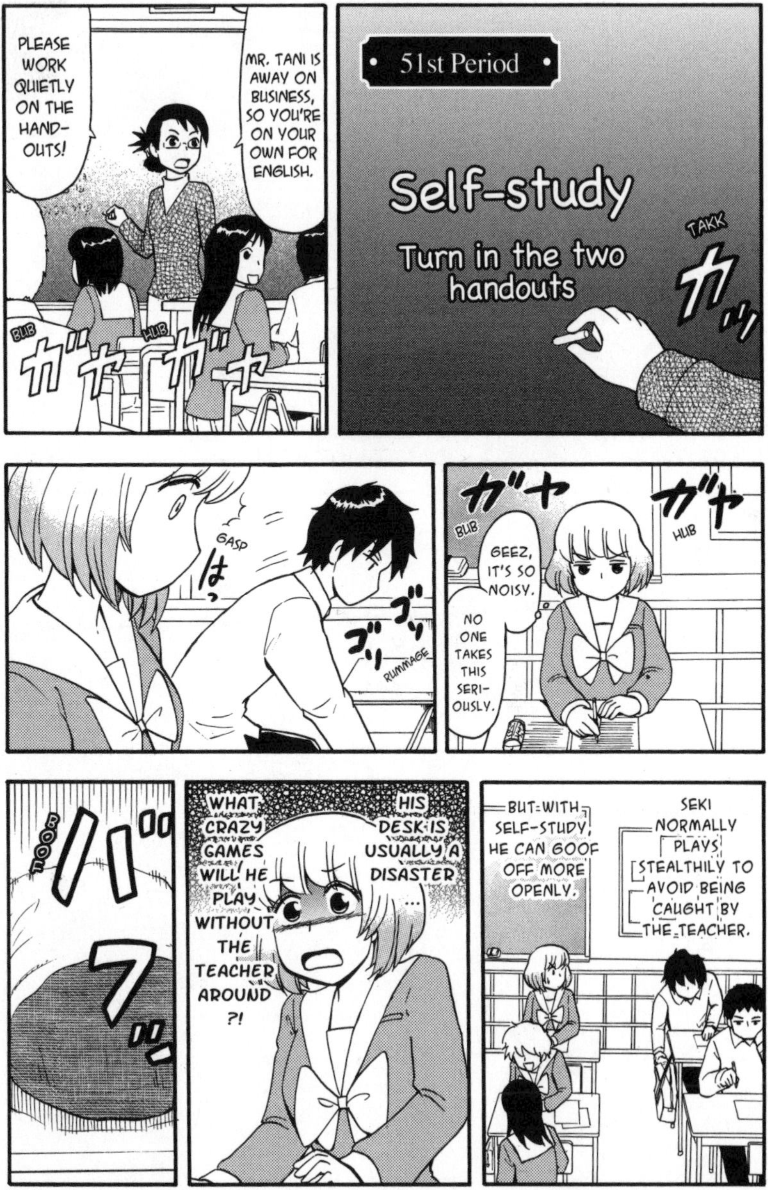
• 51st Period •
Self-study
Turn in the two handouts
TAKK
MR. TANI IS AWAY ON BUSINESS, SO YOU'RE ON YOUR OWN FOR ENGLISH.
PLEASE WORK QUIETLY ON THE HAND-OUTS!
BUB
HUB
BUB
HUB
GEEZ, IT'S SO NOISY.
NO ONE TAKES THIS SERI-OUSLY.
GASP
RUMMAGE
SEKI NORMALLY PLAYS STEALTHILY TO AVOID BEING CAUGHT BY THE TEACHER.
BUT WITH SELF-STUDY, HE CAN GOOF OFF MORE OPENLY.
HIS DESK IS USUALLY A DISASTER...
WHAT CRAZY GAMES WILL HE PLAY WITHOUT THE TEACHER AROUND ?!
BOOT

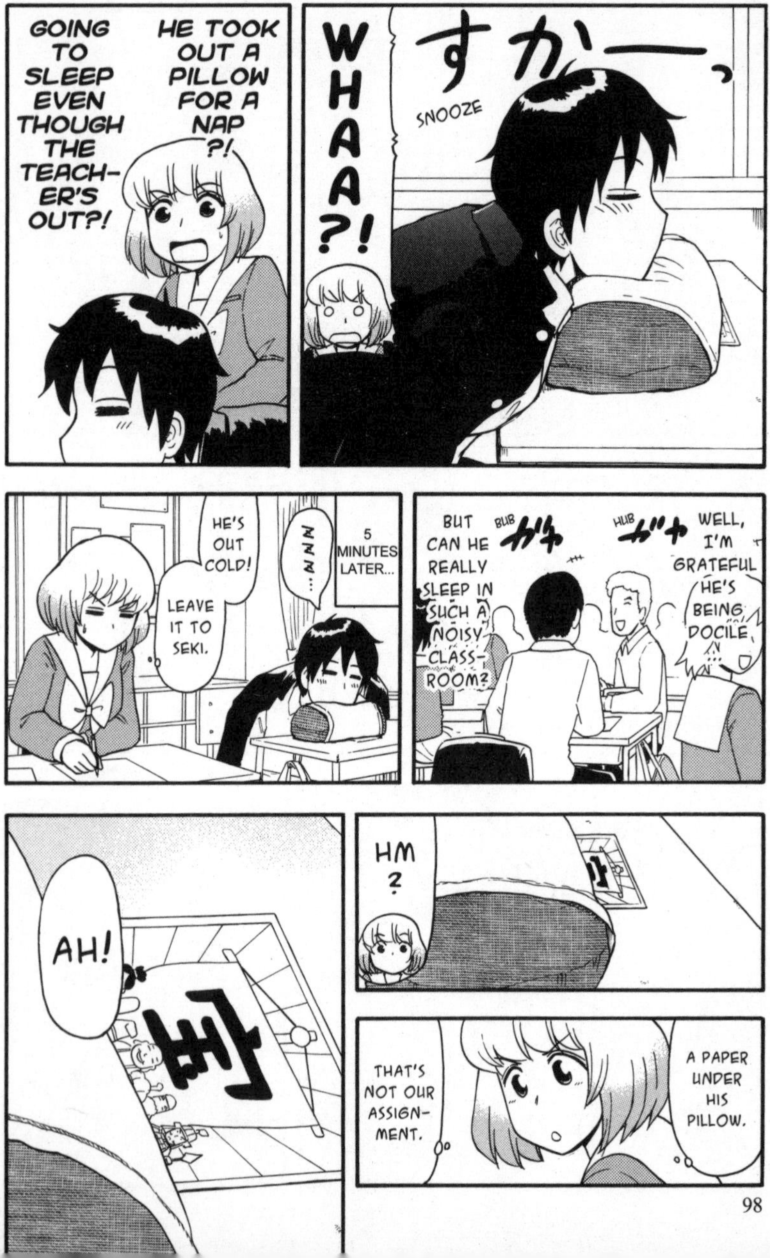
すかー
SNOOZE
WHAA?!
HE TOOK OUT A PILLOW FOR A NAP?!
GOING TO SLEEP EVEN THOUGH THE TEACHER'S OUT?!
WELL, I'M GRATEFUL HE'S BEING DOCILE.
HUB ガヤ
BUB ガヤ
BUT CAN HE REALLY SLEEP IN SUCH A NOISY CLASSROOM?
5 MINUTES LATER...
ZZZ...
HE'S OUT COLD!
LEAVE IT TO SEKI.
HM?
A PAPER UNDER HIS PILLOW.
THAT'S NOT OUR ASSIGNMENT.
AH!

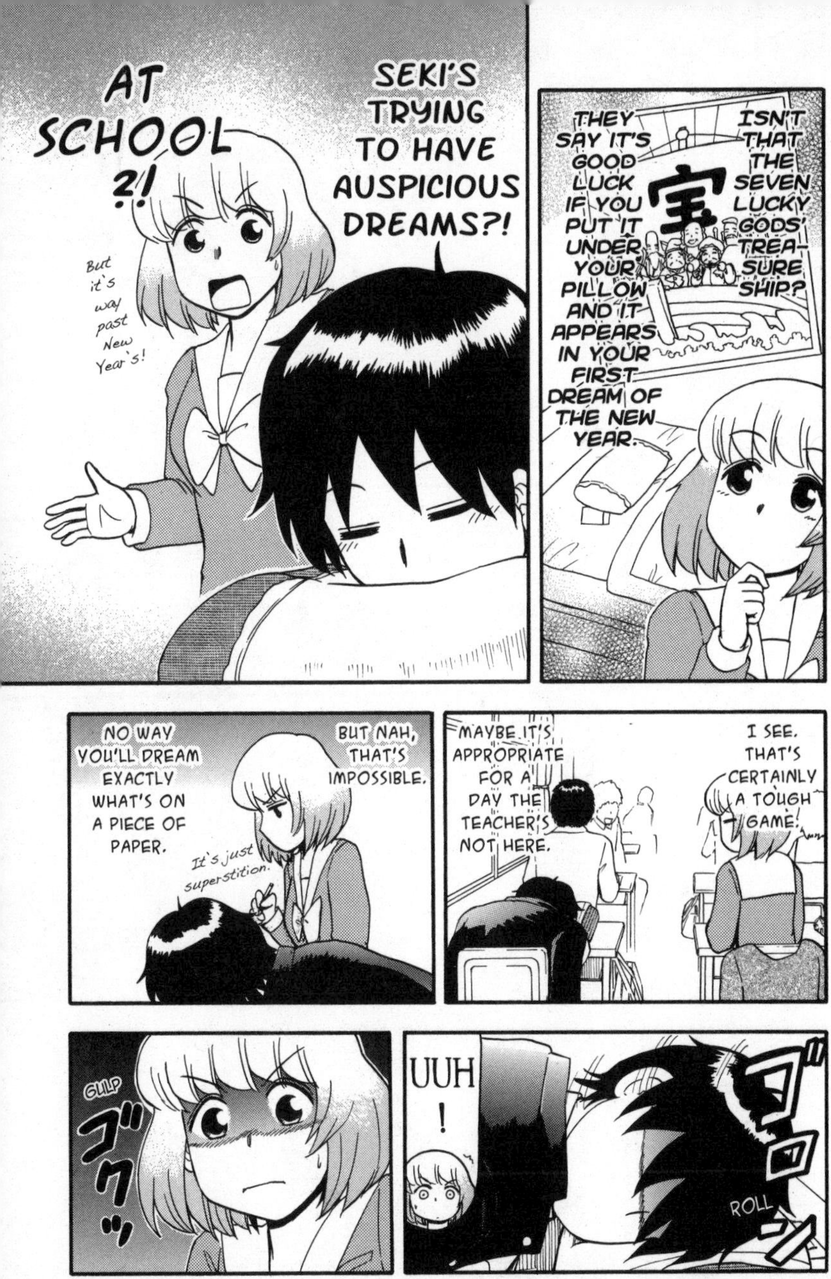
ISN'T THAT THE SEVEN LUCKY GODS' TREA-SURE SHIP?
THEY SAY IT'S GOOD LUCK IF YOU PUT IT UNDER YOUR PILLOW AND IT APPEARS IN YOUR FIRST DREAM OF THE NEW YEAR.
宝
SEKI'S TRYING TO HAVE AUSPICIOUS DREAMS?!
AT SCHOOL?!
But it's way past New Year's!
I SEE. THAT'S CERTAINLY A TOUGH GAME.
MAYBE IT'S APPROPRIATE FOR A DAY THE TEACHER'S NOT HERE.
BUT NAH, THAT'S IMPOSSIBLE.
NO WAY YOU'LL DREAM EXACTLY WHAT'S ON A PIECE OF PAPER.
It's just superstition.
UUH!
ROLL
GULP

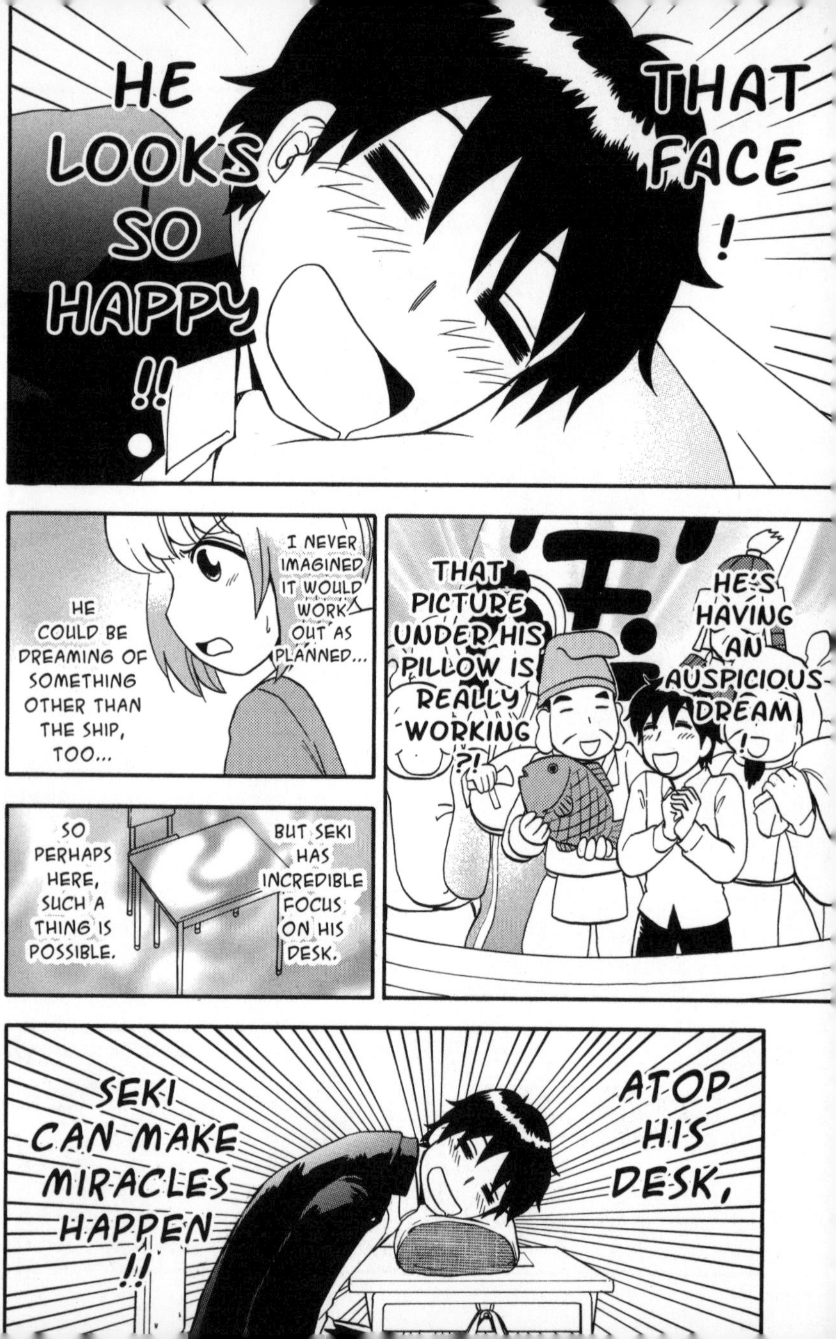
THAT FACE!
HE LOOKS SO HAPPY!!
HE'S HAVING AN AUSPICIOUS DREAM!
THAT PICTURE UNDER HIS PILLOW IS REALLY WORKING?!
I NEVER IMAGINED IT WOULD WORK OUT AS PLANNED...
HE COULD BE DREAMING OF SOMETHING OTHER THAN THE SHIP, TOO...
BUT SEKI HAS INCREDIBLE FOCUS ON HIS DESK.
SO PERHAPS HERE, SUCH A THING IS POSSIBLE.
ATOP HIS DESK,
SEKI CAN MAKE MIRACLES HAPPEN!!

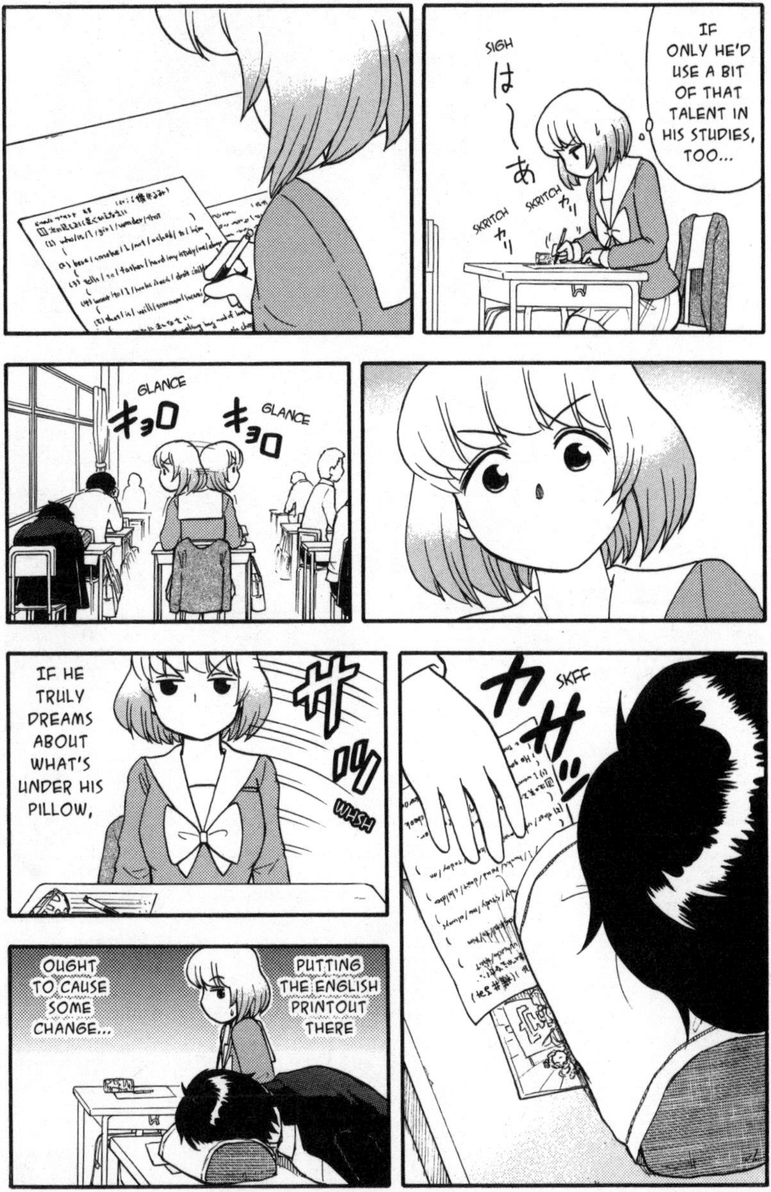
IF ONLY HE'D USE A BIT OF THAT TALENT IN HIS STUDIES, TOO...
SIGH
は～あ
SKRITCH
カリ
SKRITCH
カリ
GLANCE
キョロ
GLANCE
キョロ
SKFF
カサッ
IF HE TRULY DREAMS ABOUT WHAT'S UNDER HIS PILLOW,
ザッ
WHSH
PUTTING THE ENGLISH PRINTOUT THERE
OUGHT TO CAUSE SOME CHANGE...

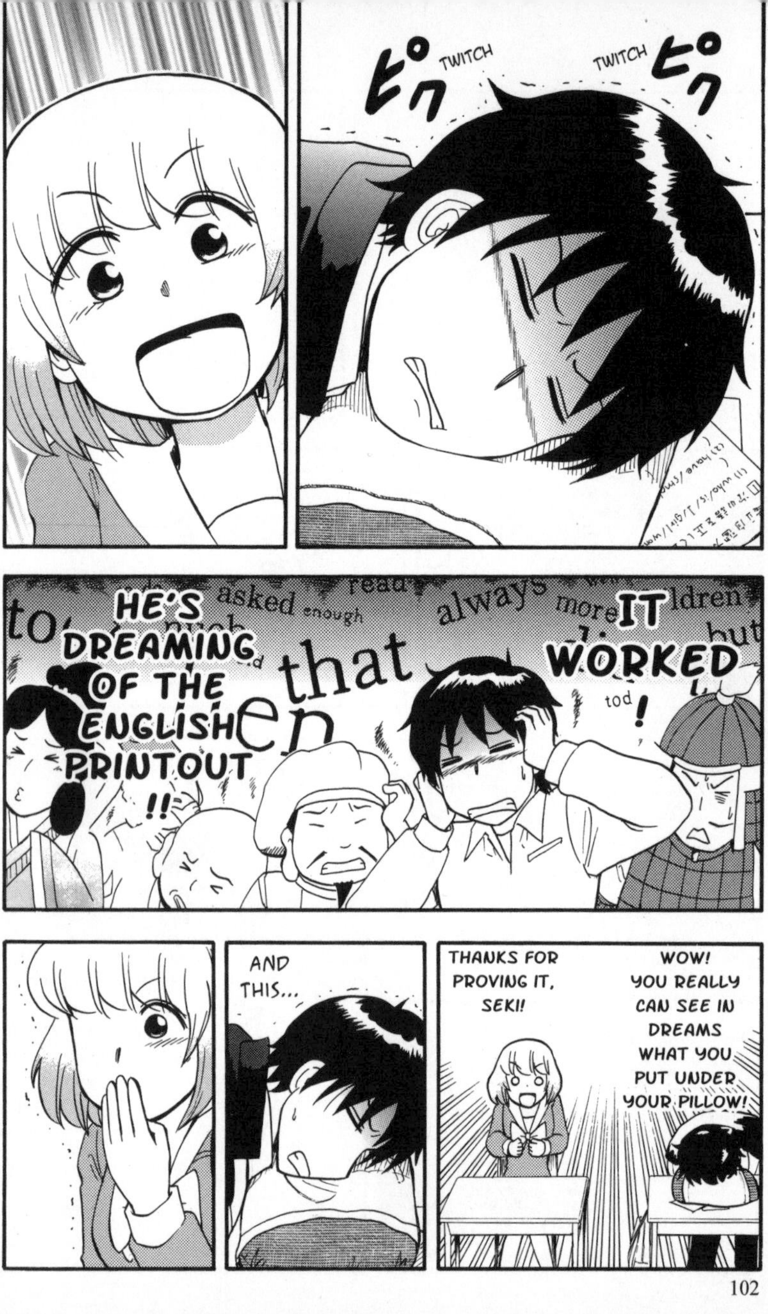
ピク TWITCH
ピク TWITCH
IT WORKED!
HE'S DREAMING OF THE ENGLISH PRINTOUT!!
asked enough read always more that
WOW! YOU REALLY CAN SEE IN DREAMS WHAT YOU PUT UNDER YOUR PILLOW!
THANKS FOR PROVING IT, SEKI!
AND THIS...

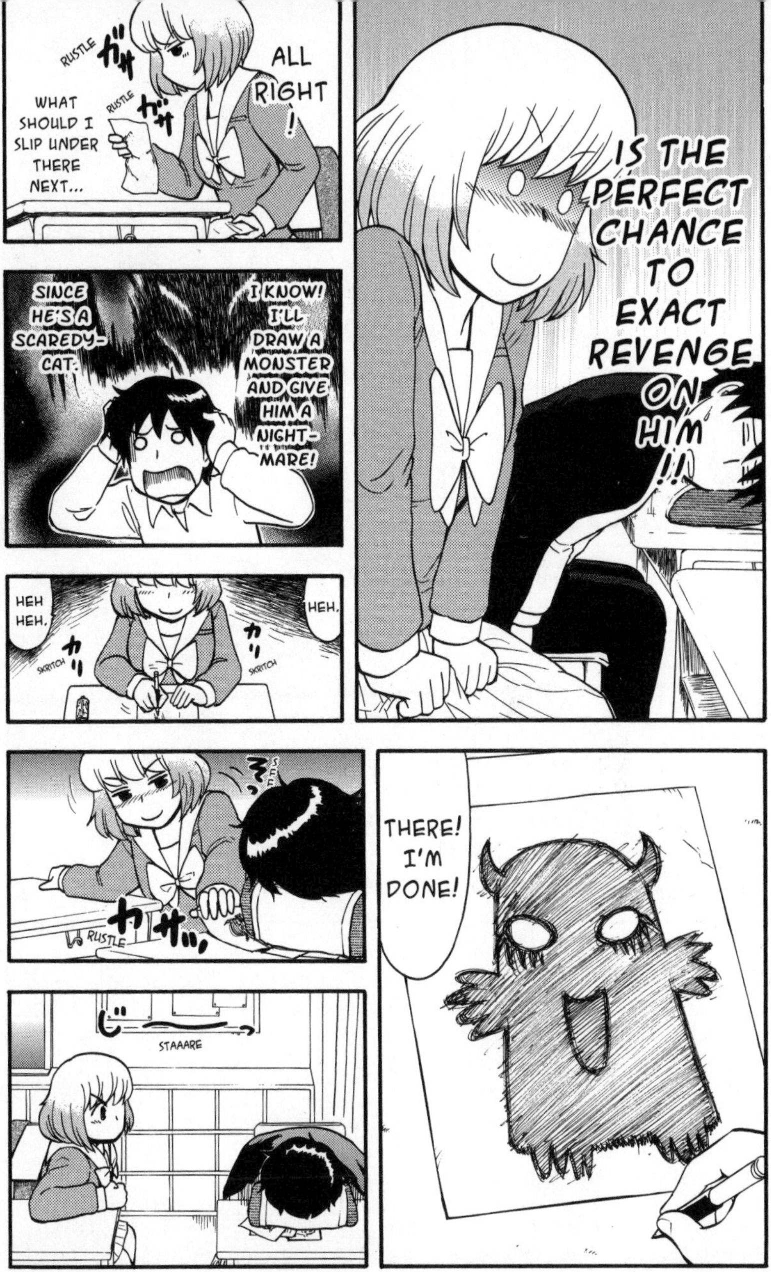
IS THE PERFECT CHANCE TO EXACT REVENGE ON HIM!!
ALL RIGHT!
RUSTLE
RUSTLE
WHAT SHOULD I SLIP UNDER THERE NEXT...
I KNOW! I'LL DRAW A MONSTER AND GIVE HIM A NIGHTMARE!
SINCE HE'S A SCAREDY-CAT:
HEH.
SKRITCH
SKRITCH
HEH HEH.
THERE! I'M DONE!
SFF
RUSTLE
STAAARE

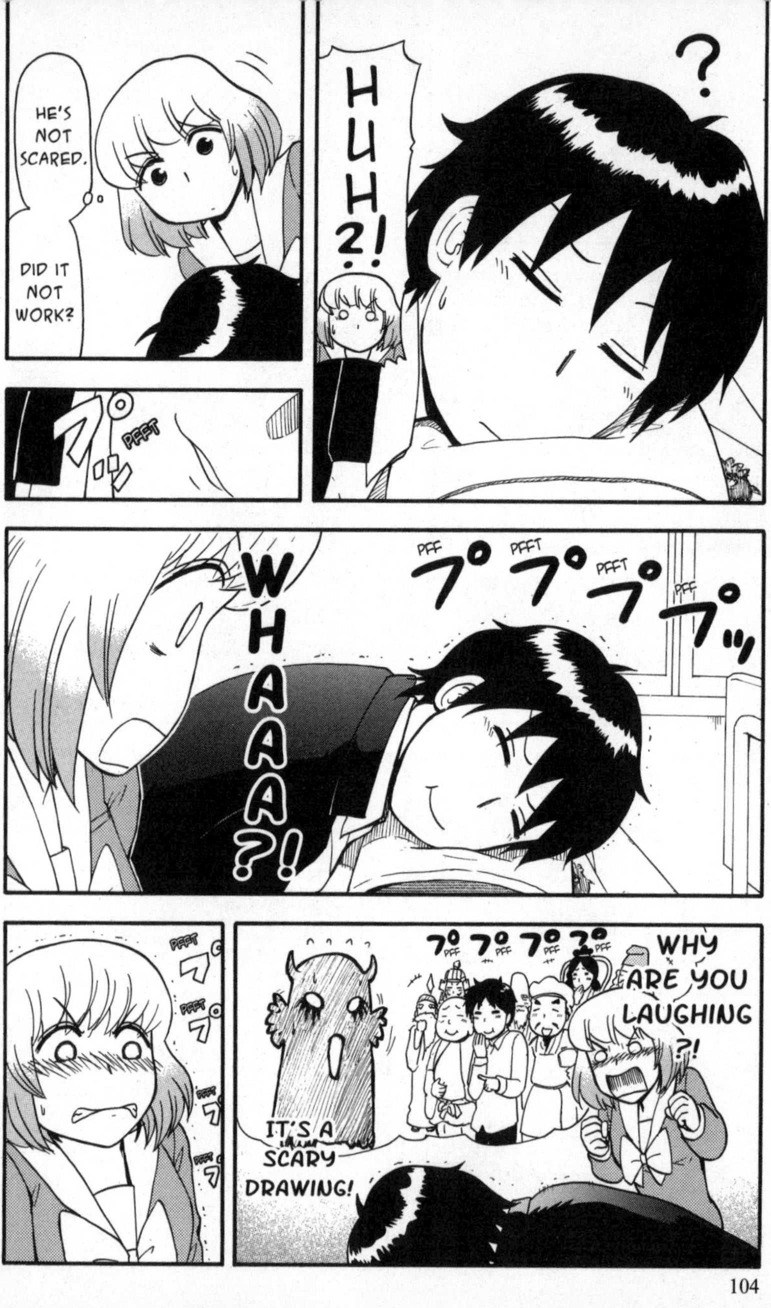
?
HUH?!
HE'S NOT SCARED.
DID IT NOT WORK?
PFFT
PFF PFFT PFFT PFF
WHAAAA?!
WHY ARE YOU LAUGHING?!
PFF PFF PFF PFF
IT'S A SCARY DRAWING!
PFFT PFFT PFFT PFFT

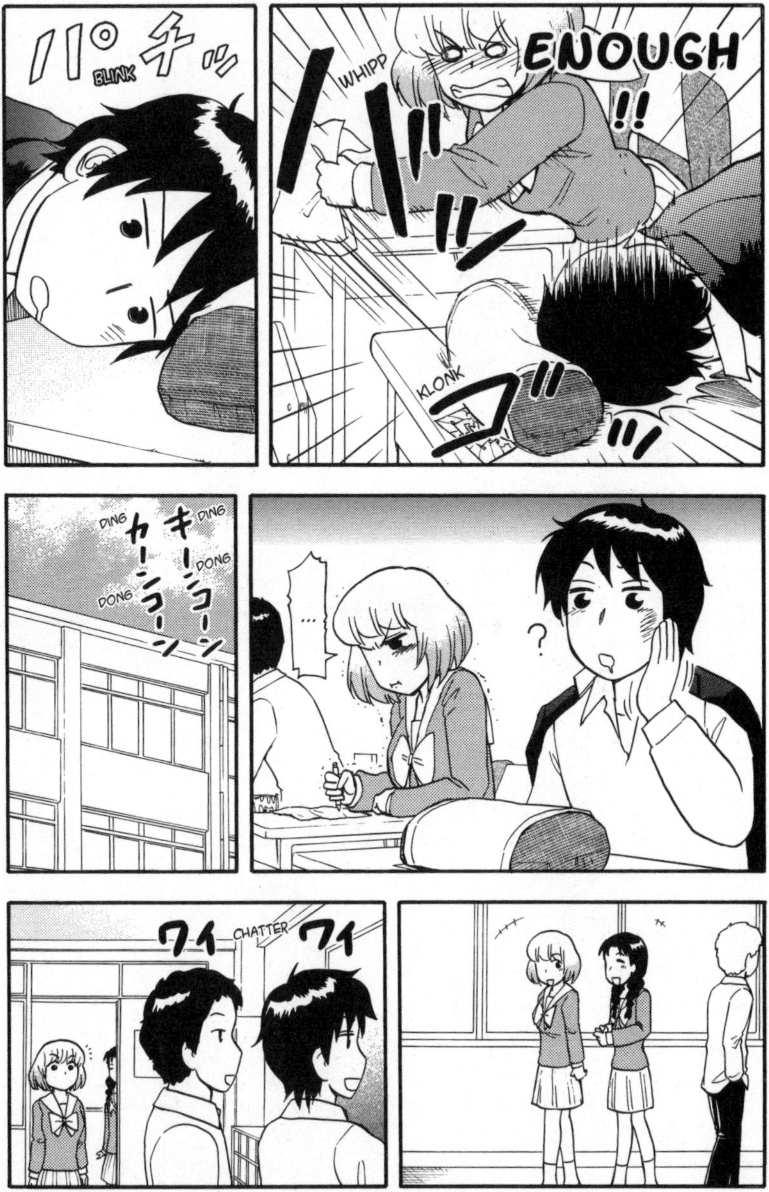
ENOUGH !!
WHIPP
バンッ
KLONK
ゴッ
パチッ
BLINK
...
?
キーンコーン
カーンコーン
DING DONG
DING DONG
ワイ ワイ
CHATTER

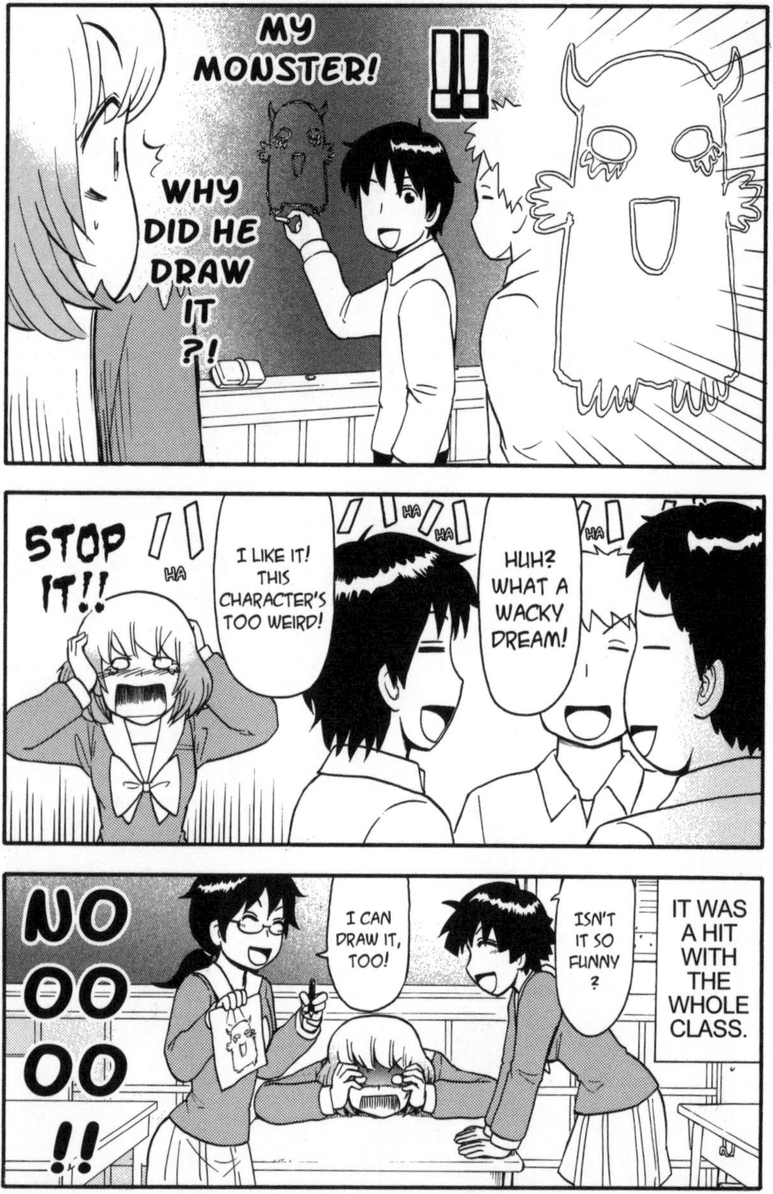
!!
MY MONSTER!
WHY DID HE DRAW IT ?!
HUH? WHAT A WACKY DREAM!
HA
HA
HA
I LIKE IT! THIS CHARACTER'S TOO WEIRD!
HA
STOP IT!!
IT WAS A HIT WITH THE WHOLE CLASS.
ISN'T IT SO FUNNY ?
I CAN DRAW IT, TOO!
NOOOOOOO !!

My Neighbor Seki

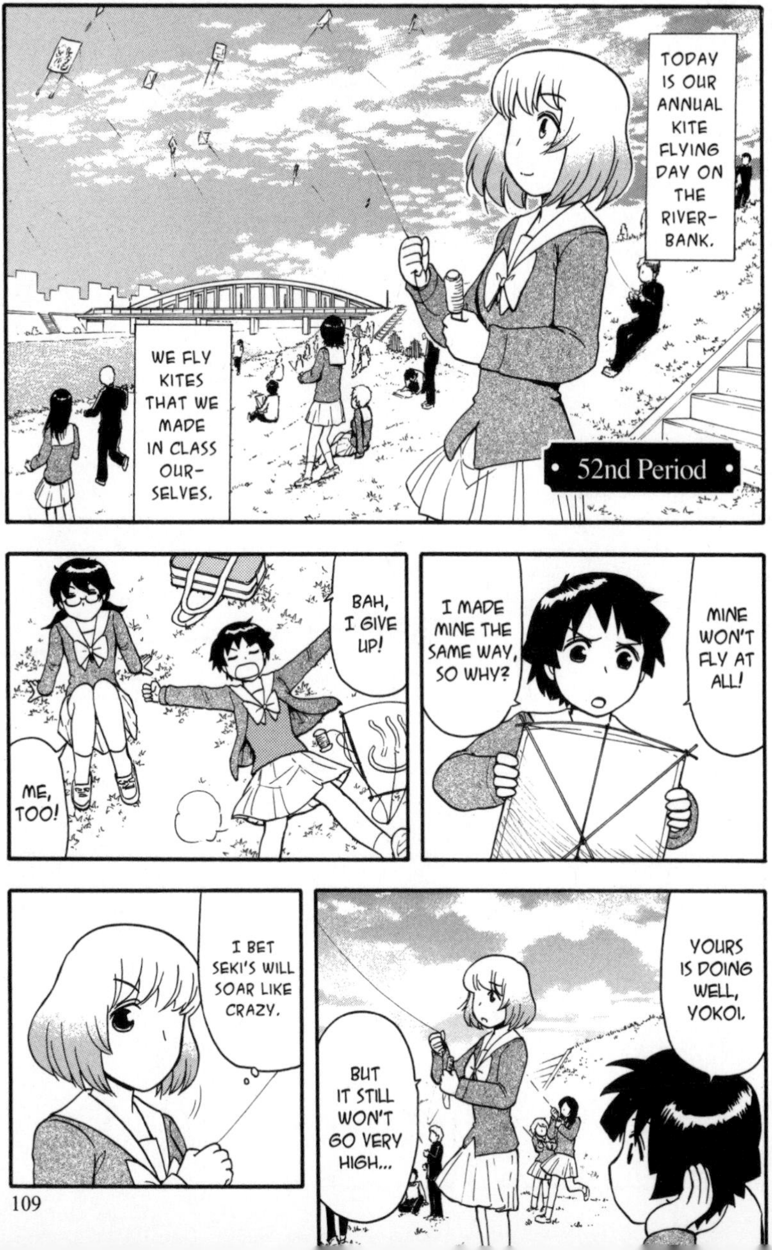
TODAY IS OUR ANNUAL KITE FLYING DAY ON THE RIVER-BANK.
WE FLY KITES THAT WE MADE IN CLASS OUR-SELVES.
52nd Period
MINE WON'T FLY AT ALL!
I MADE MINE THE SAME WAY, SO WHY?
BAH, I GIVE UP!
ME, TOO!
YOURS IS DOING WELL, YOKOI.
BUT IT STILL WON'T GO VERY HIGH...
I BET SEKI'S WILL SOAR LIKE CRAZY.

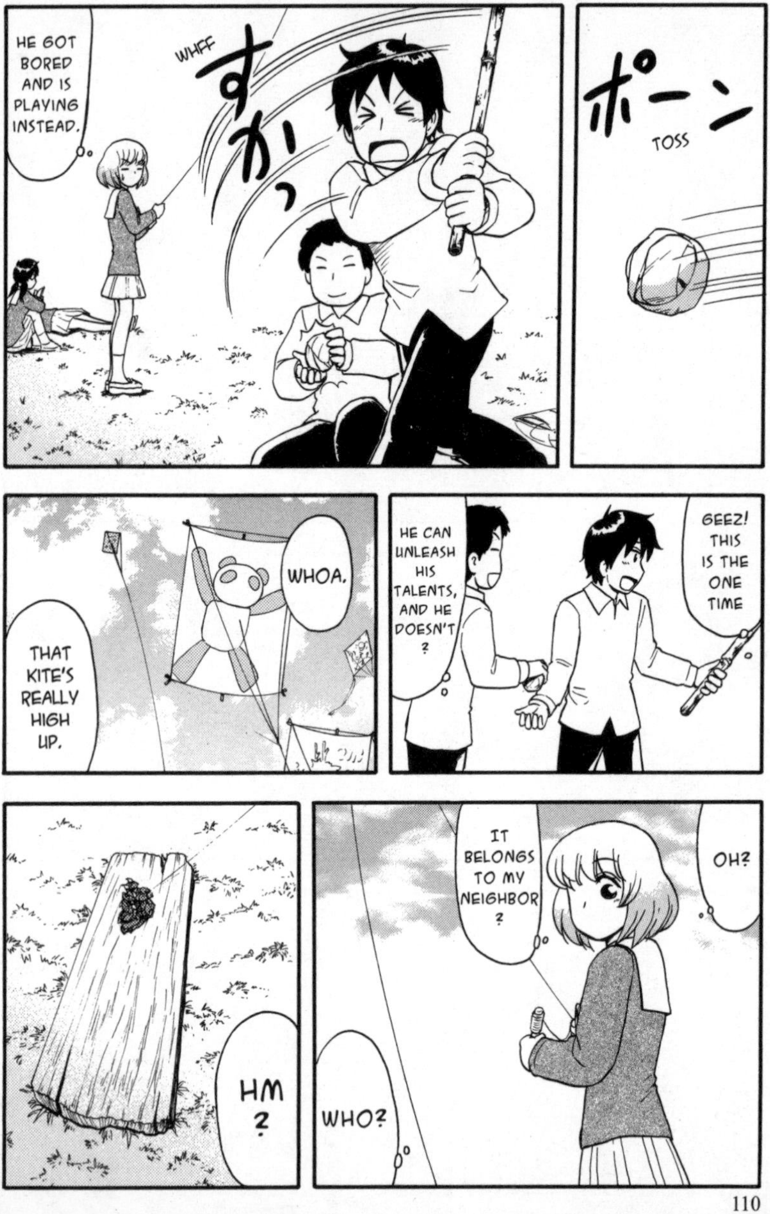
ポーン
TOSS
すかっ
WHFF
HE GOT BORED AND IS PLAYING INSTEAD.
GEEZ! THIS IS THE ONE TIME
HE CAN UNLEASH HIS TALENTS, AND HE DOESN'T?
WHOA.
THAT KITE'S REALLY HIGH UP.
OH?
IT BELONGS TO MY NEIGHBOR?
WHO?
HM?

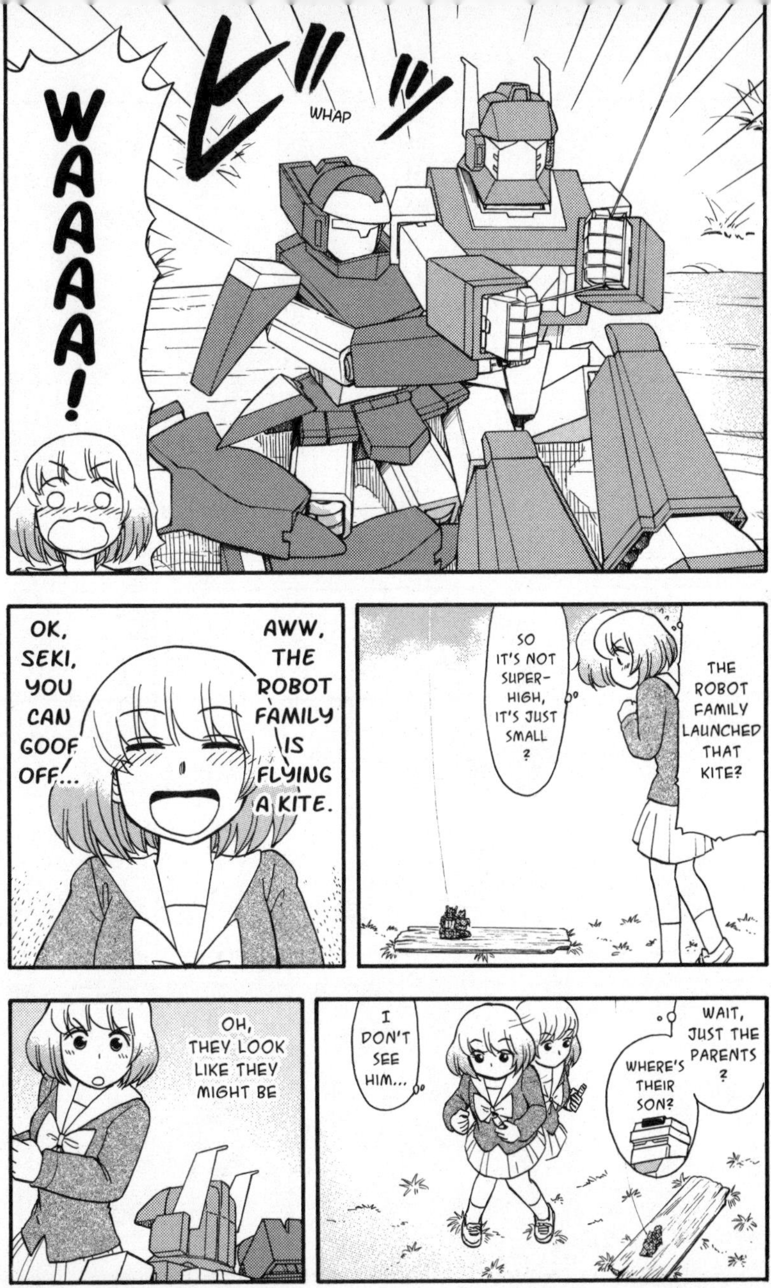

WHAP
WAAAAA!
THE ROBOT FAMILY LAUNCHED THAT KITE?
SO IT'S NOT SUPER-HIGH, IT'S JUST SMALL?
AWW, THE ROBOT FAMILY IS FLYING A KITE.
OK, SEKI, YOU CAN GOOF OFF...
WAIT, JUST THE PARENTS?
WHERE'S THEIR SON?
I DON'T SEE HIM...
OH, THEY LOOK LIKE THEY MIGHT BE

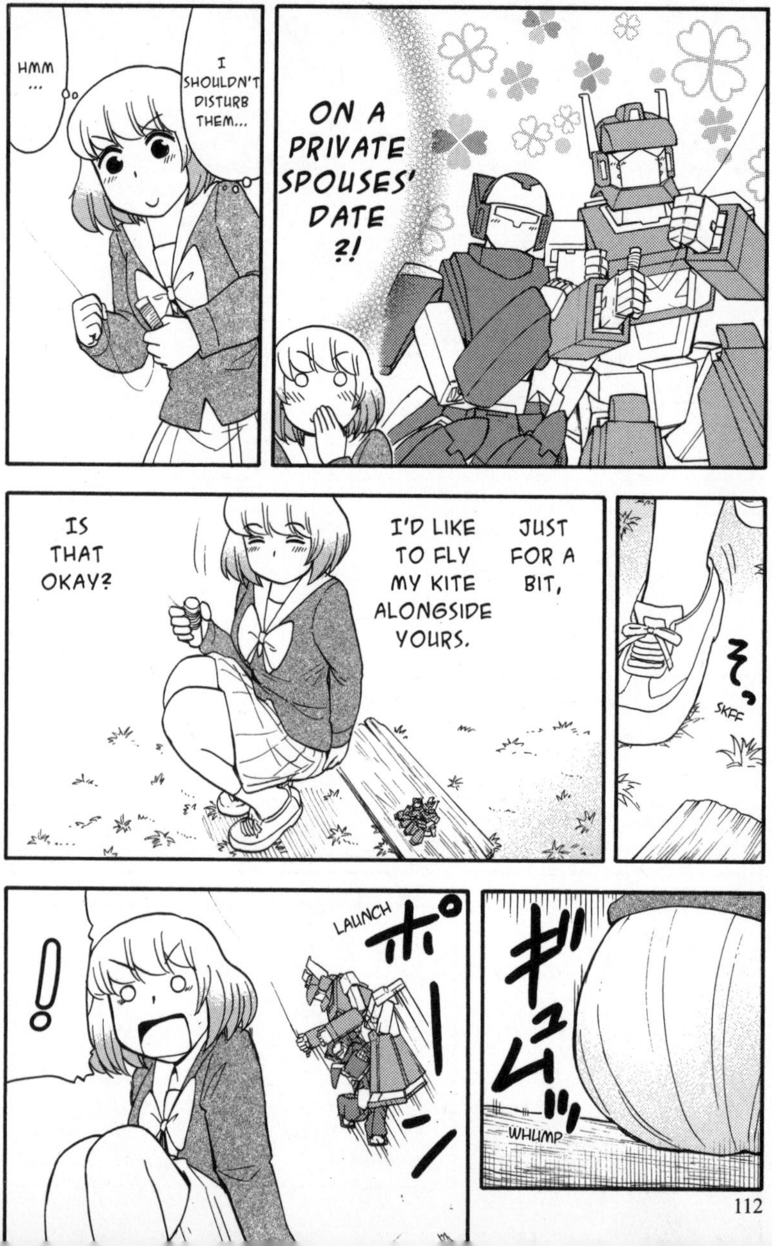
ON A PRIVATE SPOUSES' DATE ?!
I SHOULDN'T DISTURB THEM...
HMM ...
SKFF
JUST FOR A BIT,
I'D LIKE TO FLY MY KITE ALONGSIDE YOURS.
IS THAT OKAY?
ギュムッ
WHUMP
ポーン
LAUNCH
!

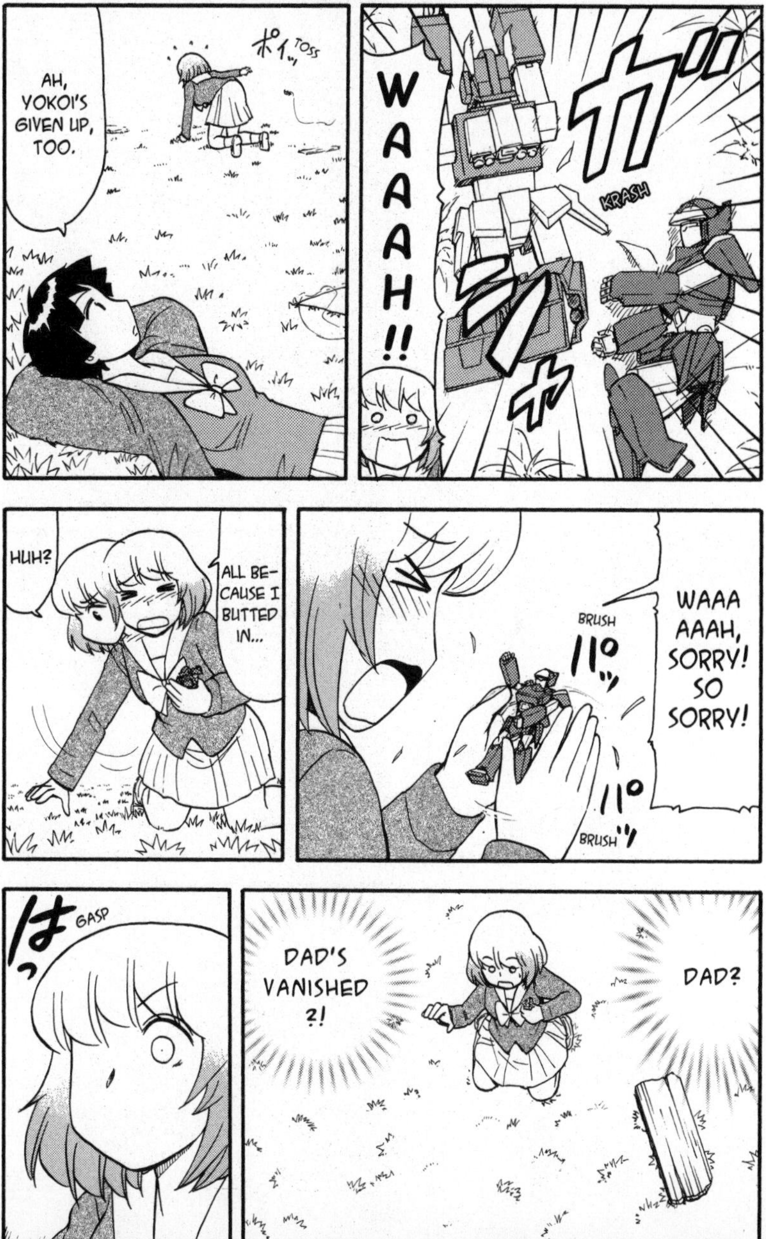
WAAAAH!!
KRASH
ポイッ TOSS
AH, YOKOI'S GIVEN UP, TOO.
WAAA AAAH, SORRY! SO SORRY!
パッ BRUSH
パッ BRUSH
ALL BE- CAUSE I BUTTED IN...
HUH?
DAD?
DAD'S VANISHED ?!
はっ GASP

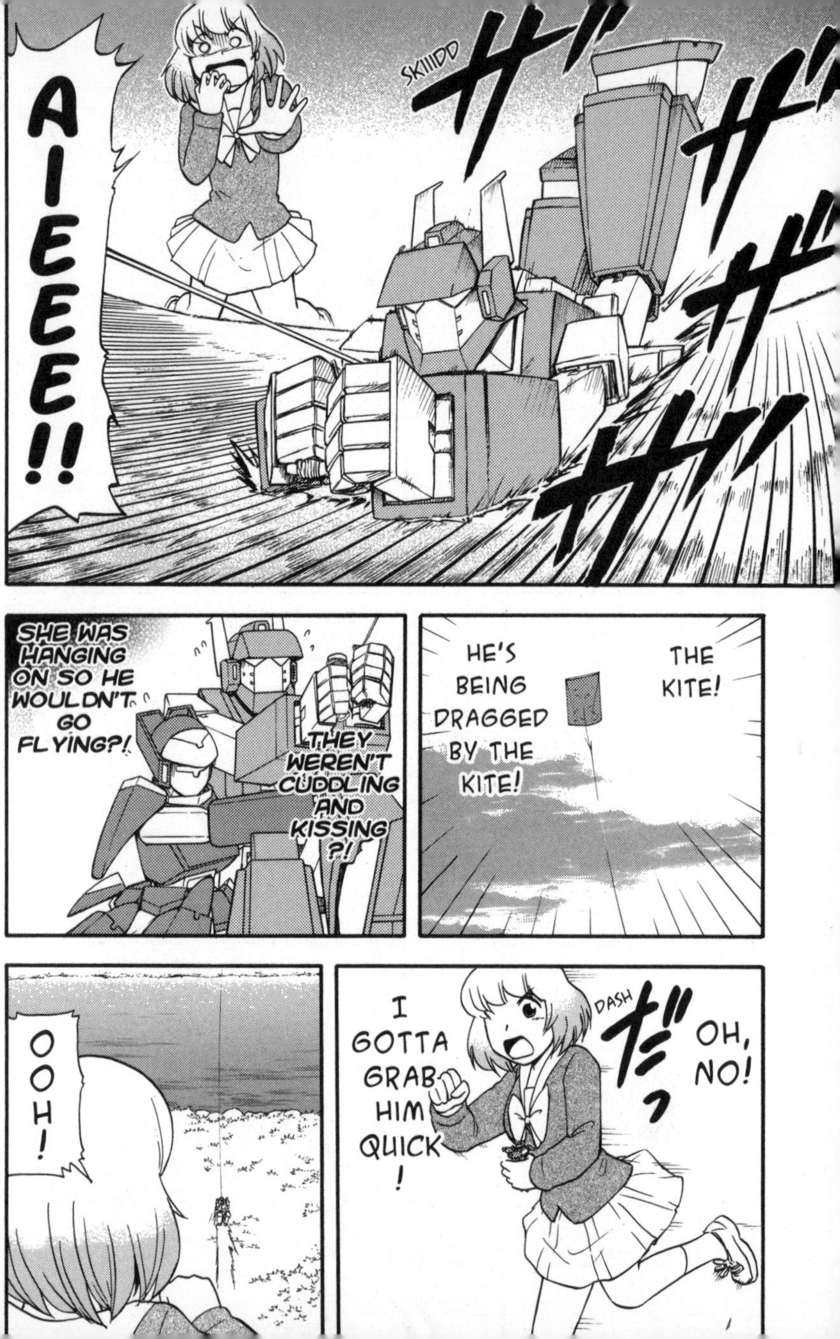
SKIIIDD
AIEEEE!!
THE KITE!
HE'S BEING DRAGGED BY THE KITE!
THEY WEREN'T CUDDLING AND KISSING?!
SHE WAS HANGING ON SO HE WOULDN'T GO FLYING?!
OH, NO!
DASH
I GOTTA GRAB HIM QUICK!
OOH!

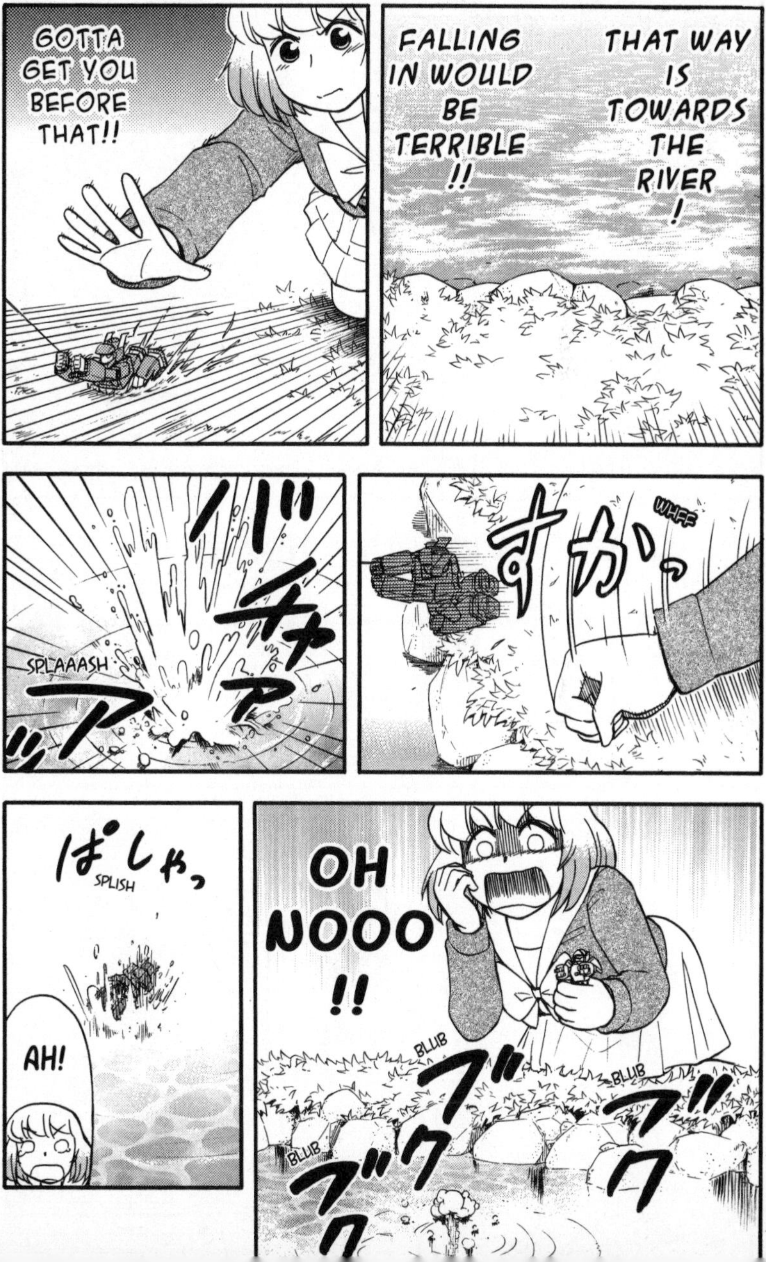
THAT WAY IS TOWARDS THE RIVER!
FALLING IN WOULD BE TERRIBLE!!
GOTTA GET YOU BEFORE THAT!!
すかっ
WHFF
バチャアッ
SPLAAASH
OH NOOO!!
ブクブク
BLUB
BLUB
BLUB
ぱしゃっ
SPLISH
AH!

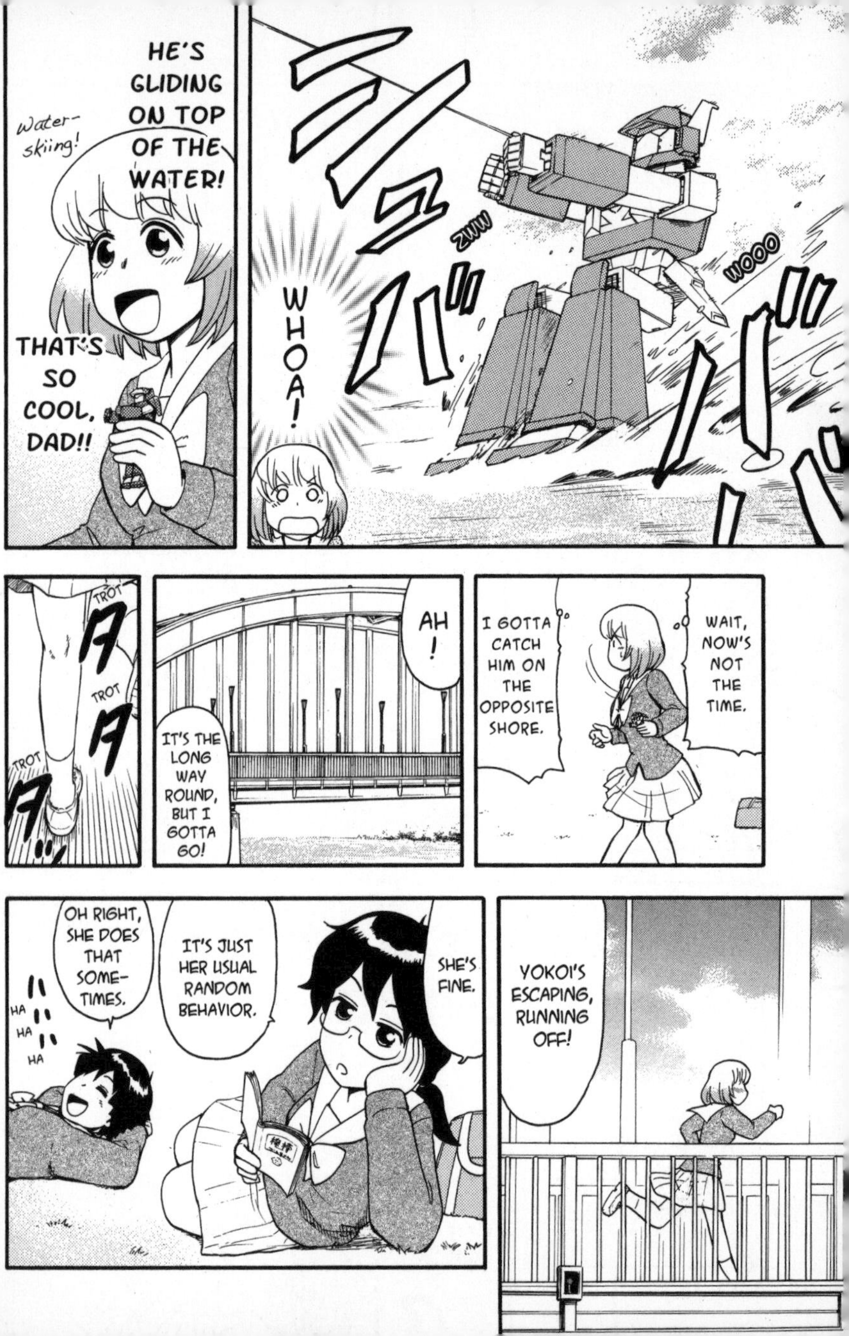
WOOO
ZWW
WHOA!
HE'S GLIDING ON TOP OF THE WATER!
Water-skiing!
THAT'S SO COOL, DAD!!
WAIT, NOW'S NOT THE TIME.
I GOTTA CATCH HIM ON THE OPPOSITE SHORE.
AH!
IT'S THE LONG WAY ROUND, BUT I GOTTA GO!
TROT
TROT
TROT
YOKOI'S ESCAPING, RUNNING OFF!
SHE'S FINE.
IT'S JUST HER USUAL RANDOM BEHAVIOR.
OH RIGHT, SHE DOES THAT SOME-TIMES.
HA
HA
HA

SMILE
ぱぁ あぁ

SPLISH
チャプッ

SPLISH
チャプッ

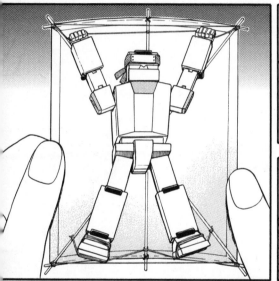

REEL
ぐい

REEL
ぐい

THIS KITE IS NOT SAFE!

LET'S BRING IT DOWN, STAT.

HM?

ガ

バサッ

GACHAK

FWAP

チ

TROT
た っ

TROT
た っ

TROT
た っ

GET READY TO HEAD BACK!

TIME'S UP!

HUB
がや

HUB
がや

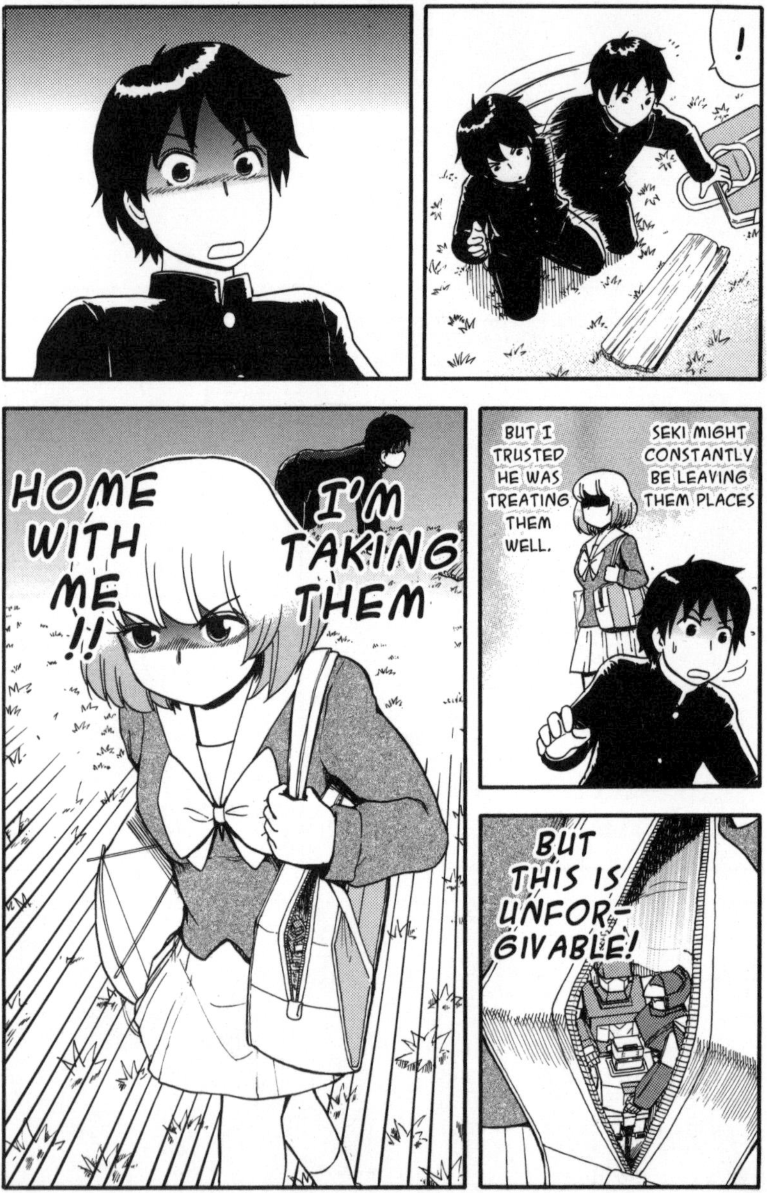
!
SEKI MIGHT CONSTANTLY BE LEAVING THEM PLACES
BUT I TRUSTED HE WAS TREATING THEM WELL.
BUT THIS IS UNFOR-GIVABLE!
I'M TAKING THEM HOME WITH ME!!

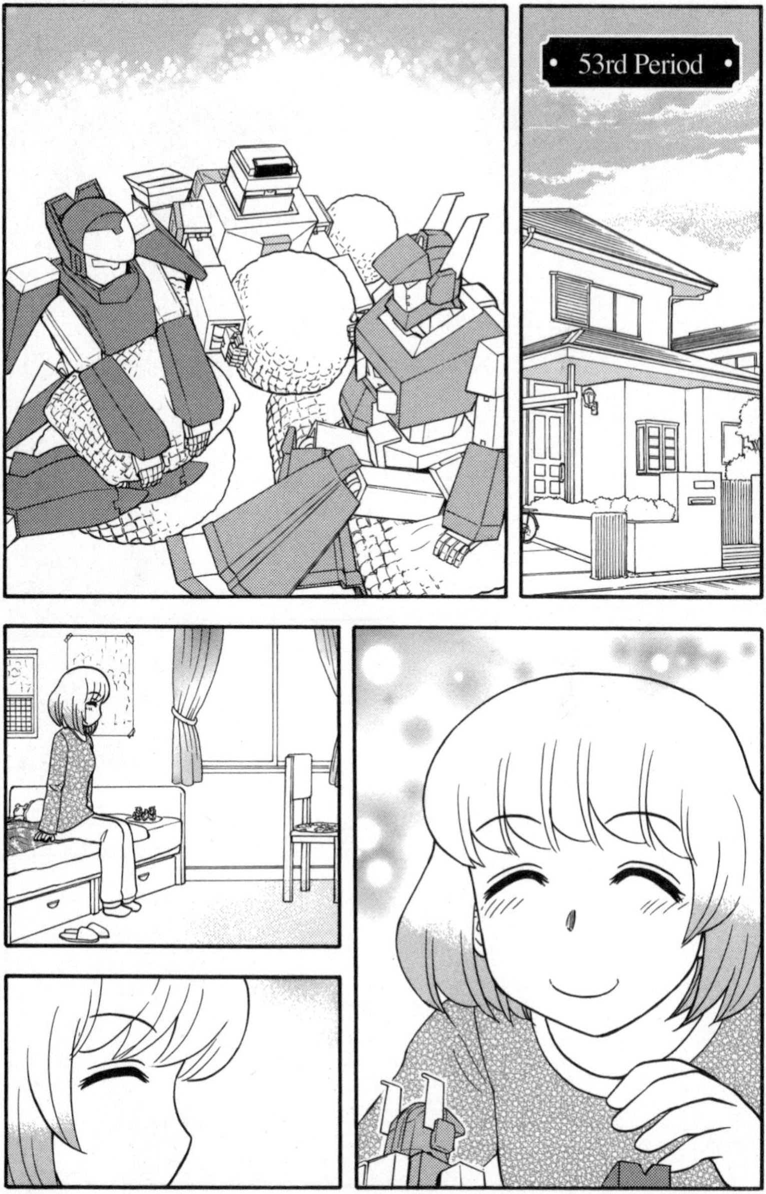
53rd Period

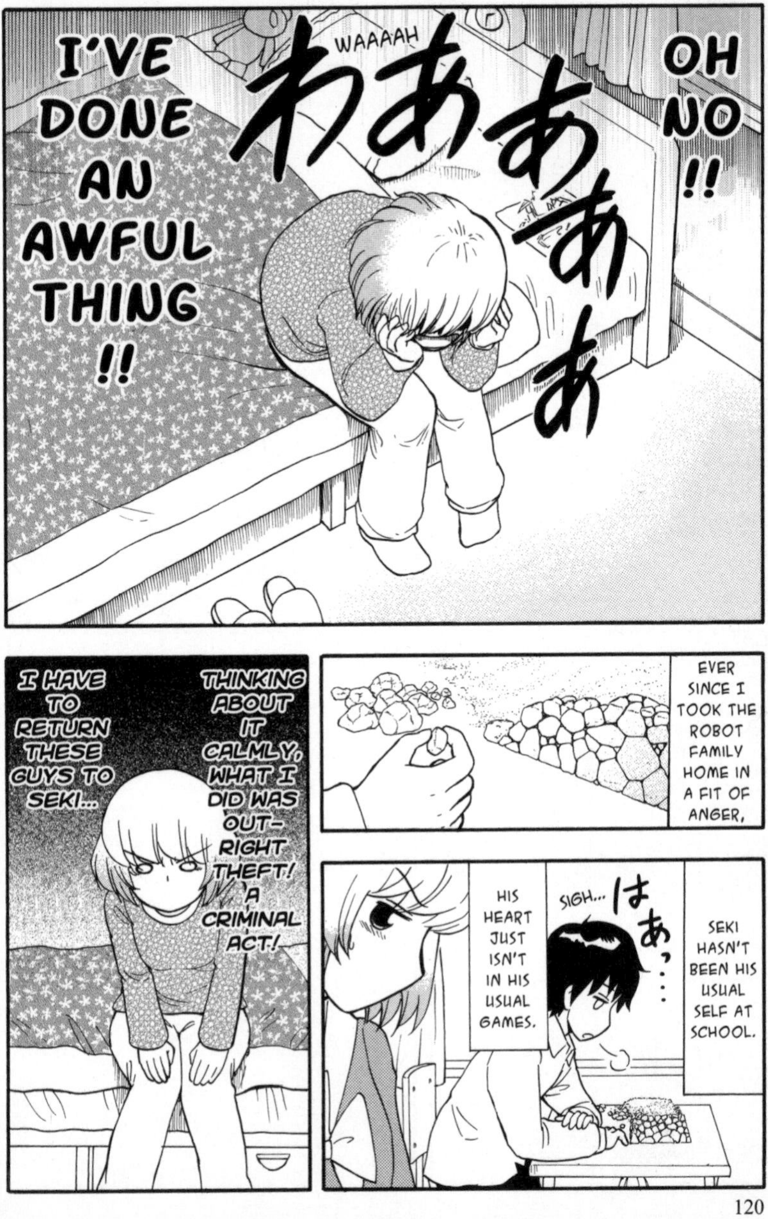
OH NO!!
WAAAAH
わあああああ
I'VE DONE AN AWFUL THING!!
EVER SINCE I TOOK THE ROBOT FAMILY HOME IN A FIT OF ANGER,
SEKI HASN'T BEEN HIS USUAL SELF AT SCHOOL.
SIGH...
はあっ…
HIS HEART JUST ISN'T IN HIS USUAL GAMES.
THINKING ABOUT IT CALMLY, WHAT I DID WAS OUT-RIGHT THEFT! A CRIMINAL ACT!
I HAVE TO RETURN THESE GUYS TO SEKI...

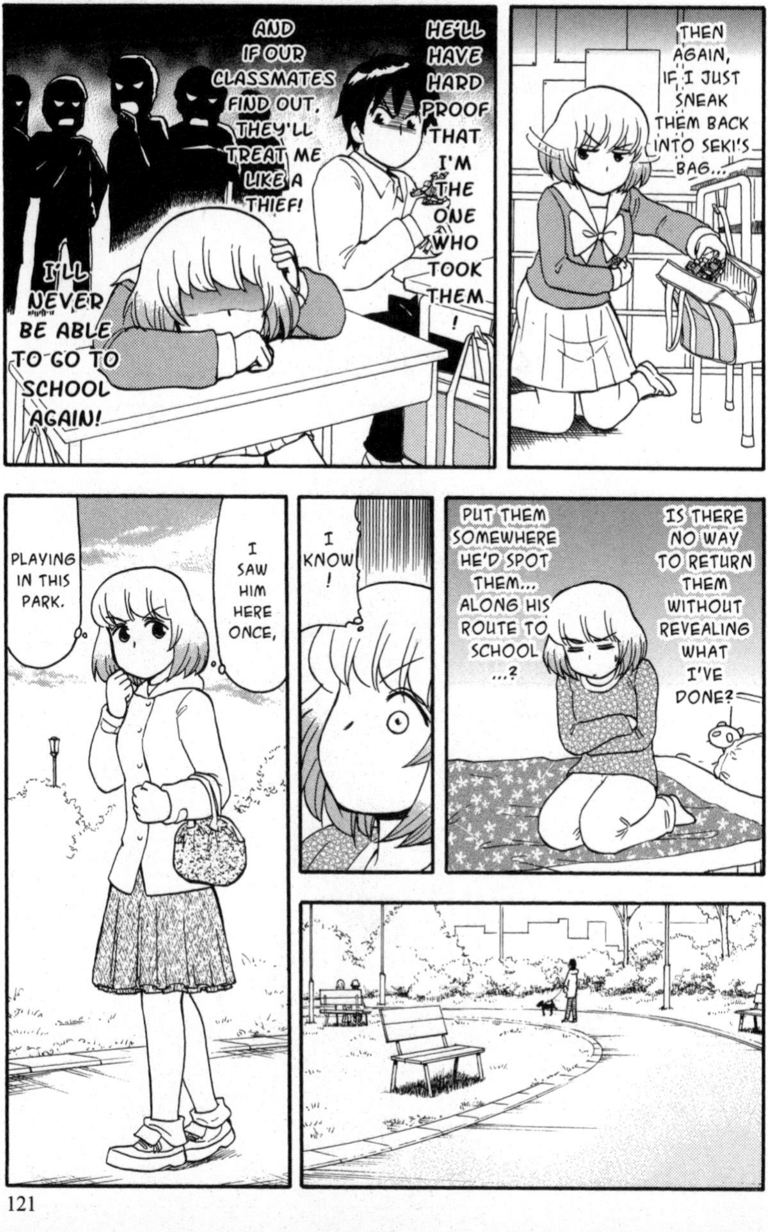
THEN AGAIN, IF I JUST SNEAK THEM BACK INTO SEKI'S BAG...
HE'LL HAVE HARD PROOF THAT I'M THE ONE WHO TOOK THEM!
AND IF OUR CLASSMATES FIND OUT, THEY'LL TREAT ME LIKE A THIEF!
I'LL NEVER BE ABLE TO GO TO SCHOOL AGAIN!
IS THERE NO WAY TO RETURN THEM WITHOUT REVEALING WHAT I'VE DONE?
PUT THEM SOMEWHERE HE'D SPOT THEM... ALONG HIS ROUTE TO SCHOOL ...?
I KNOW!
I SAW HIM HERE ONCE,
PLAYING IN THIS PARK.

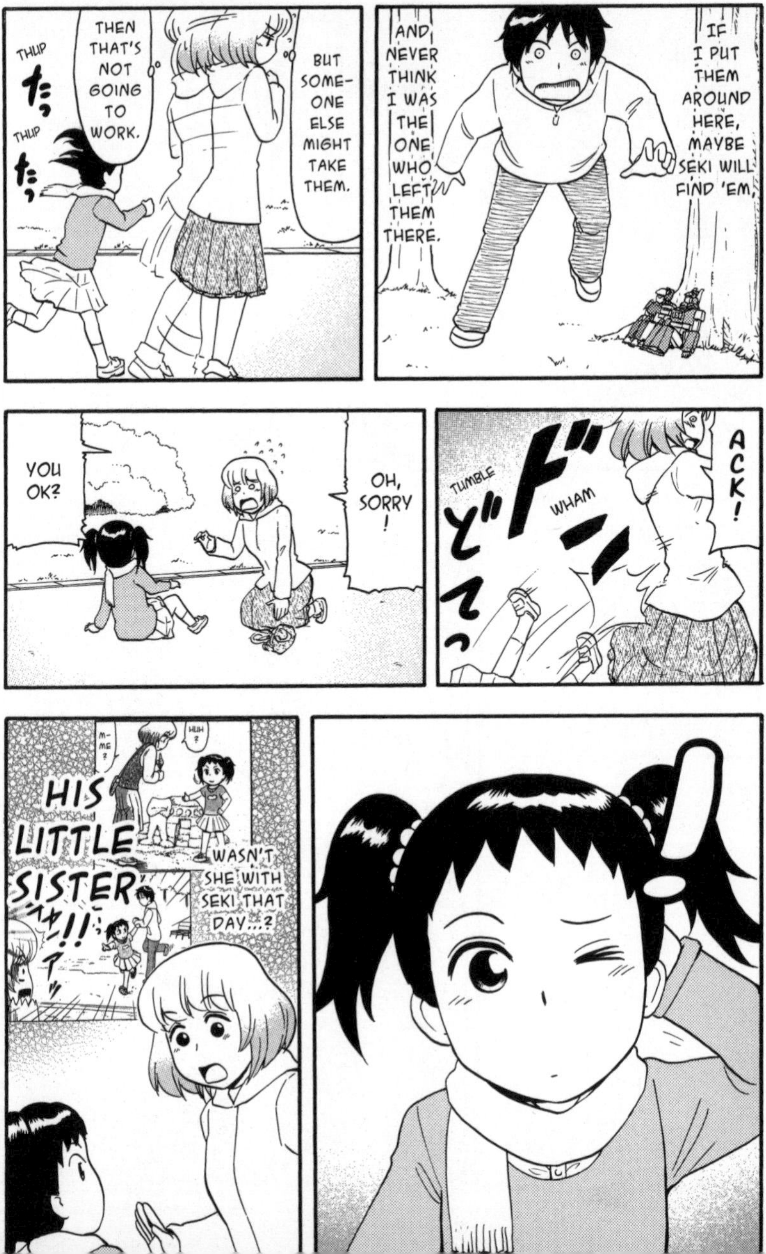
IF I PUT THEM AROUND HERE, MAYBE SEKI WILL FIND 'EM,
AND NEVER THINK I WAS THE ONE WHO LEFT THEM THERE.
BUT SOMEONE ELSE MIGHT TAKE THEM.
THEN THAT'S NOT GOING TO WORK.
THUP
たっ
THUP
たっ
ACK!
TUMBLE
どてっ
WHAM
ドン
OH, SORRY!
YOU OK?
HUH?
M-ME?
WASN'T SHE WITH SEKI THAT DAY...?
HIS LITTLE SISTER!!

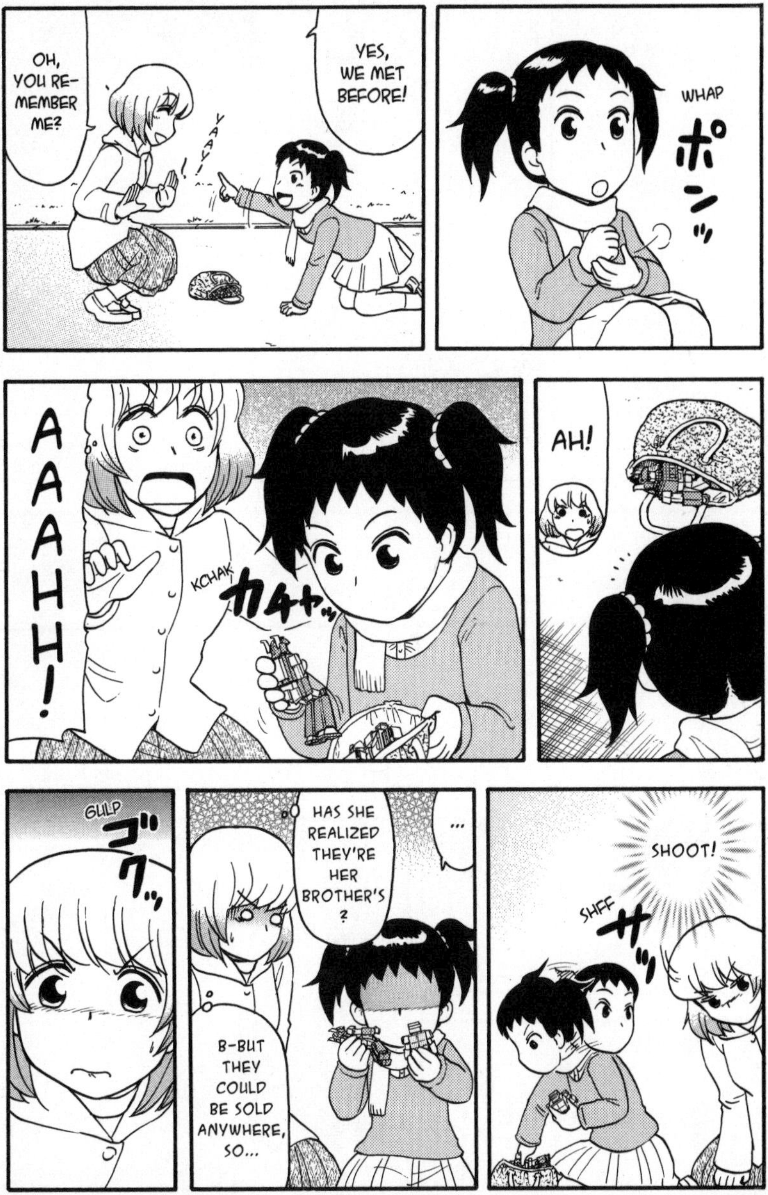
WHAP
ポンッ
YES, WE MET BEFORE!
YAAY!
OH, YOU RE-MEMBER ME?
AH!
KCHAK
カチャッ
AAAAHH!
SHOOT!
SHFF
サッ
...
HAS SHE REALIZED THEY'RE HER BROTHER'S?
B-BUT THEY COULD BE SOLD ANYWHERE, SO...
GULP
ゴクッ

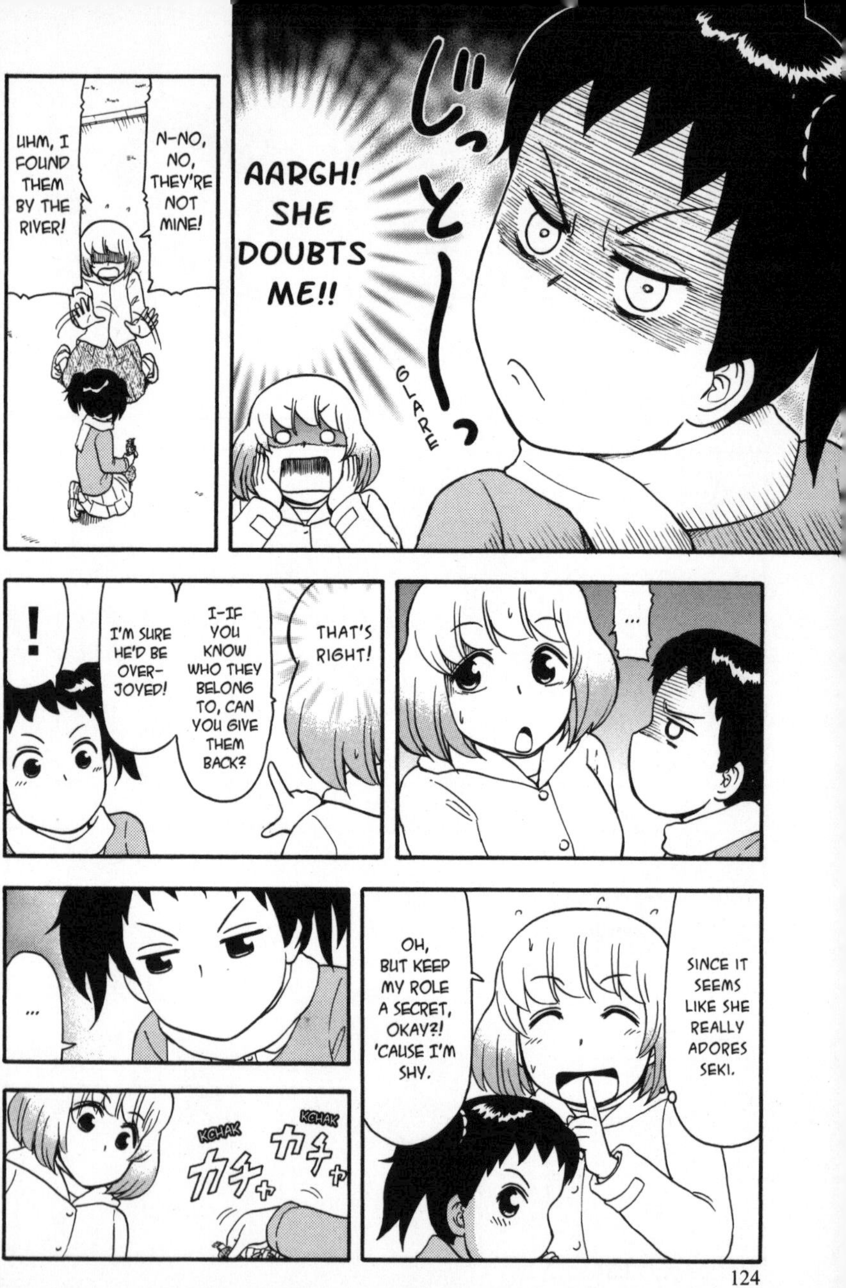
じっとーっ
GLARE
AARGH! SHE DOUBTS ME!!
N-NO, NO, THEY'RE NOT MINE!
UHM, I FOUND THEM BY THE RIVER!
...
THAT'S RIGHT!
I-IF YOU KNOW WHO THEY BELONG TO, CAN YOU GIVE THEM BACK?
I'M SURE HE'D BE OVER-JOYED!
!
SINCE IT SEEMS LIKE SHE REALLY ADORES SEKI.
OH, BUT KEEP MY ROLE A SECRET, OKAY?! 'CAUSE I'M SHY.
...
KCHAK
カチャ
KCHAK
カチャ

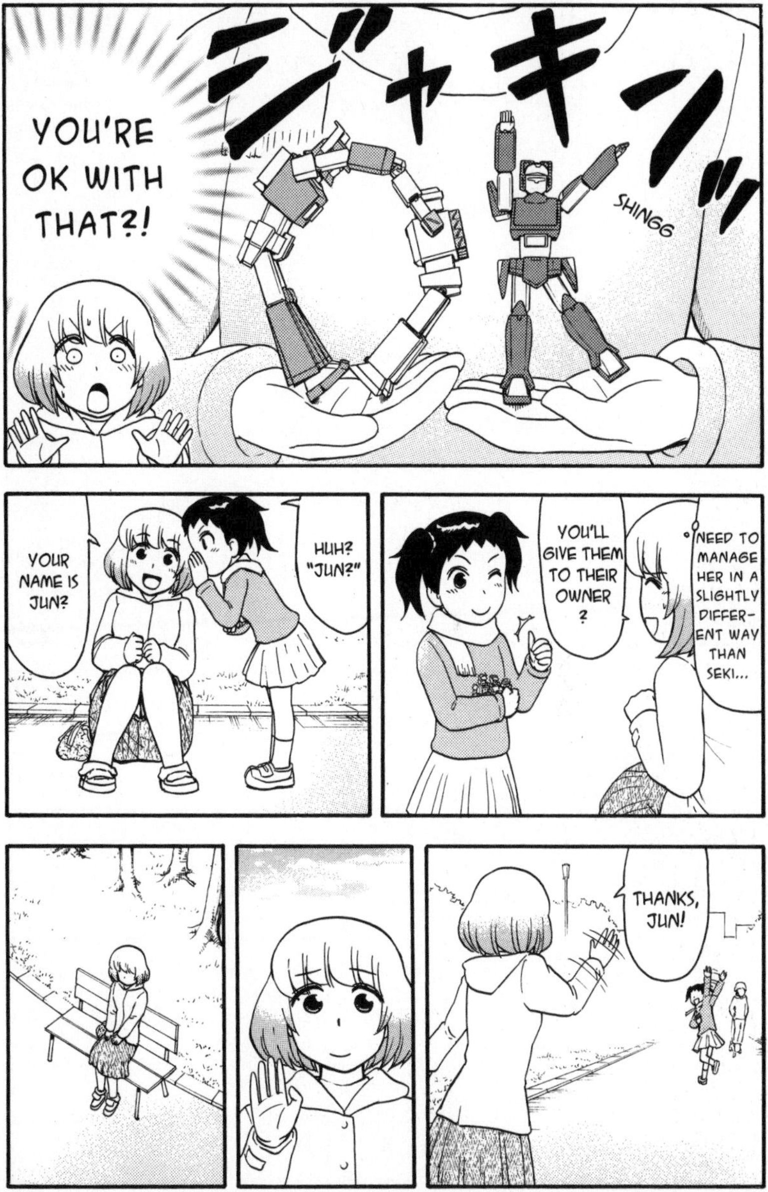
ジャキンッ
SHINGG
YOU'RE OK WITH THAT?!
NEED TO MANAGE HER IN A SLIGHTLY DIFFER-ENT WAY THAN SEKI...
YOU'LL GIVE THEM TO THEIR OWNER?
HUH? "JUN?"
YOUR NAME IS JUN?
THANKS, JUN!

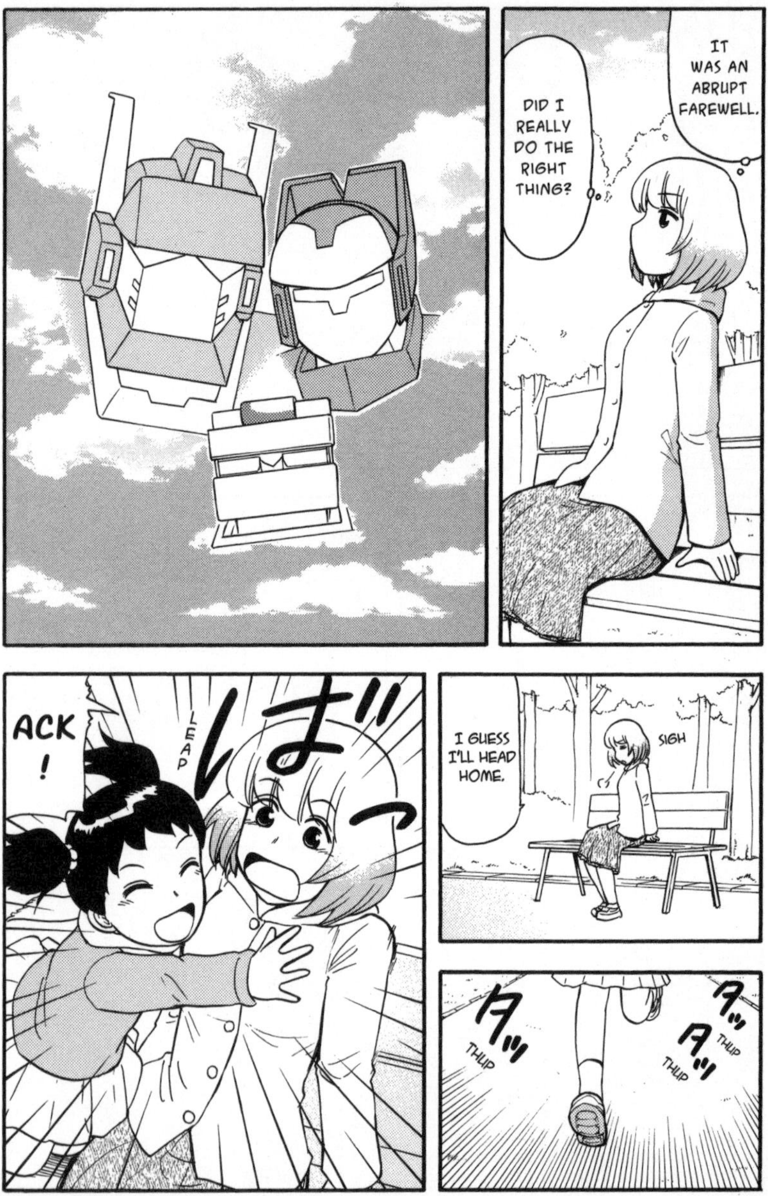
IT WAS AN ABRUPT FAREWELL.
DID I REALLY DO THE RIGHT THING?
SIGH
I GUESS I'LL HEAD HOME.
タッ
THUP
タッ
THUP
タッ
THUP
ばっ
LEAP
ACK!

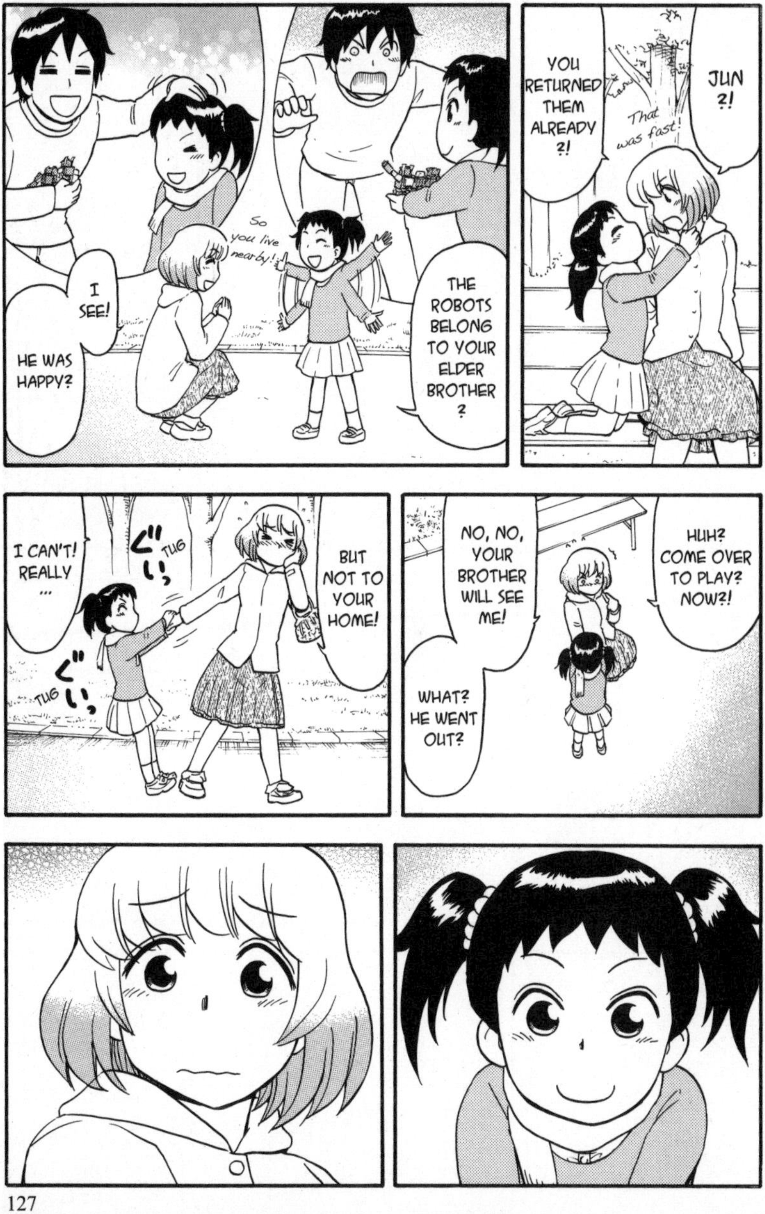

JUN ?!
That was fast!
YOU RETURNED THEM ALREADY ?!
THE ROBOTS BELONG TO YOUR ELDER BROTHER ?
So you live nearby!
I SEE!
HE WAS HAPPY?
HUH? COME OVER TO PLAY? NOW?!
NO, NO, YOUR BROTHER WILL SEE ME!
WHAT? HE WENT OUT?
BUT NOT TO YOUR HOME!
ぐいっ TUG
I CAN'T! REALLY ...
ぐいっ TUG

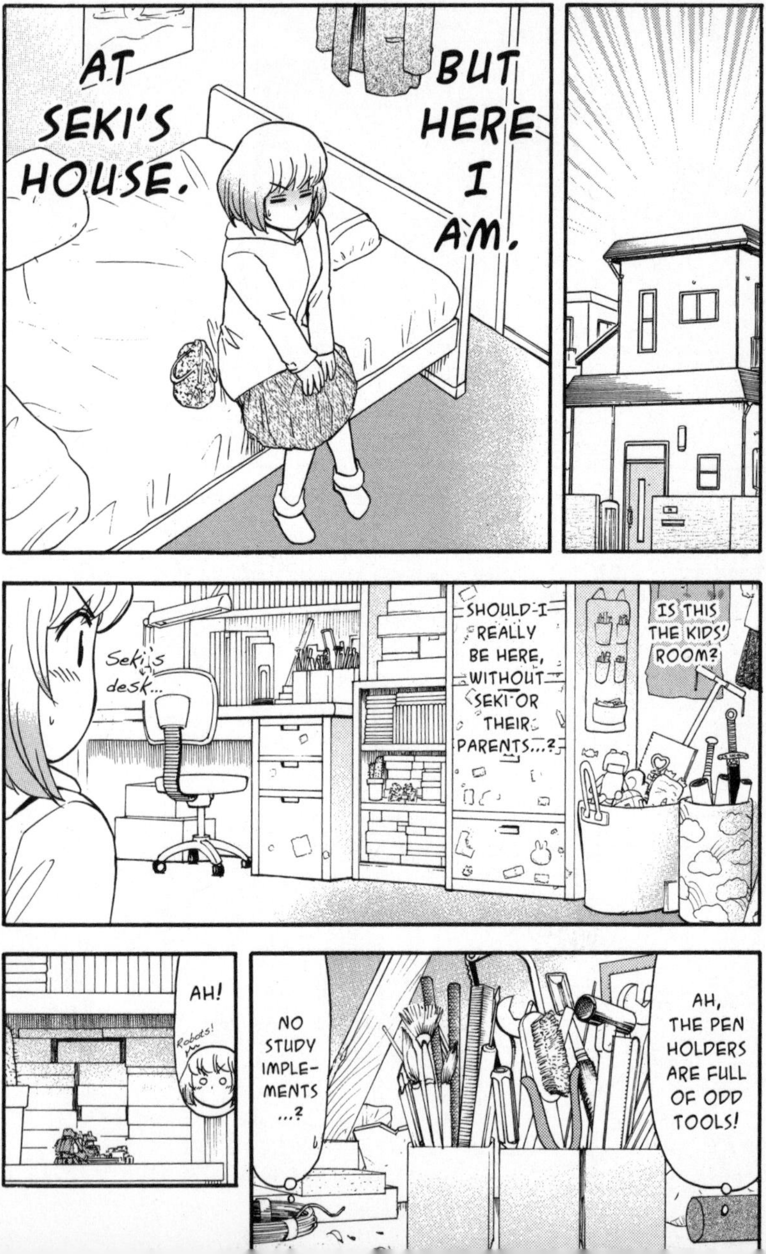
BUT HERE I AM.
AT SEKI'S HOUSE.
IS THIS THE KIDS' ROOM?
SHOULD I REALLY BE HERE, WITHOUT SEKI OR THEIR PARENTS...?
Seki's desk...
AH, THE PEN HOLDERS ARE FULL OF ODD TOOLS!
NO STUDY IMPLE-MENTS...?
AH!
Robots!

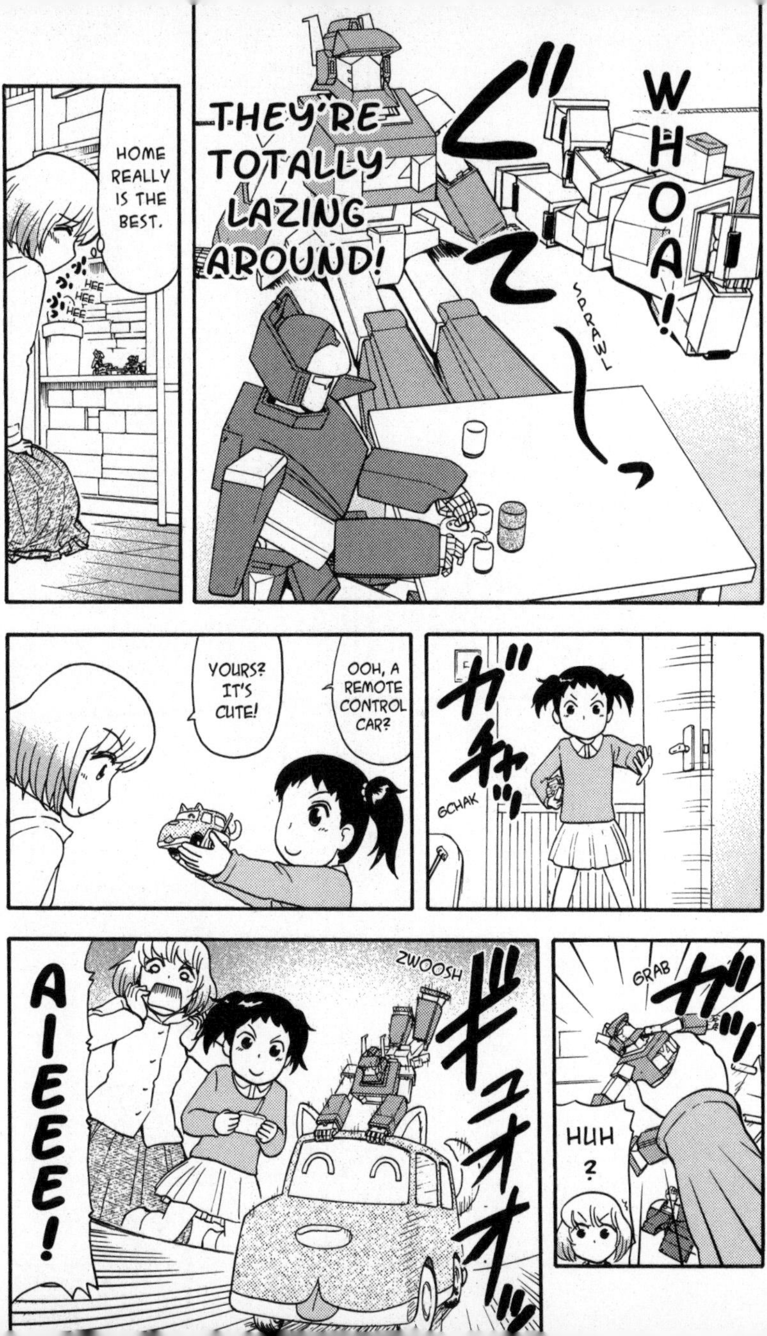
WHOA!
THEY'RE TOTALLY LAZING AROUND!
SPRAWL
HOME REALLY IS THE BEST.
HEE HEE HEE
GCHAK
OOH, A REMOTE CONTROL CAR?
YOURS? IT'S CUTE!
GRAB
HUH?
ZWOOSH
AIEEE!

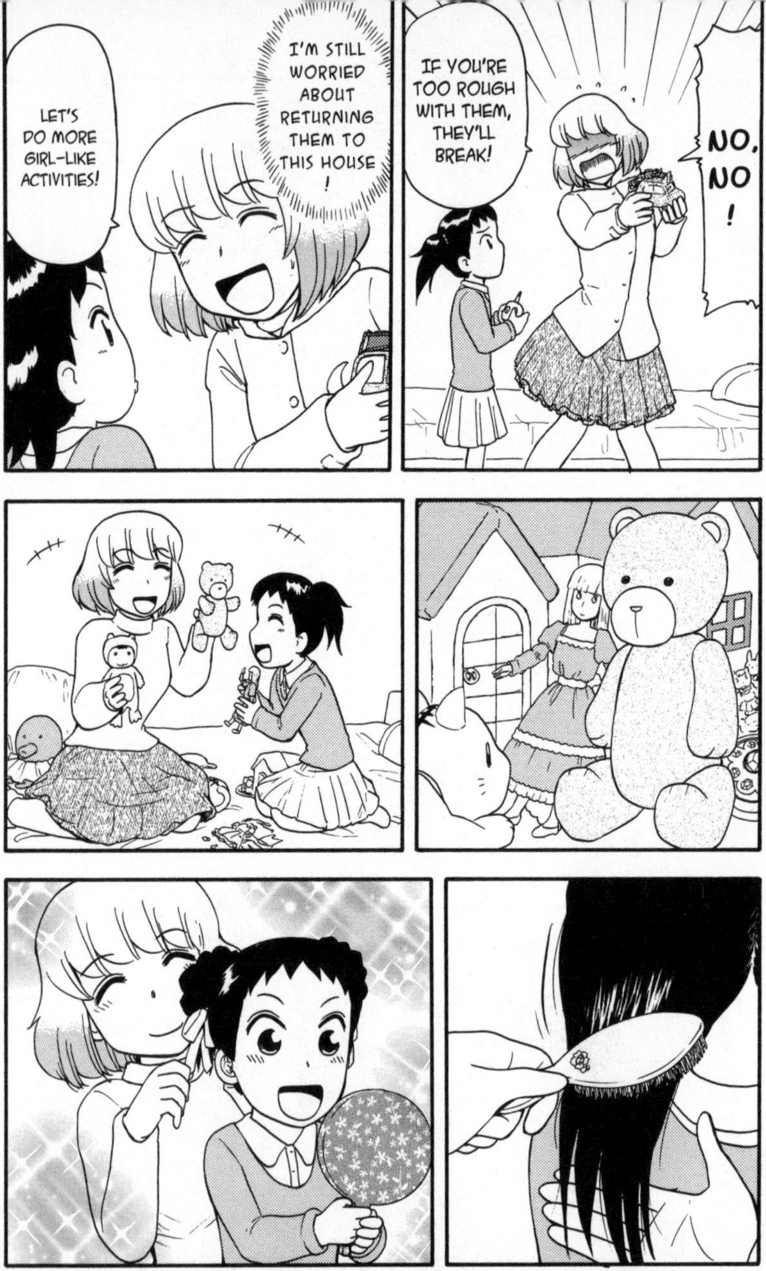
NO, NO!
IF YOU'RE TOO ROUGH WITH THEM, THEY'LL BREAK!
I'M STILL WORRIED ABOUT RETURNING THEM TO THIS HOUSE!
LET'S DO MORE GIRL-LIKE ACTIVITIES!

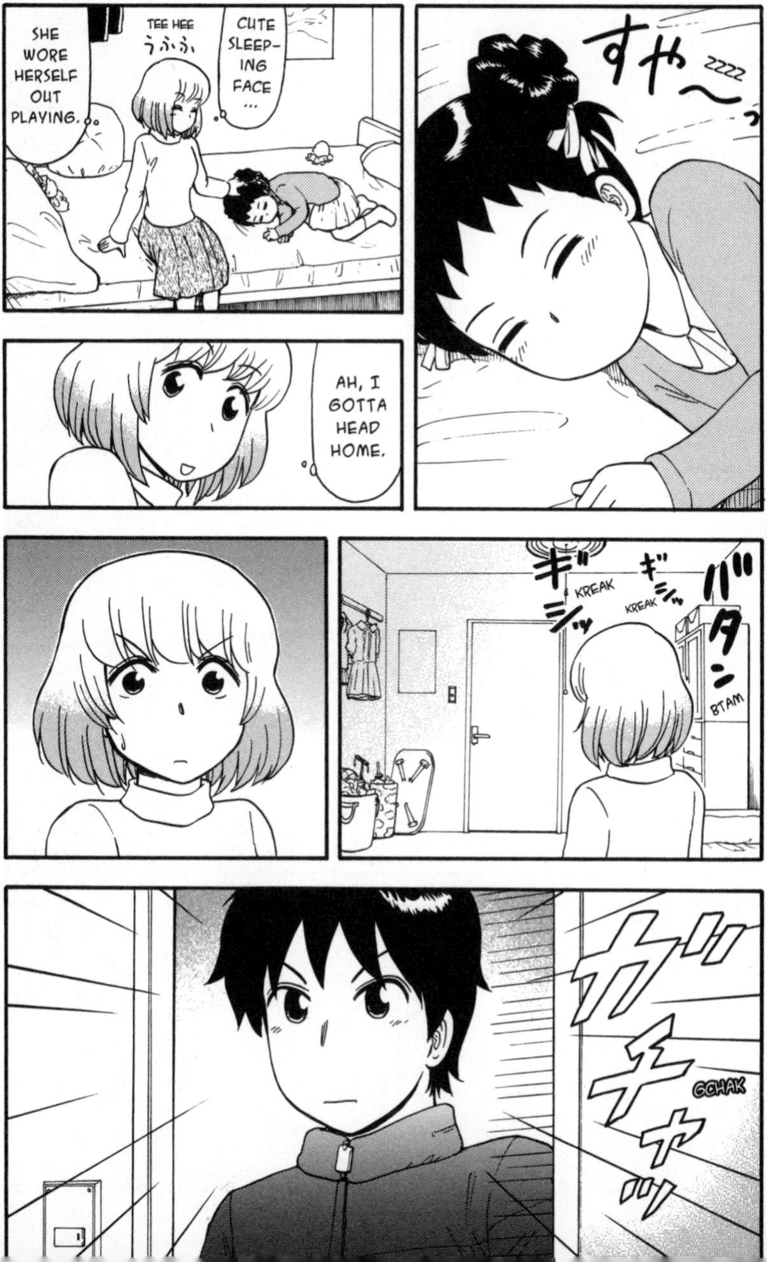
すや〜っ
ZZZZ
CUTE SLEEPING FACE...
TEE HEE
うふふ
SHE WORE HERSELF OUT PLAYING.
AH, I GOTTA HEAD HOME.
バタン
BTAM
ギシッ
KREAK
ギシッ
KREAK
ガチャッ
GCHAK

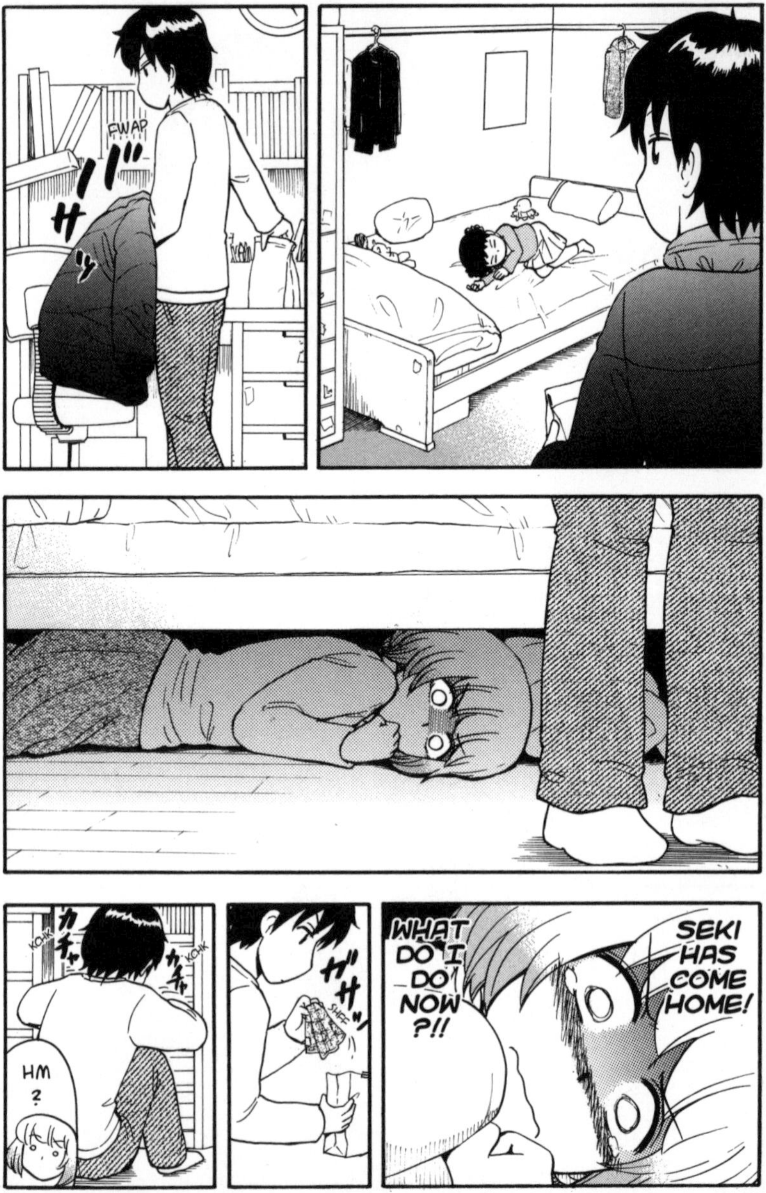
FWAP
SEKI HAS COME HOME!
WHAT DO I DO NOW?!!
ガサッ
SHFF
カチャ
KCHK
カチャ
KCHK
HM ?

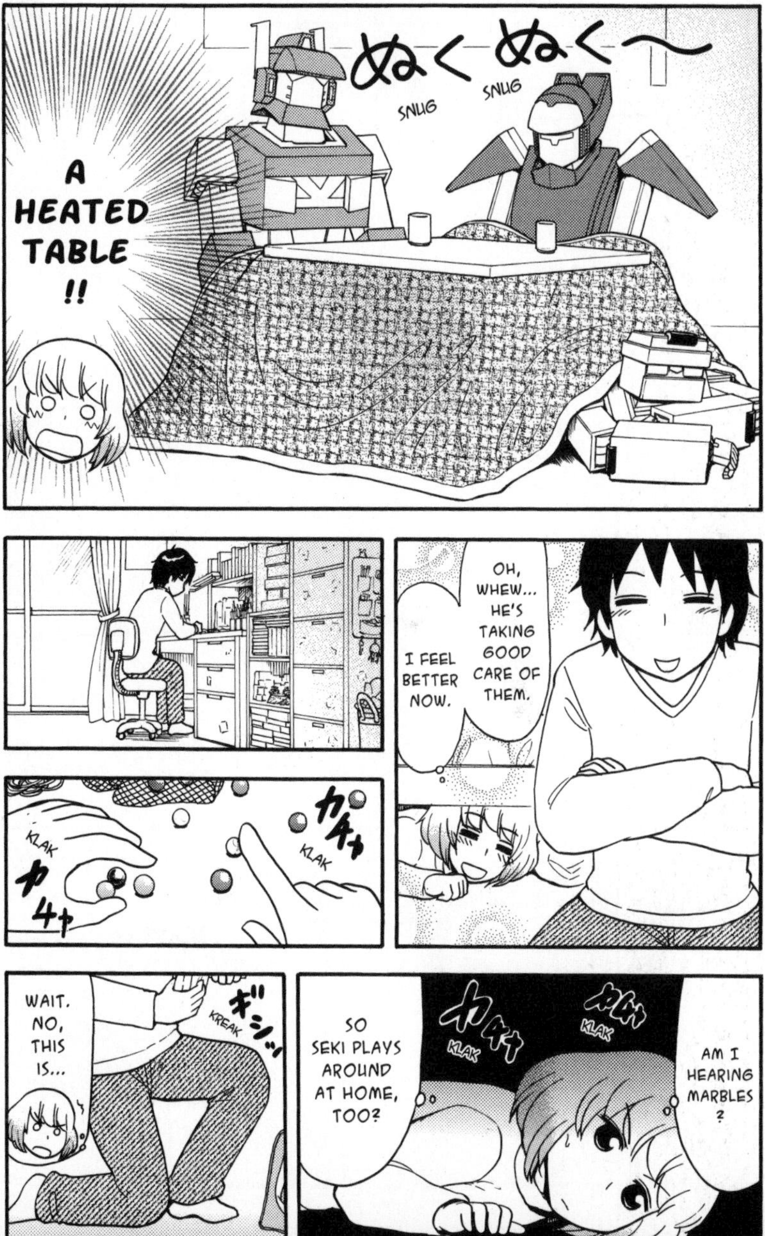
ぬくぬく〜
SNUG
SNUG
A HEATED TABLE !!
OH, WHEW... HE'S TAKING GOOD CARE OF THEM.
I FEEL BETTER NOW.
カチャ
KLAK
KLAK
カチャ
AM I HEARING MARBLES ?
カチャ
KLAK
カチャ
KLAK
SO SEKI PLAYS AROUND AT HOME, TOO?
ギシッ
KREAK
WAIT. NO, THIS IS...

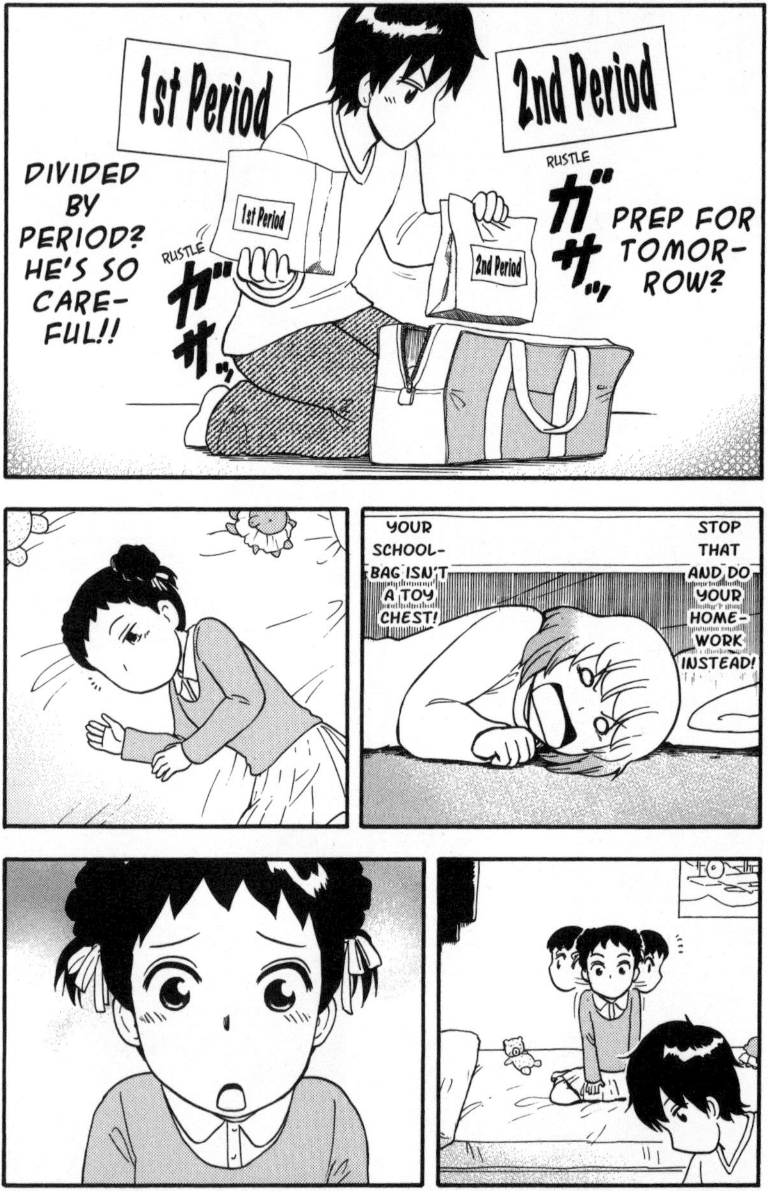
PREP FOR TOMORROW?
2nd Period
RUSTLE
ガサッ
2nd Period
1st Period
1st Period
RUSTLE
ガサッ
DIVIDED BY PERIOD? HE'S SO CAREFUL!!
STOP THAT AND DO YOUR HOMEWORK INSTEAD!
YOUR SCHOOLBAG ISN'T A TOY CHEST!

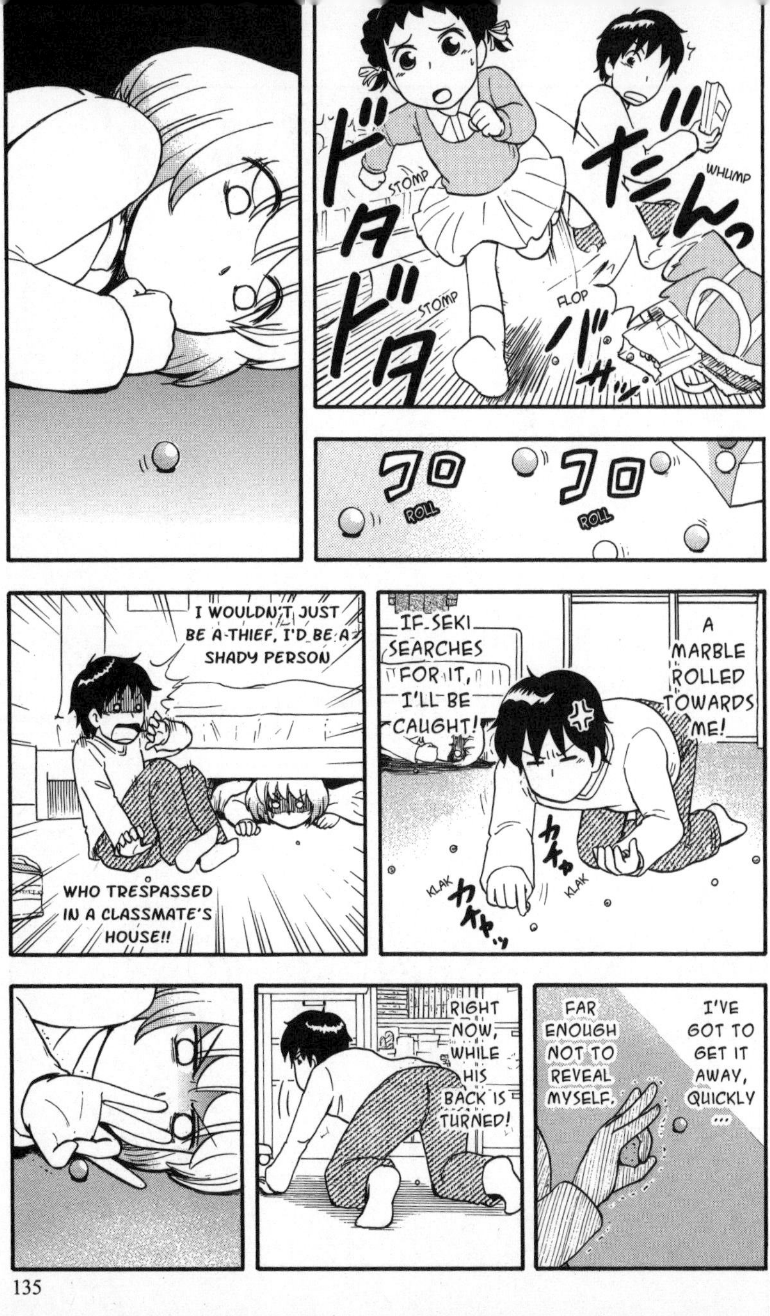
ドタドタ
STOMP
STOMP
だんっ
WHUMP
バサッ
FLOP
コロコロ
ROLL
ROLL
A MARBLE ROLLED TOWARDS ME!
IF SEKI SEARCHES FOR IT, I'LL BE CAUGHT!
カチャカチャッ
KLAK
KLAK
I WOULDN'T JUST BE A THIEF, I'D BE A SHADY PERSON
WHO TRESPASSED IN A CLASSMATE'S HOUSE!!
I'VE GOT TO GET IT AWAY, QUICKLY ...
FAR ENOUGH NOT TO REVEAL MYSELF.
RIGHT NOW, WHILE HIS BACK IS TURNED!

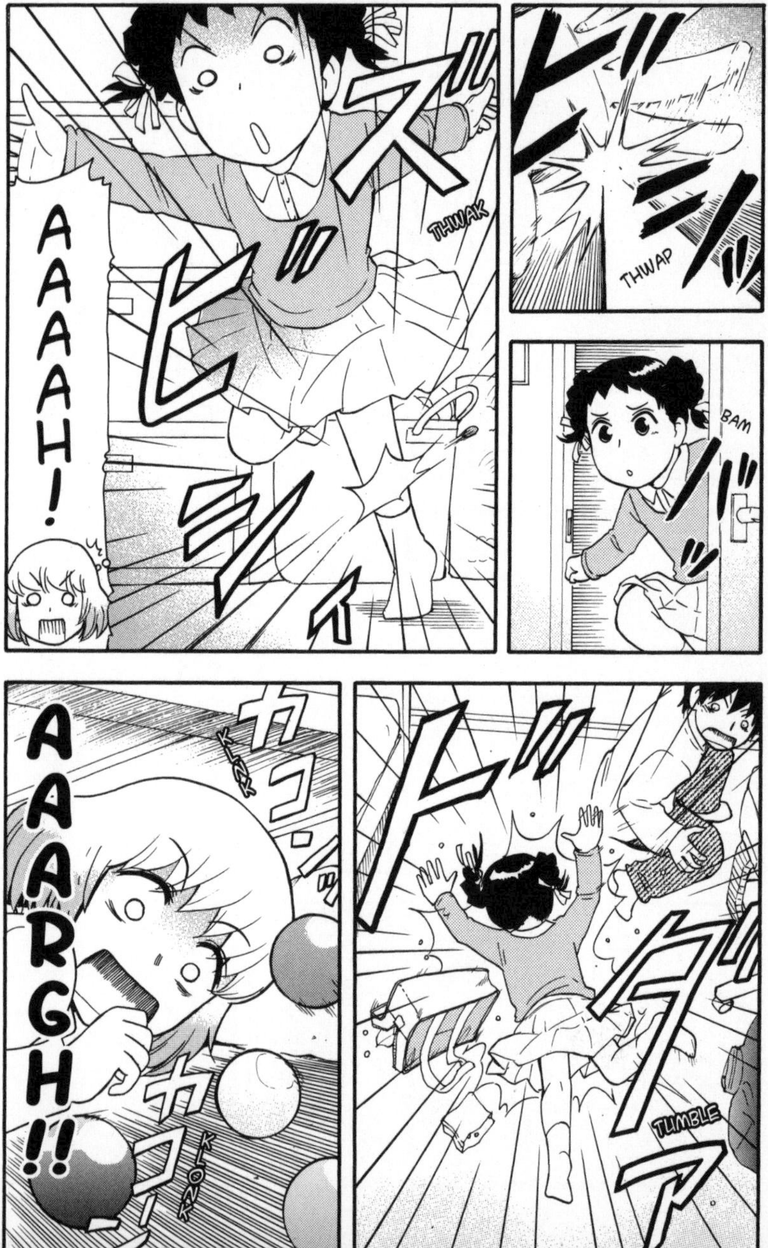
THWAP
BAM
THWAK
AAAAAH!
TUMBLE
KLICK
AAARGH!!
KLONK

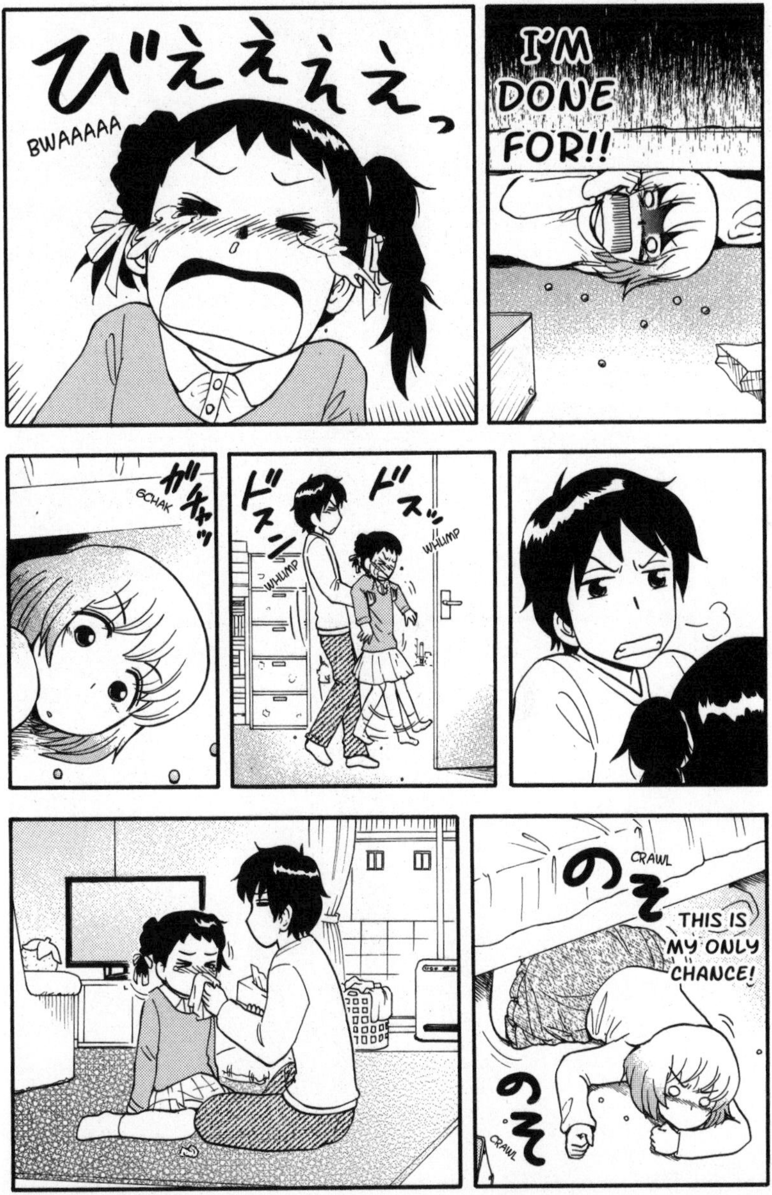
I'M DONE FOR!!
びえええええっ
BWAAAAA
ドスッ
WHUMP
ドスン
WHUMP
ガチャッ
GCHAK
のそ
CRAWL
THIS IS MY ONLY CHANCE!
のそ
CRAWL

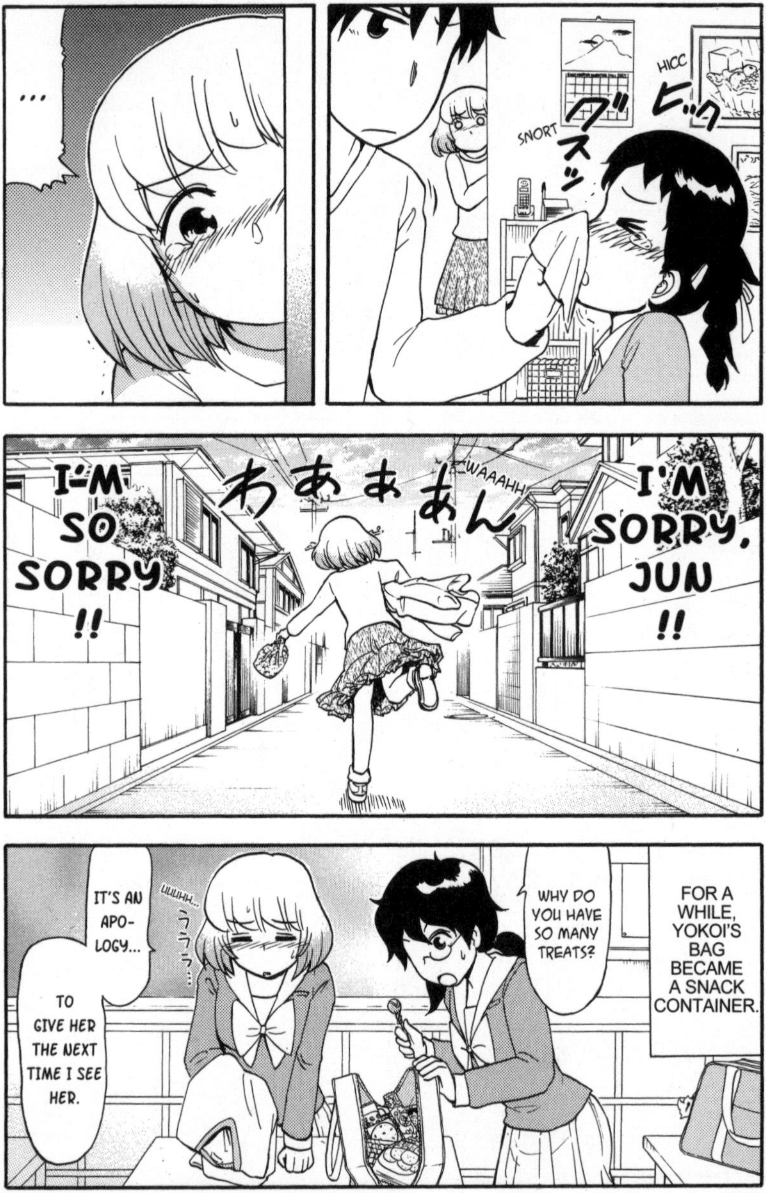
HICC
ヒック
SNORT
グズッ
...
I'M SORRY, JUN!!
わあああん
WAAAHH
I'M SO SORRY!!
FOR A WHILE, YOKOI'S BAG BECAME A SNACK CONTAINER.
WHY DO YOU HAVE SO MANY TREATS?
IT'S AN APOLOGY...
UUUHH...
TO GIVE HER THE NEXT TIME I SEE HER.

My Neighbor Seki

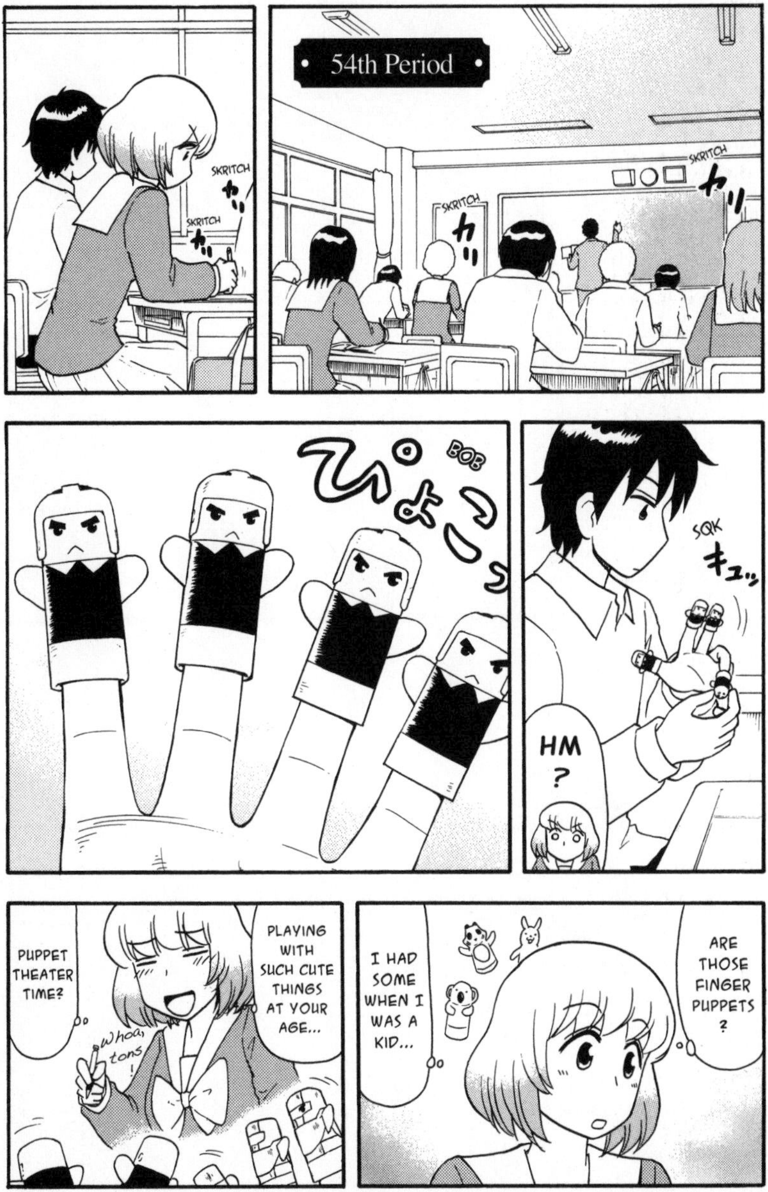
54th Period
SKRITCH
カリ
SKRITCH
カリ
SKRITCH
カリ
SKRITCH
ガリ
SQK
キュッ
HM ?
ぴょこーっ
BOB
ARE THOSE FINGER PUPPETS?
I HAD SOME WHEN I WAS A KID...
PLAYING WITH SUCH CUTE THINGS AT YOUR AGE...
PUPPET THEATER TIME?
Whoa, tons!

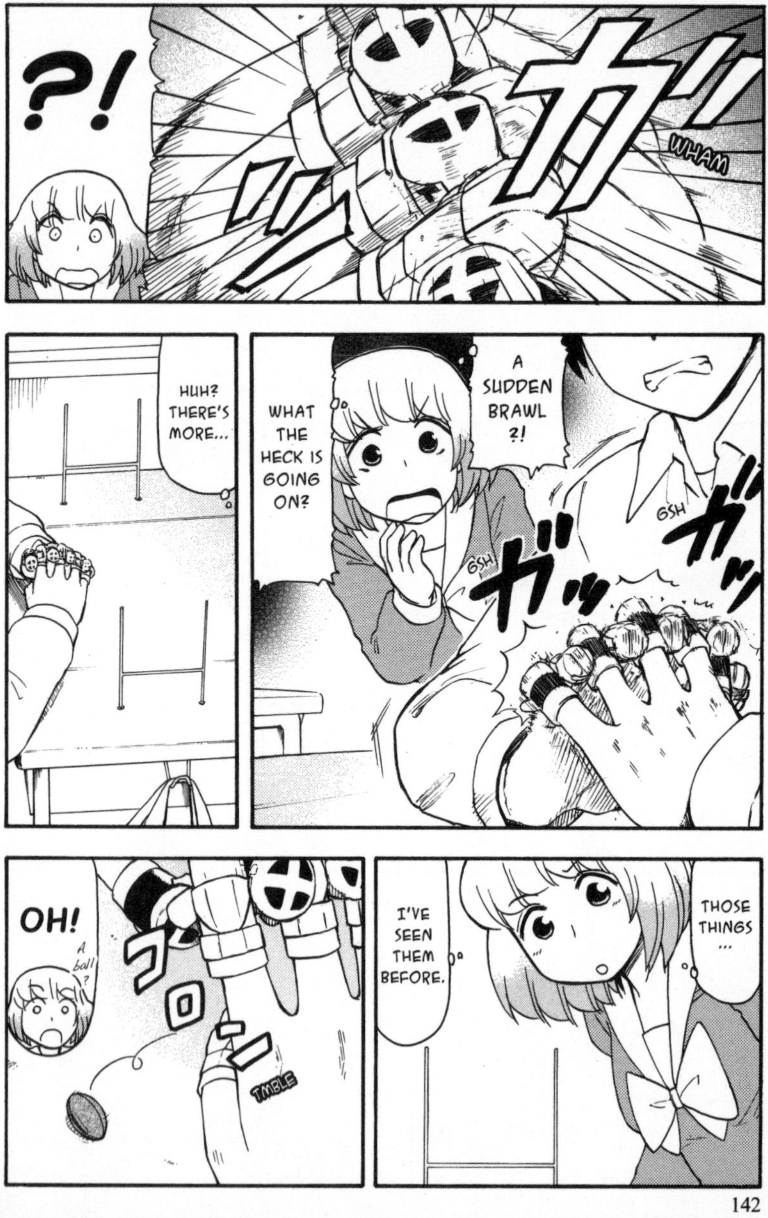
?!
WHAM
A SUDDEN BRAWL ?!
WHAT THE HECK IS GOING ON?
GSH
GSH
HUH? THERE'S MORE...
THOSE THINGS ...
I'VE SEEN THEM BEFORE.
OH!
A ball?
TMBLE

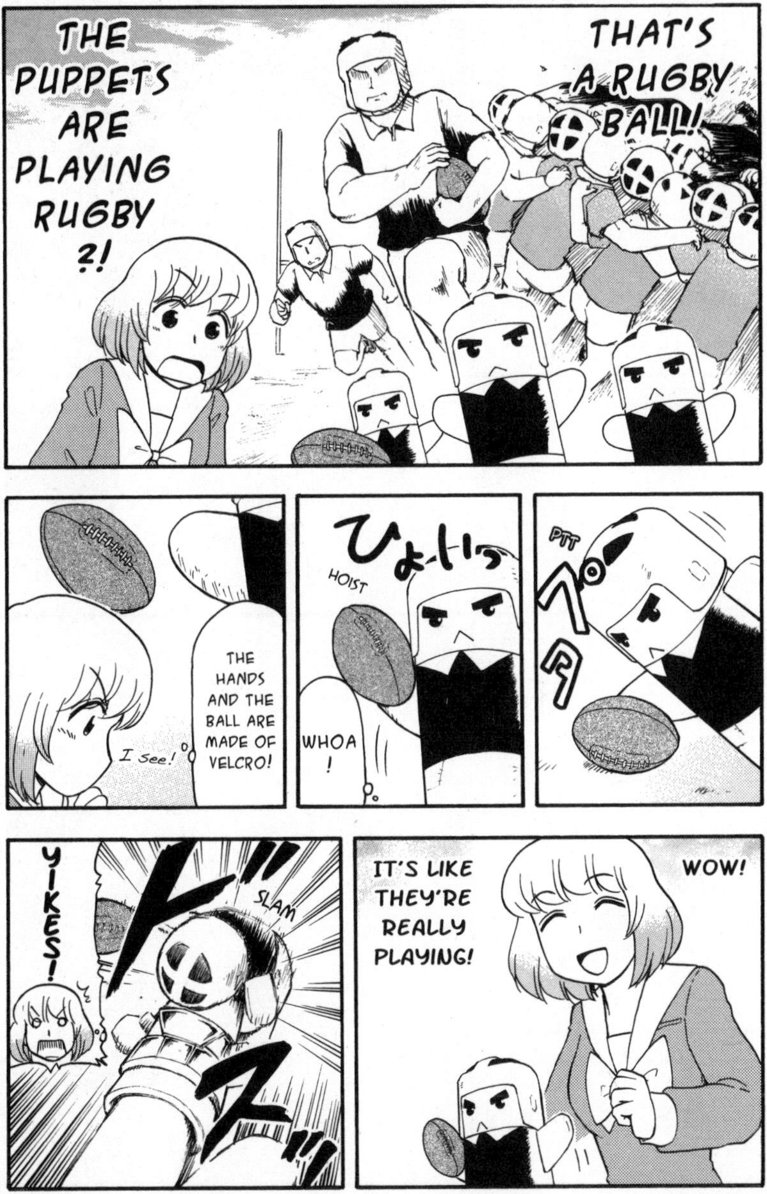
THAT'S A RUGBY BALL!
THE PUPPETS ARE PLAYING RUGBY?!
PTT
ペタ
ひょーいっ
HOIST
WHOA!
THE HANDS AND THE BALL ARE MADE OF VELCRO!
I see!
WOW!
IT'S LIKE THEY'RE REALLY PLAYING!
SLAM
YIKES!

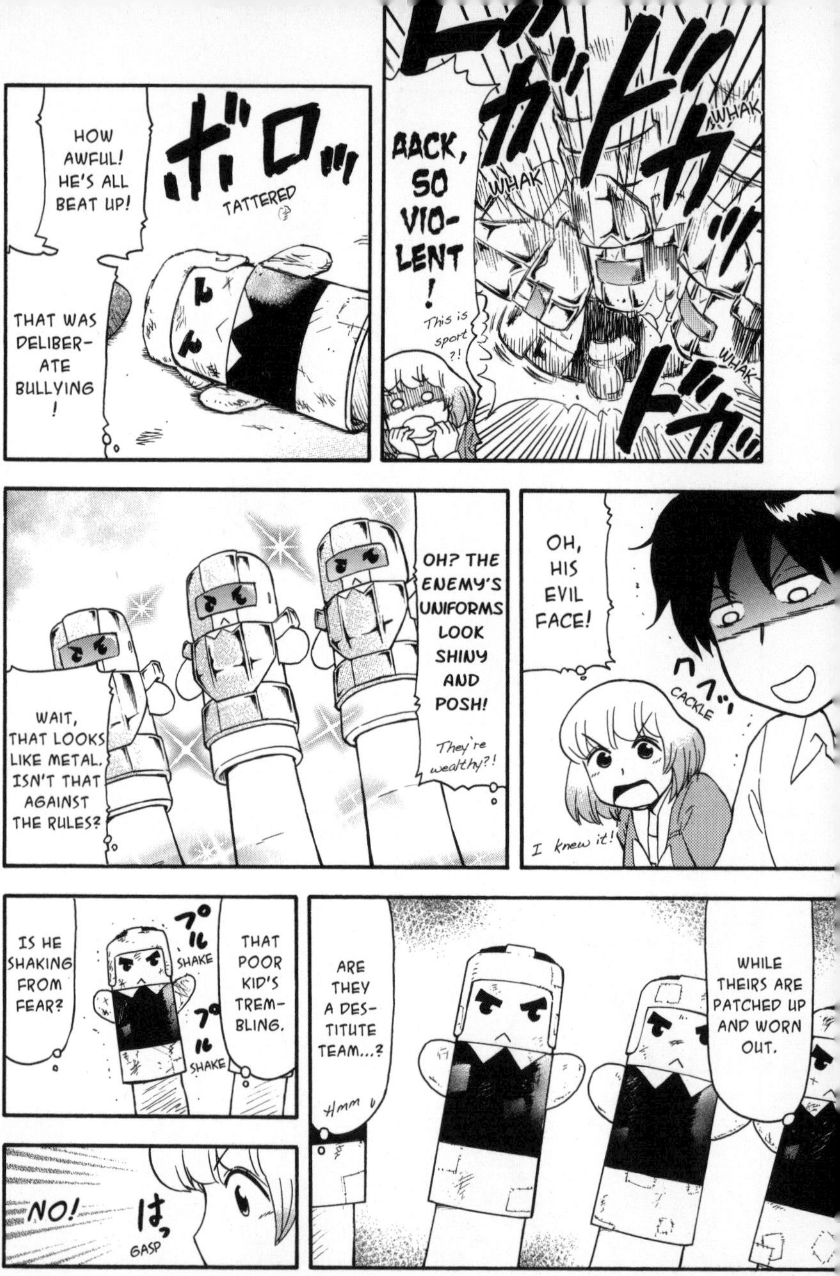
WHAK
WHAK
WHAK
AACK, SO VIO-LENT!
This is sport?!
HOW AWFUL! HE'S ALL BEAT UP!
TATTERED
THAT WAS DELIBER-ATE BULLYING!
OH, HIS EVIL FACE!
CACKLE
I knew it!
OH? THE ENEMY'S UNIFORMS LOOK SHINY AND POSH!
They're wealthy?!
WAIT, THAT LOOKS LIKE METAL. ISN'T THAT AGAINST THE RULES?
WHILE THEIRS ARE PATCHED UP AND WORN OUT.
ARE THEY A DES-TITUTE TEAM...?
Hmm
THAT POOR KID'S TREM-BLING.
SHAKE
SHAKE
IS HE SHAKING FROM FEAR?
GASP
NO!

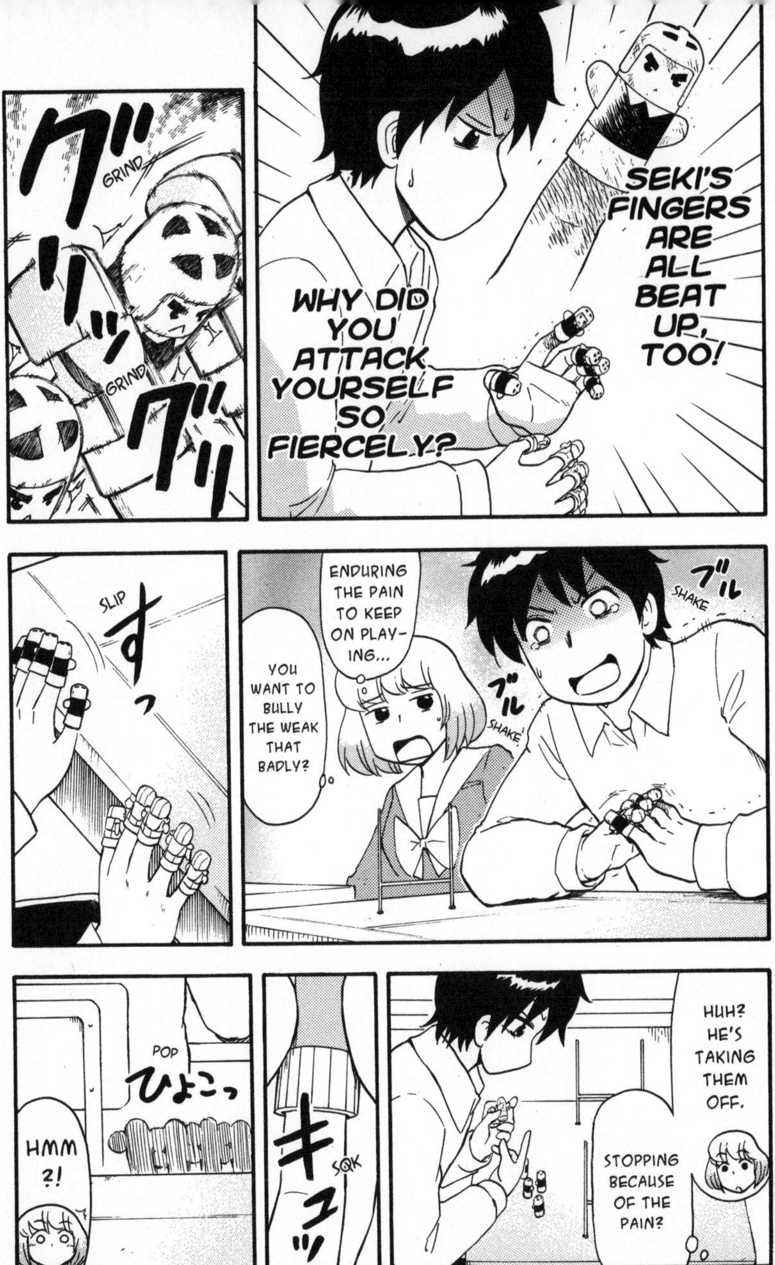
SEKI'S FINGERS ARE ALL BEAT UP, TOO!
WHY DID YOU ATTACK YOURSELF SO FIERCELY?
グリッ
GRIND
GRIND
グリ
ブル
SHAKE
ENDURING THE PAIN TO KEEP ON PLAY-ING...
YOU WANT TO BULLY THE WEAK THAT BADLY?
ブル
SHAKE
SLIP
すっ
HUH? HE'S TAKING THEM OFF.
STOPPING BECAUSE OF THE PAIN?
キュッ
SQK
POP
ひょこっ
HMM ?!

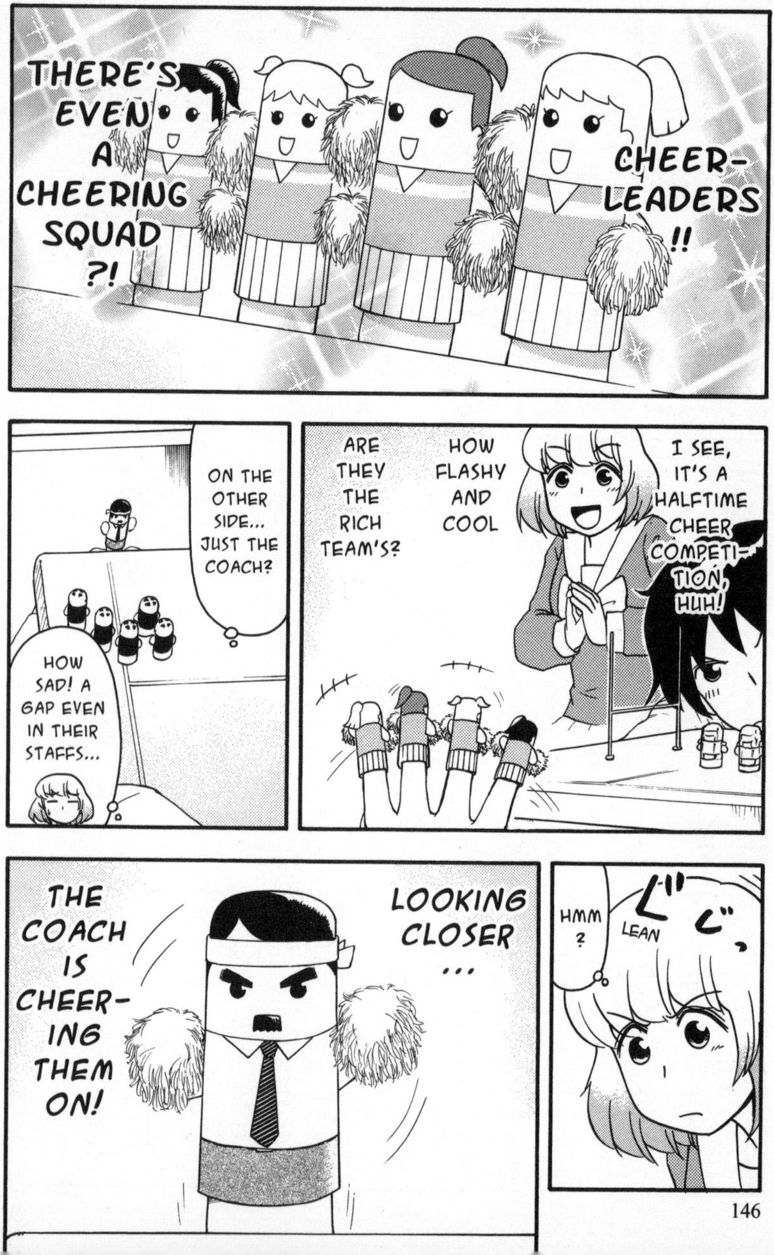
CHEER-LEADERS!!
THERE'S EVEN A CHEERING SQUAD?!
I SEE, IT'S A HALFTIME CHEER COMPETITION, HUH!
HOW FLASHY AND COOL
ARE THEY THE RICH TEAM'S?
ON THE OTHER SIDE... JUST THE COACH?
HOW SAD! A GAP EVEN IN THEIR STAFFS...
HMM?
LEAN
LOOKING CLOSER...
THE COACH IS CHEERING THEM ON!

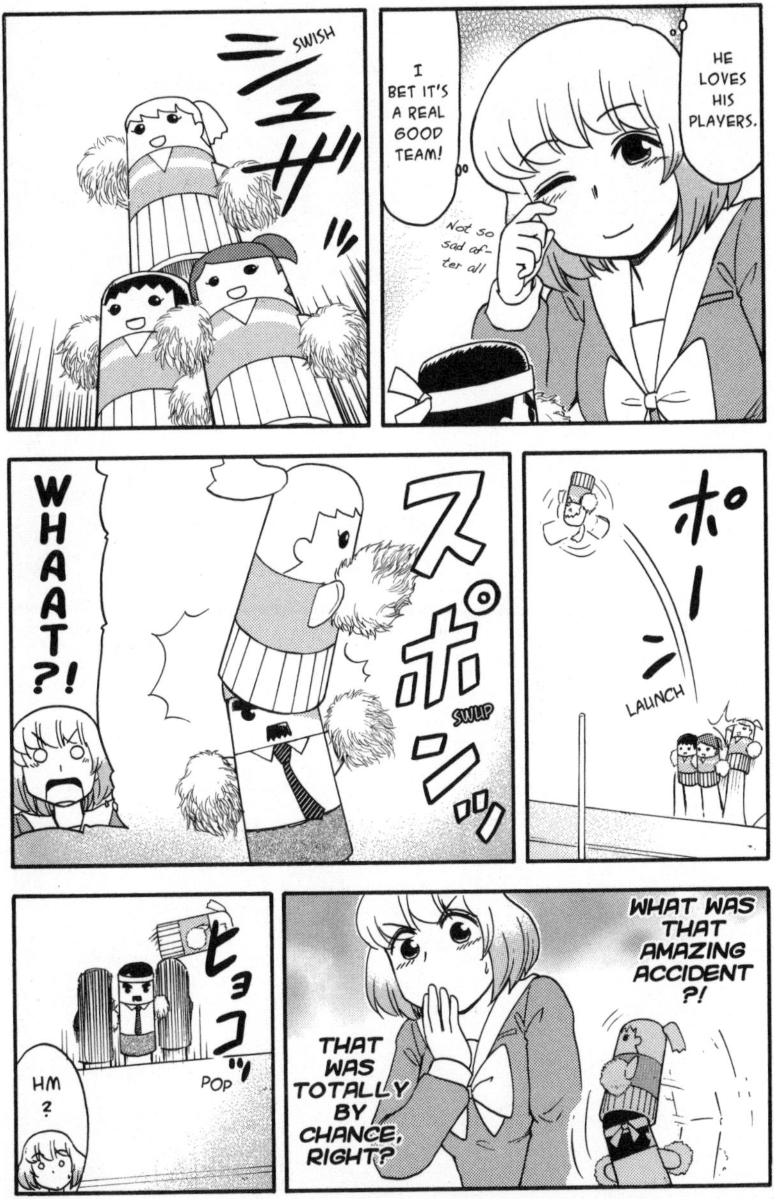
HE LOVES HIS PLAYERS.
I BET IT'S A REAL GOOD TEAM!
Not so sad after all
シュザッ
SWISH
ポーン
LAUNCH
スポンッ
SWUP
WHAAAT?!
WHAT WAS THAT AMAZING ACCIDENT?!
THAT WAS TOTALLY BY CHANCE, RIGHT?
ヒョコッ
POP
HM?

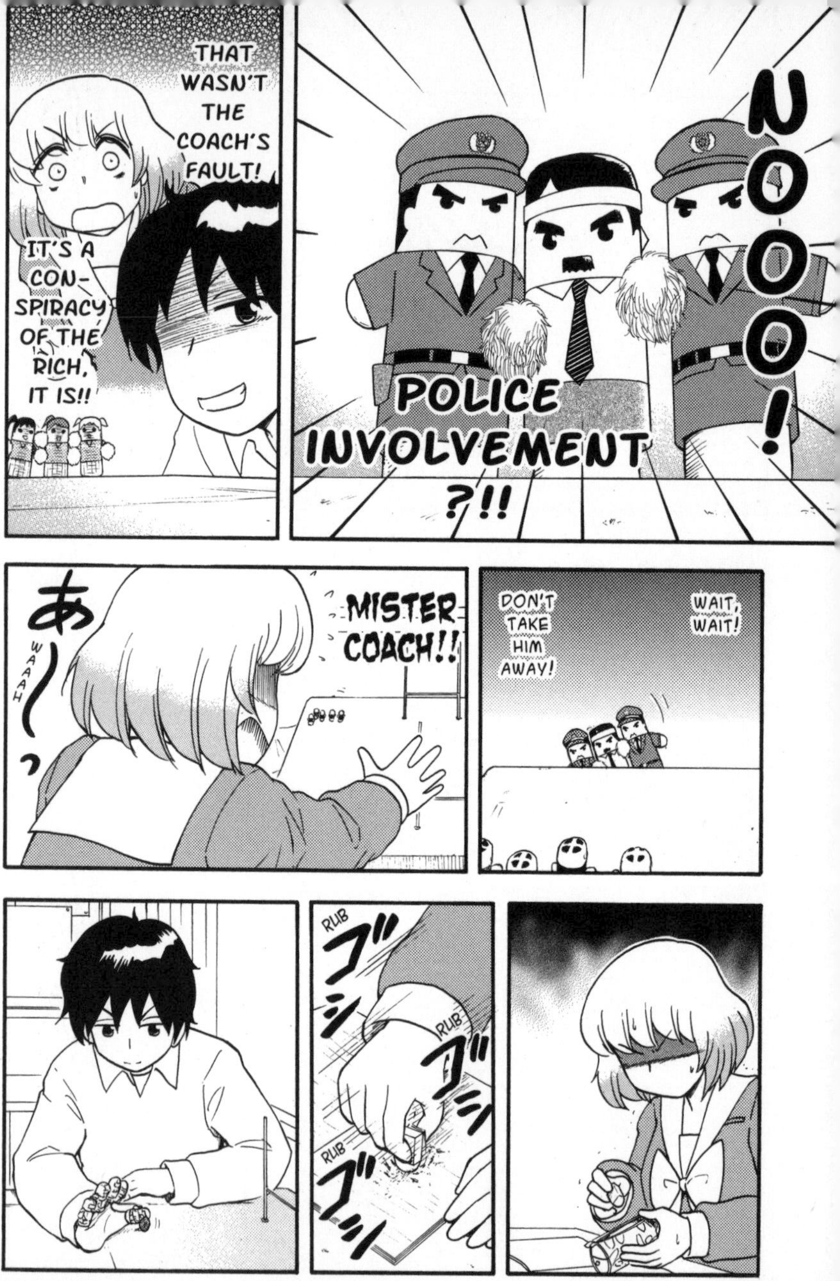
NOOOO!
POLICE INVOLVEMENT ?!!
THAT WASN'T THE COACH'S FAULT!
IT'S A CON-SPIRACY OF THE RICH, IT IS!!
WAIT, WAIT!
DON'T TAKE HIM AWAY!
MISTER COACH!!
あ～っ
WAAAH
RUB
ゴシ
RUB
ゴシ
RUB
ゴシ

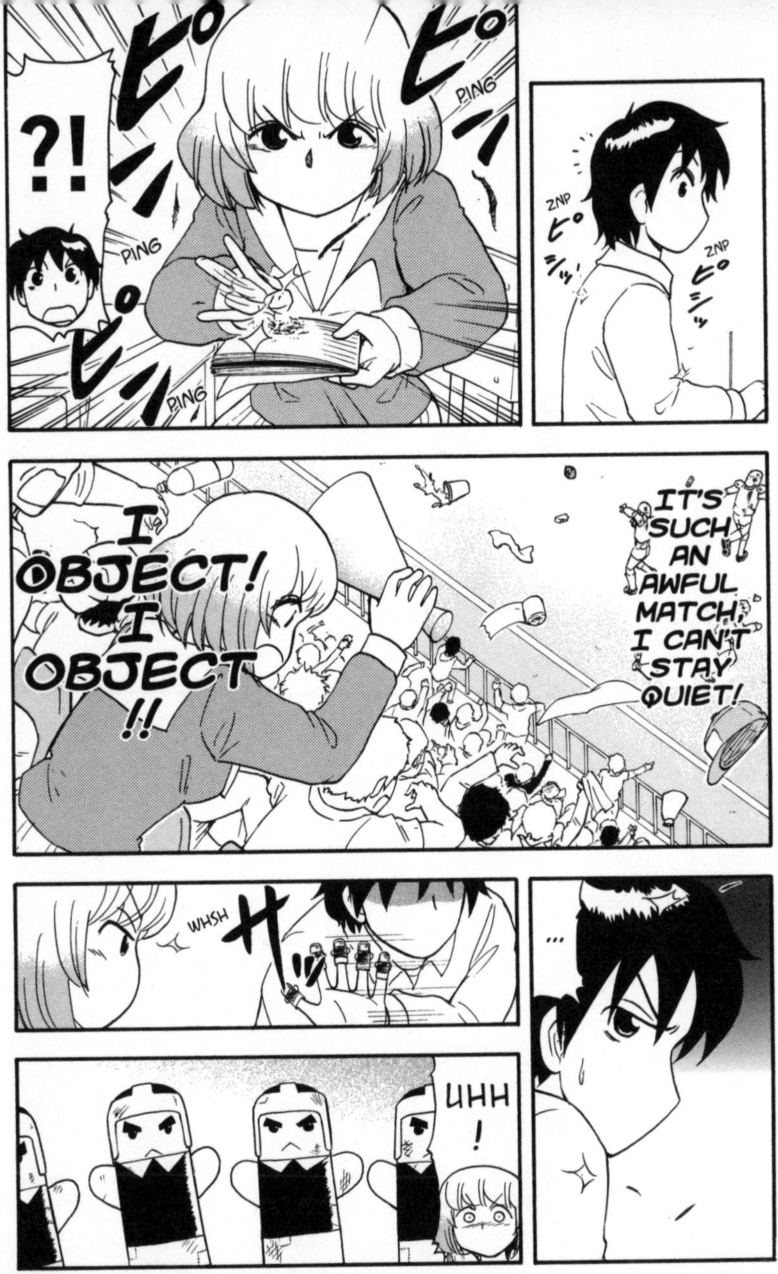
ZNP
ZNP
PING
PING
?!
PING
PING
IT'S SUCH AN AWFUL MATCH, I CAN'T STAY QUIET!
I OBJECT! I OBJECT!!
...
WHSH
UHH!

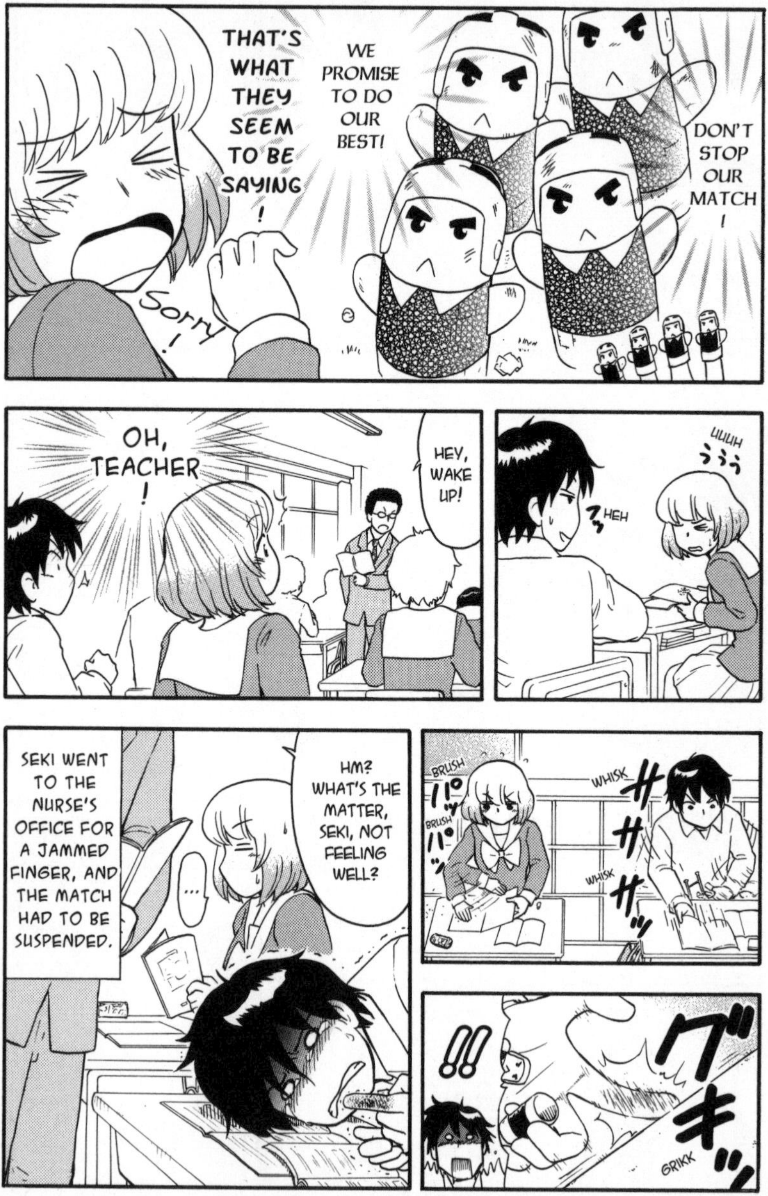
DON'T STOP OUR MATCH!
WE PROMISE TO DO OUR BEST!
THAT'S WHAT THEY SEEM TO BE SAYING!
Sorry!
UUUH
うぅぅ
HEH
HEY, WAKE UP!
OH, TEACHER!
WHISK
ザ
WHISK
ザ
ザッ
BRUSH
パッ
BRUSH
パッ
グギッ
GRIKK
!!!
HM? WHAT'S THE MATTER, SEKI, NOT FEELING WELL?
...
SEKI WENT TO THE NURSE'S OFFICE FOR A JAMMED FINGER, AND THE MATCH HAD TO BE SUSPENDED.

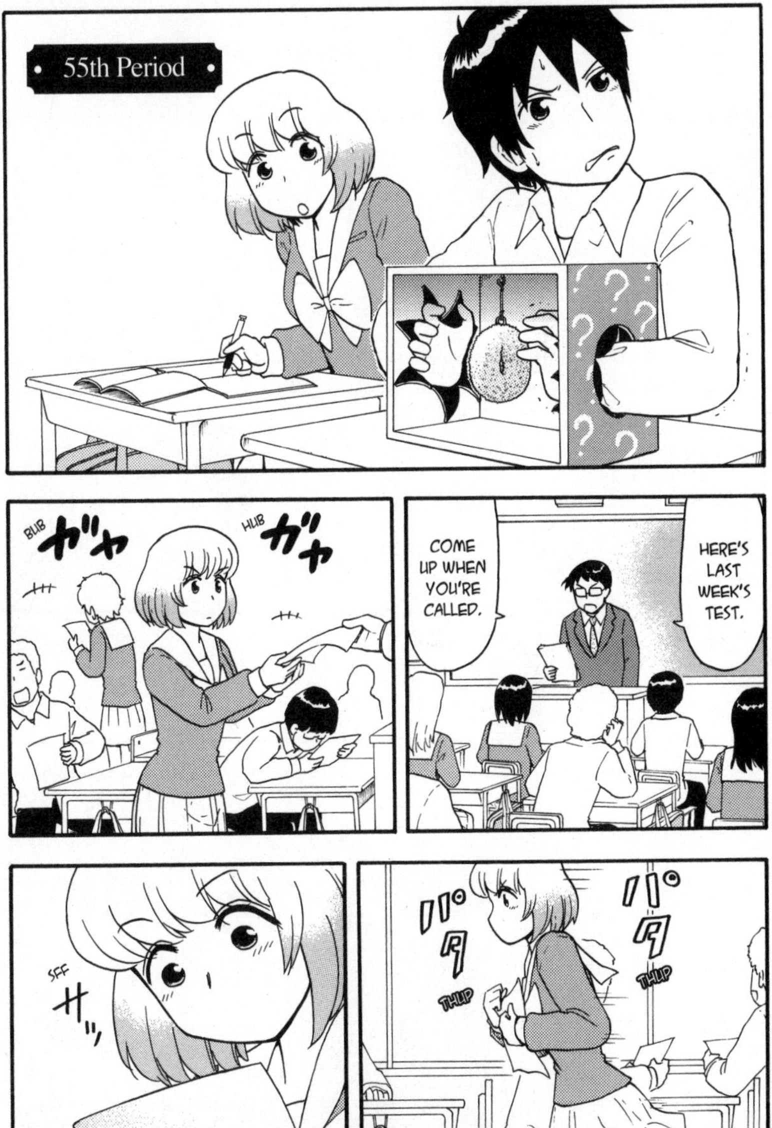

55th Period
HERE'S LAST WEEK'S TEST.
COME UP WHEN YOU'RE CALLED.
HUB ガヤ
BUB ガヤ
パタ THUP
パタ THUP
SFF サッ

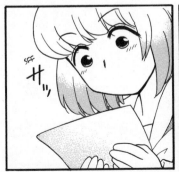

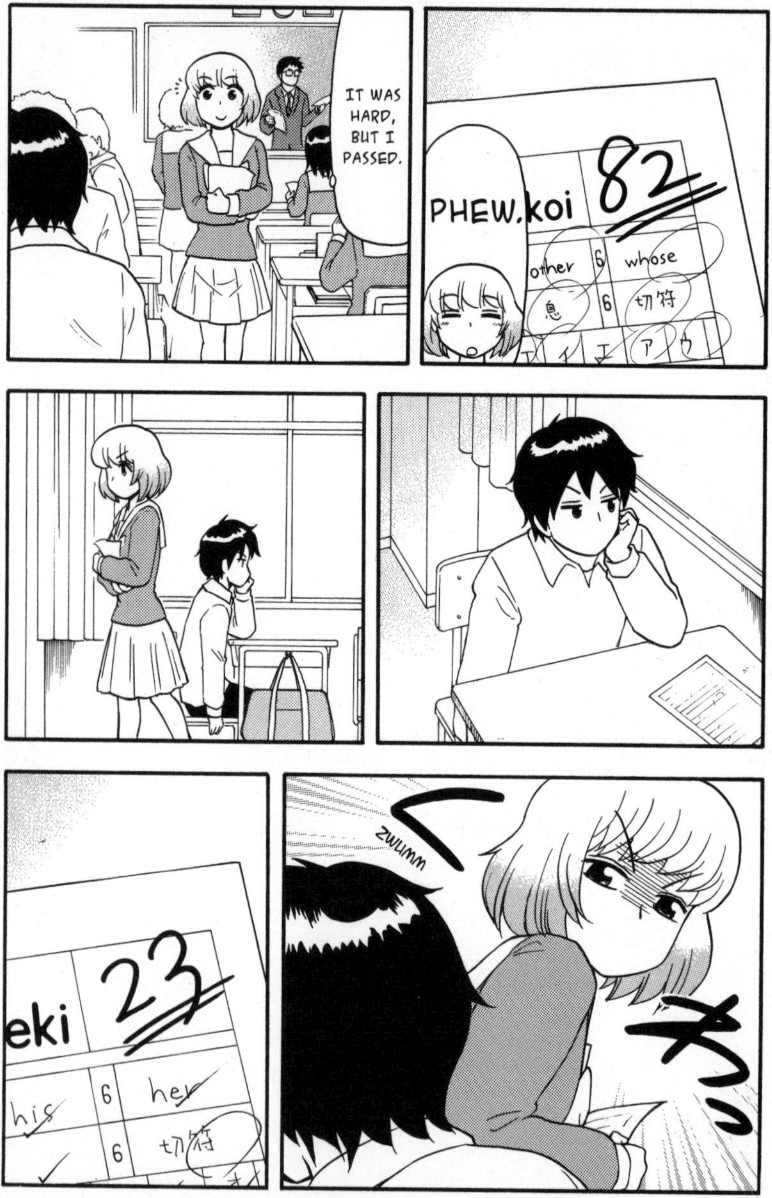
PHEW.
koi
82
other
6
whose
息
6
切符
IT WAS HARD, BUT I PASSED.
zwumm
eki
23
his
6
her
6
切符

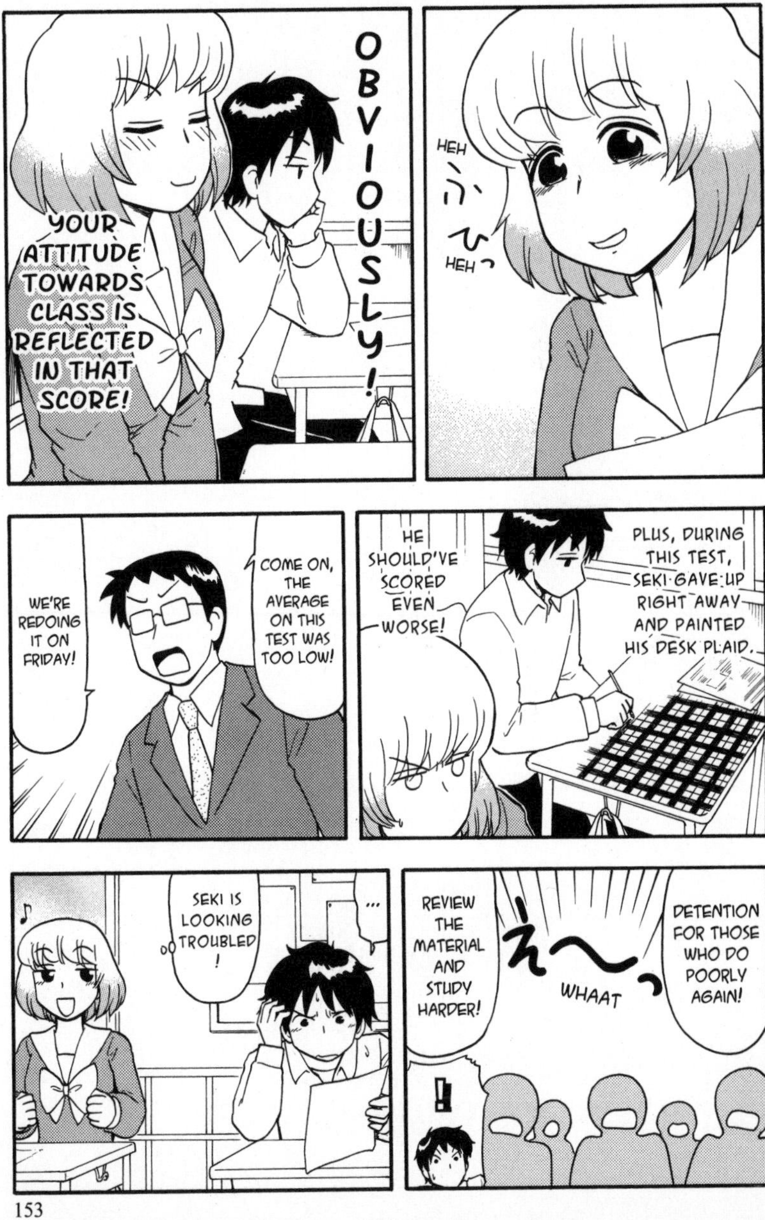
ふひっ
HEH HEH
OBVIOUSLY!
YOUR ATTITUDE TOWARDS CLASS IS REFLECTED IN THAT SCORE!
PLUS, DURING THIS TEST, SEKI GAVE UP RIGHT AWAY AND PAINTED HIS DESK PLAID.
HE SHOULD'VE SCORED EVEN WORSE!
COME ON, THE AVERAGE ON THIS TEST WAS TOO LOW!
WE'RE REDOING IT ON FRIDAY!
DETENTION FOR THOSE WHO DO POORLY AGAIN!
えへ～っ
WHAAT
REVIEW THE MATERIAL AND STUDY HARDER!
!
...
SEKI IS LOOKING TROUBLED!
♪

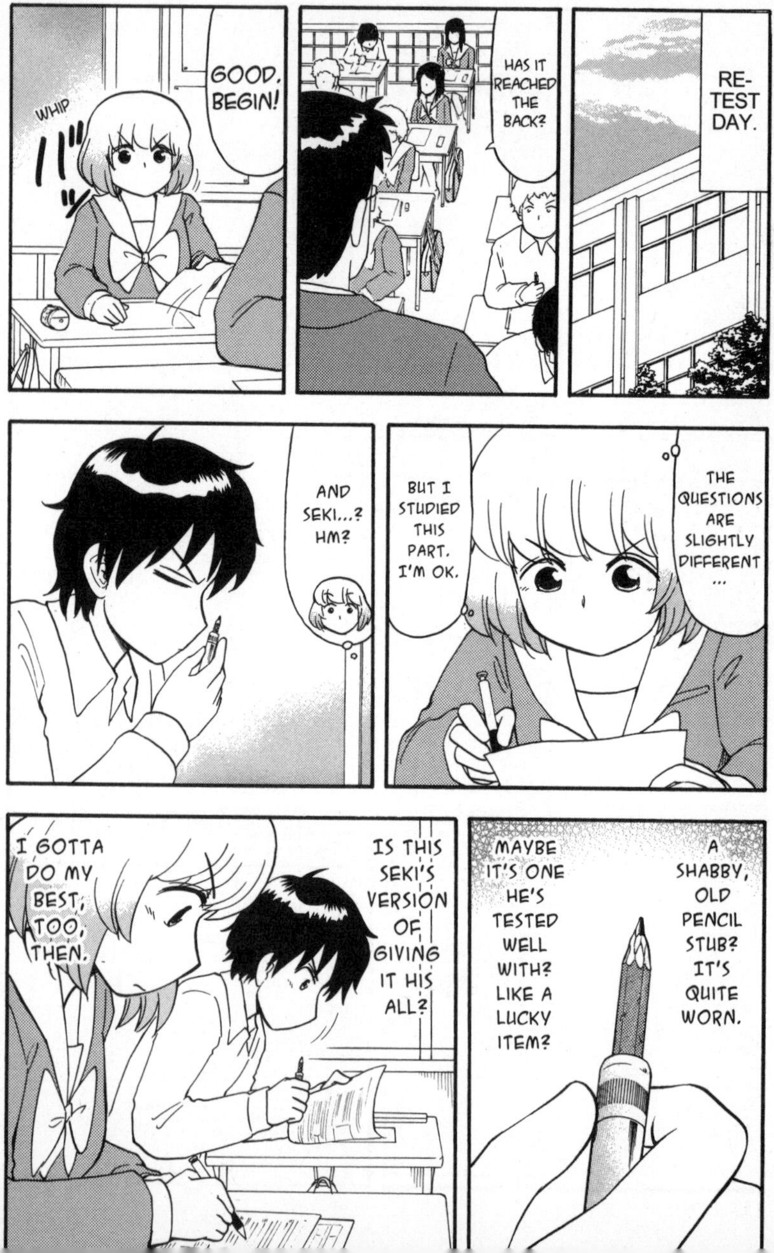
RE-TEST DAY.
HAS IT REACHED THE BACK?
GOOD, BEGIN!
WHIP
THE QUESTIONS ARE SLIGHTLY DIFFERENT ...
BUT I STUDIED THIS PART. I'M OK.
AND SEKI...? HM?
A SHABBY, OLD PENCIL STUB? IT'S QUITE WORN.
MAYBE IT'S ONE HE'S TESTED WELL WITH? LIKE A LUCKY ITEM?
IS THIS SEKI'S VERSION OF GIVING IT HIS ALL?
I GOTTA DO MY BEST, TOO, THEN.

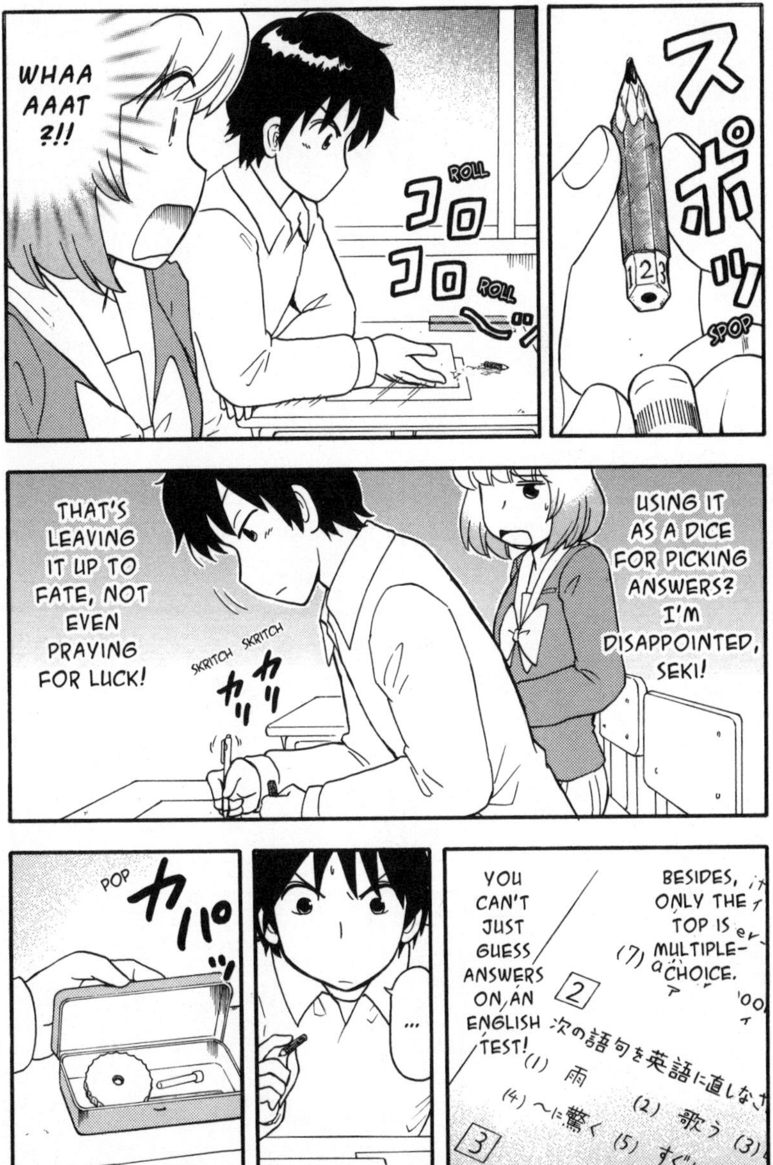
スポッ
SPOP
WHAA AAAT ?!!
コロコロ
ROLL
ROLL
～ッ
USING IT AS A DICE FOR PICKING ANSWERS? I'M DISAPPOINTED, SEKI!
THAT'S LEAVING IT UP TO FATE, NOT EVEN PRAYING FOR LUCK!
SKRITCH SKRITCH
カリカリ
BESIDES, ONLY THE TOP IS MULTIPLE-CHOICE.
YOU CAN'T JUST GUESS ANSWERS ON AN ENGLISH TEST!
(7)
2
次の語句を英語に直しな
(1) 雨
(2) 歌う
(4) ～に驚く
(5) すぐに
3
...
POP
カパッ

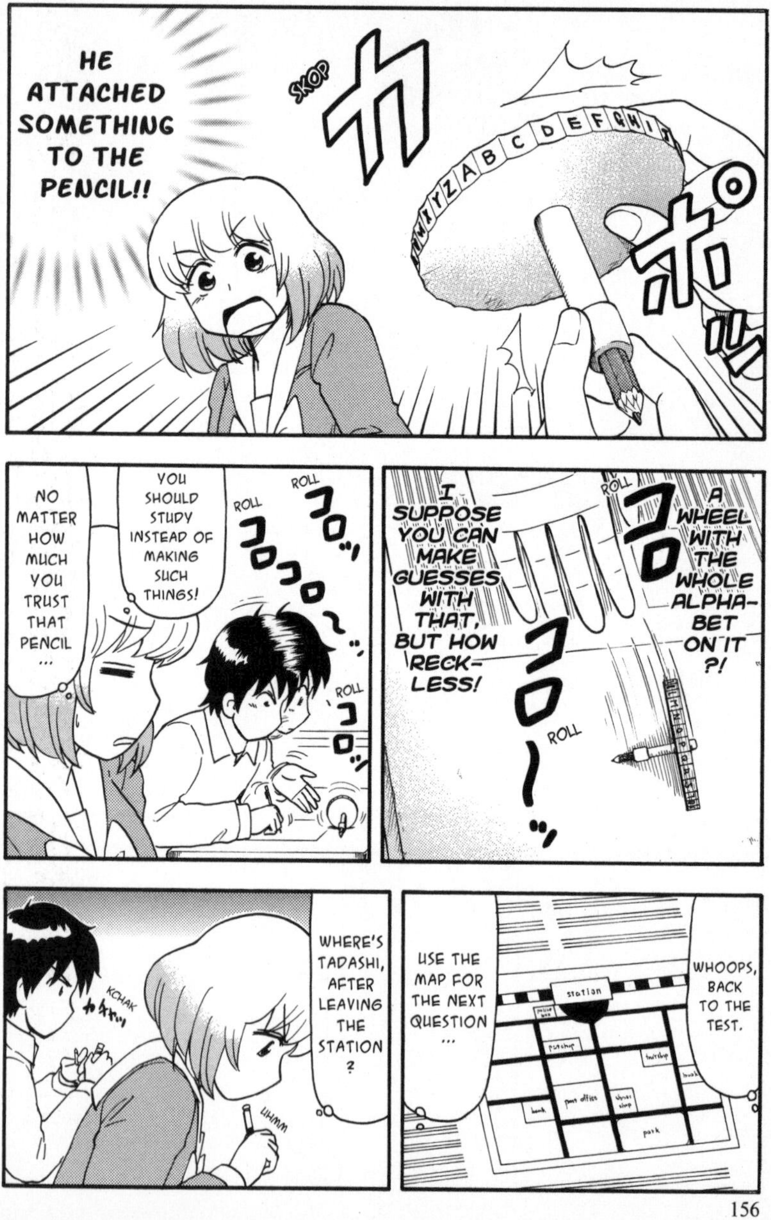
SKOP
HE ATTACHED SOMETHING TO THE PENCIL!!
A WHEEL WITH THE WHOLE ALPHA-BET ON IT ?!
ROLL
I SUPPOSE YOU CAN MAKE GUESSES WITH THAT, BUT HOW RECK-LESS!
ROLL
ROLL
ROLL
YOU SHOULD STUDY INSTEAD OF MAKING SUCH THINGS!
NO MATTER HOW MUCH YOU TRUST THAT PENCIL ...
ROLL
WHOOPS, BACK TO THE TEST.
USE THE MAP FOR THE NEXT QUESTION ...
station
post office
bank
park
WHERE'S TADASHI, AFTER LEAVING THE STATION ?
KCHAK
UHMM

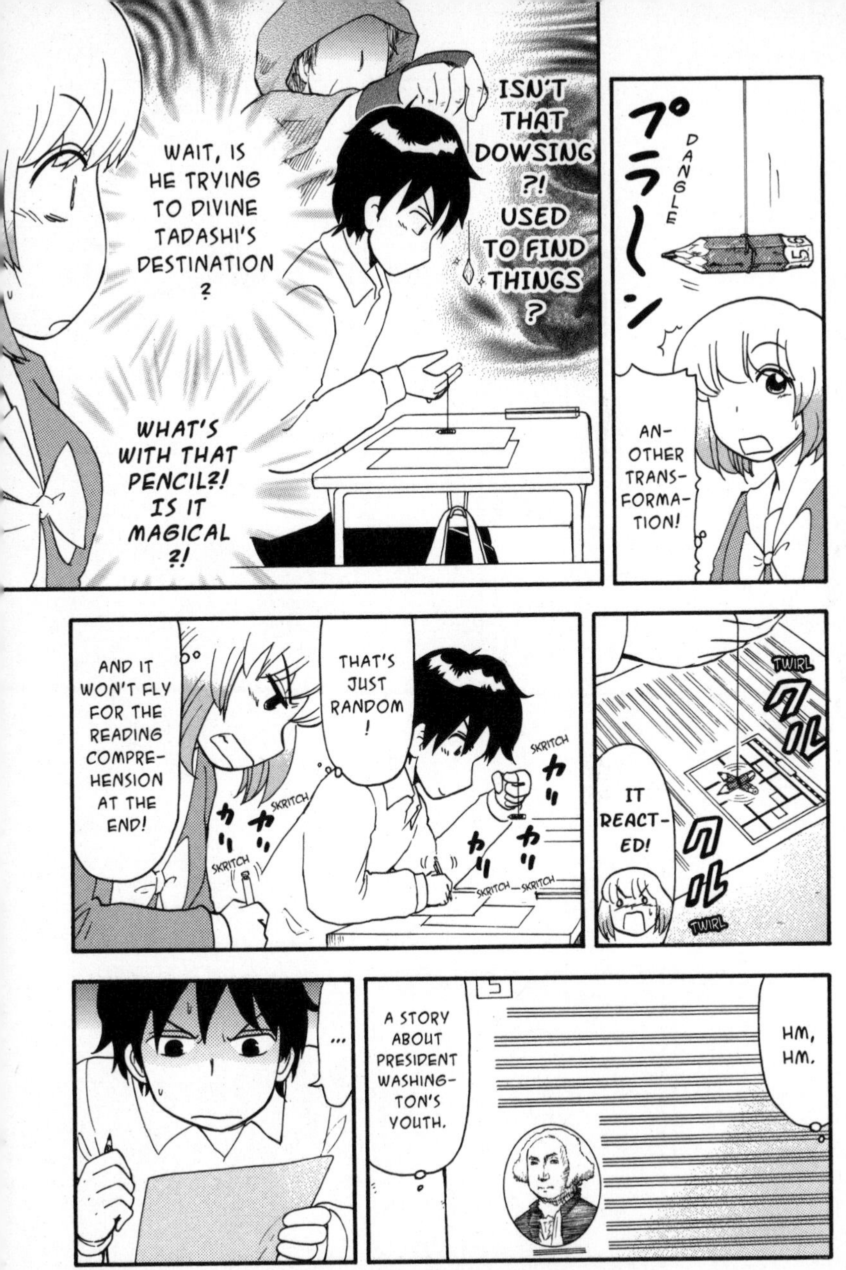
プラ〜ン
DANGLE
ANOTHER TRANSFORMATION!
ISN'T THAT DOWSING?! USED TO FIND THINGS?
WAIT, IS HE TRYING TO DIVINE TADASHI'S DESTINATION?
WHAT'S WITH THAT PENCIL?! IS IT MAGICAL?!
TWIRL
IT REACTED!
TWIRL
THAT'S JUST RANDOM!
AND IT WON'T FLY FOR THE READING COMPREHENSION AT THE END!
SKRITCH
SKRITCH
SKRITCH
SKRITCH
SKRITCH
HM, HM.
A STORY ABOUT PRESIDENT WASHINGTON'S YOUTH.
...

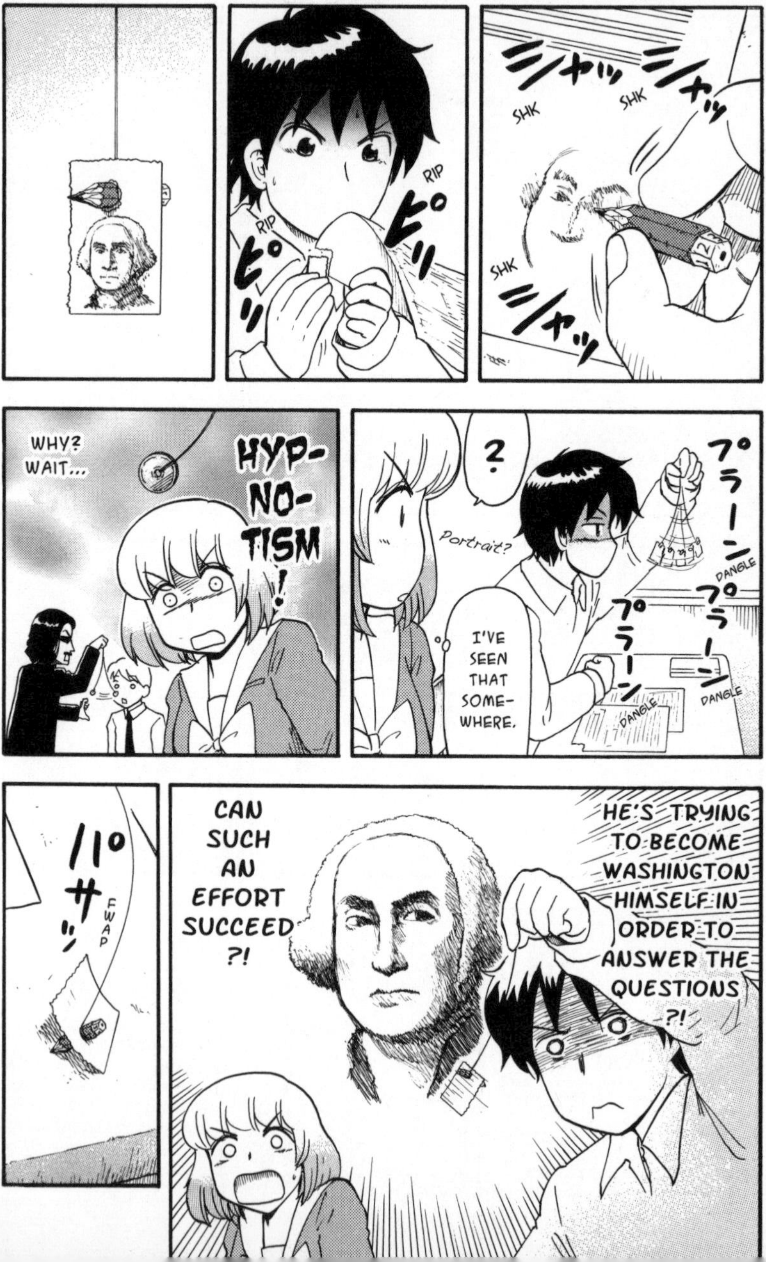
シャッ
SHK
シャッ
SHK
シャッ
SHK
ピッ
RIP
ピッ
RIP
?
Portrait?
I'VE SEEN THAT SOME-WHERE.
プラーン
DANGLE
プラーン
DANGLE
プラーン
DANGLE
HYP-NO-TISM!
WHY? WAIT...
HE'S TRYING TO BECOME WASHINGTON HIMSELF IN ORDER TO ANSWER THE QUESTIONS?!
CAN SUCH AN EFFORT SUCCEED?!
パサッ
FWAP

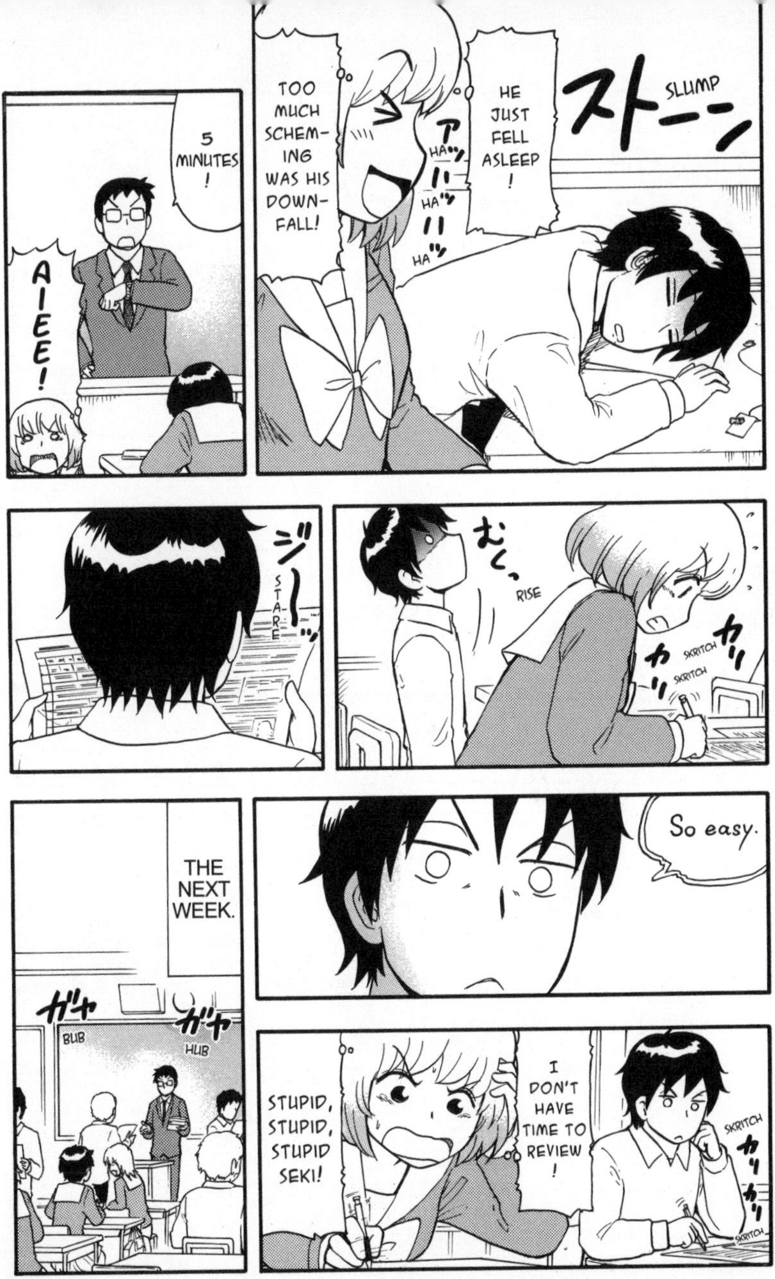
ストーン
SLUMP
HE JUST FELL ASLEEP!
アハハ
HA HA HA
TOO MUCH SCHEM-ING WAS HIS DOWN-FALL!
5 MINUTES!
AIEEE!
むく
RISE
カリカリ
SKRITCH SKRITCH
ジー
STARE
So easy.
I DON'T HAVE TIME TO REVIEW!
STUPID, STUPID, STUPID SEKI!
SKRITCH
カリカリ
SKRITCH
THE NEXT WEEK.
ガヤガヤ
BUB HUB

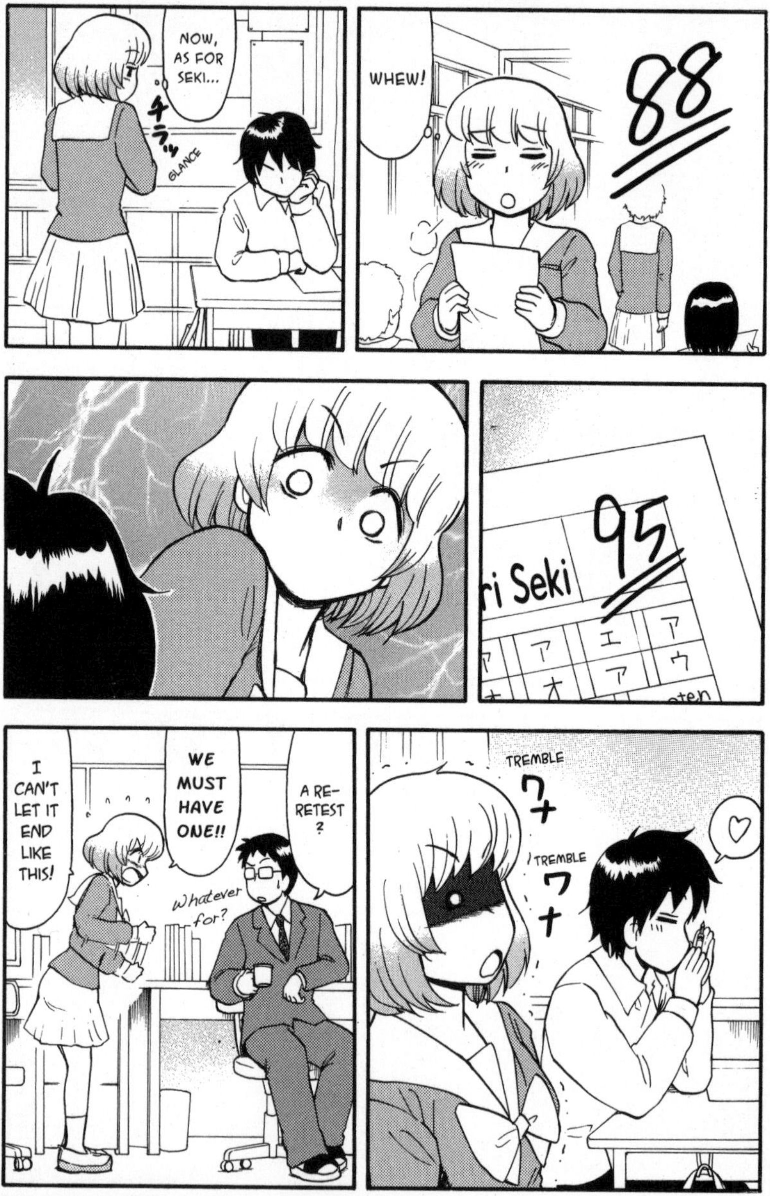

WHEW!
88
NOW, AS FOR SEKI...
チラッ
GLANCE
95
ri Seki
TREMBLE
ワナ
TREMBLE
ワナ
♡
A RE-RETEST?
WE MUST HAVE ONE!!
I CAN'T LET IT END LIKE THIS!
Whatever for?

Continued in My Neighbor Seki Volume 5

My Neighbor Seki

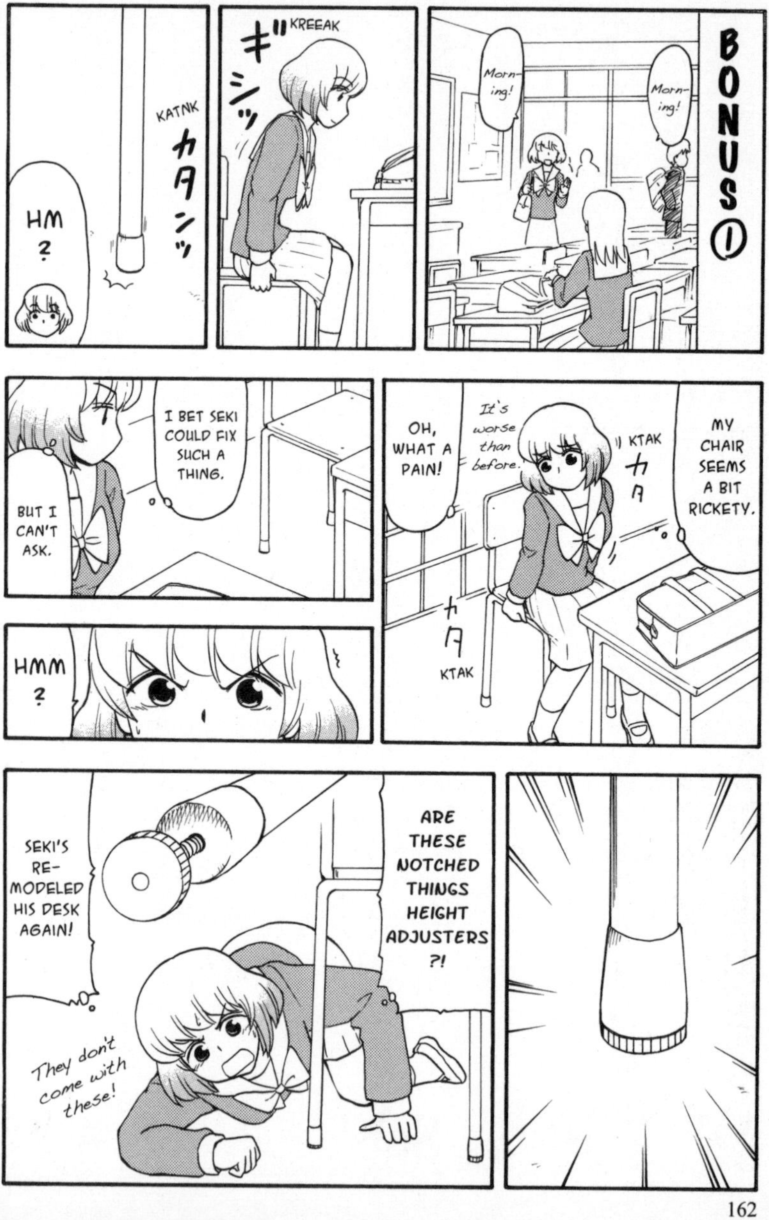
BONUS ①
Morning!
Morning!
ギシッ
KREEAK
KATNK
カタンッ
HM?
MY CHAIR SEEMS A BIT RICKETY.
KTAK
カタ
It's worse than before.
OH, WHAT A PAIN!
カタ
KTAK
I BET SEKI COULD FIX SUCH A THING.
BUT I CAN'T ASK.
HMM?
ARE THESE NOTCHED THINGS HEIGHT ADJUSTERS?!
SEKI'S RE-MODELED HIS DESK AGAIN!
They don't come with these!

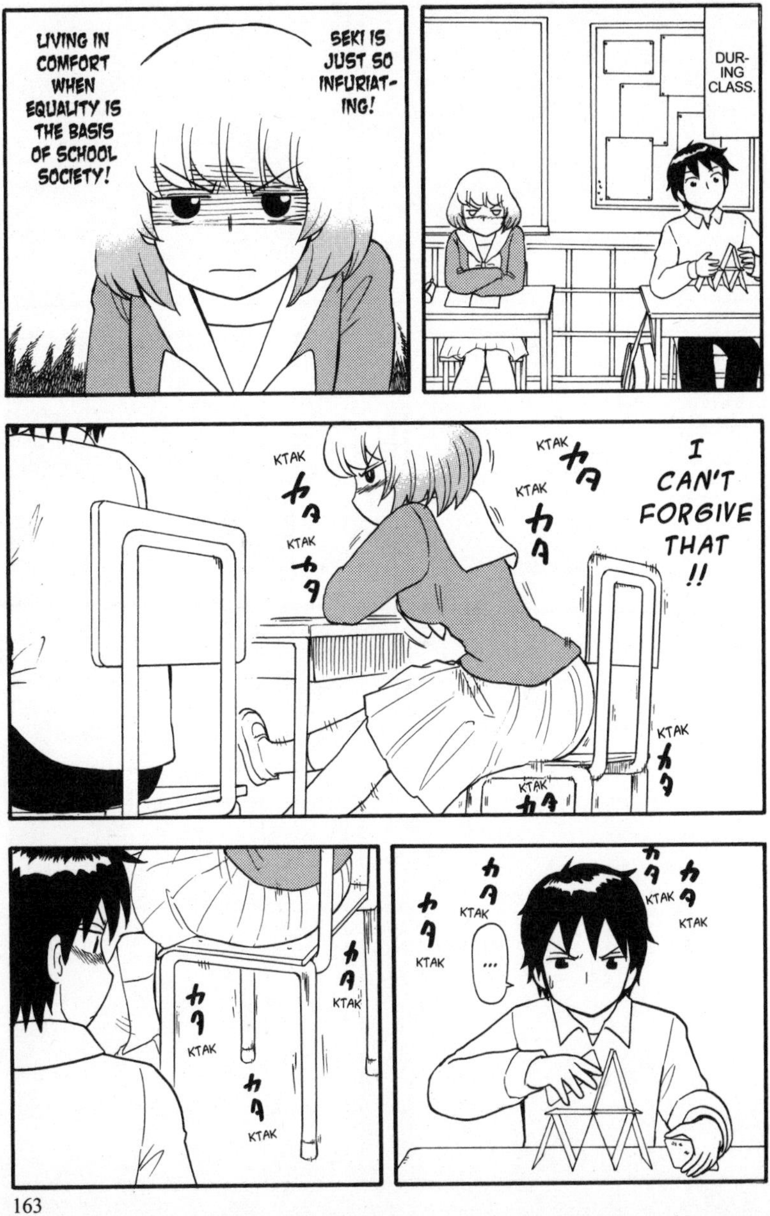

DURING CLASS.
SEKI IS JUST SO INFURIATING!
LIVING IN COMFORT WHEN EQUALITY IS THE BASIS OF SCHOOL SOCIETY!
I CAN'T FORGIVE THAT!!
KTAK
KTAK
KTAK
KTAK
KTAK
KTAK
KTAK
KTAK
...
KTAK
KTAK
KTAK
KTAK
KTAK

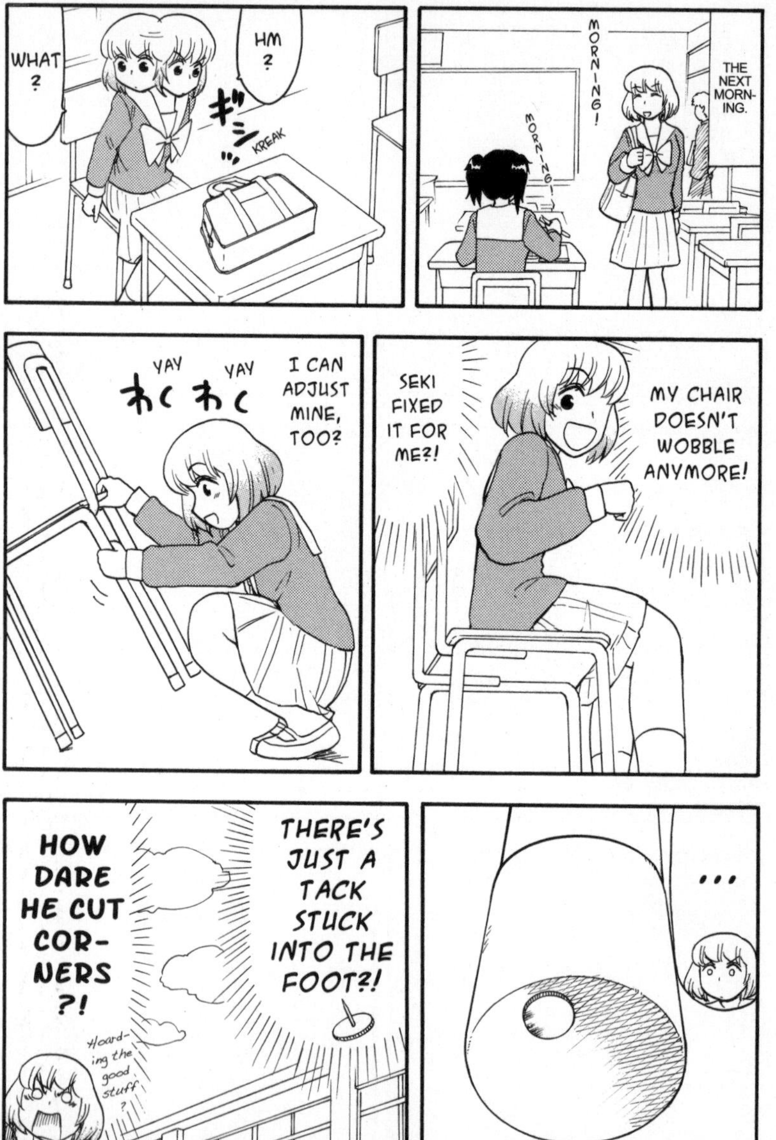
THE NEXT MORNING.
MORNING!
MORNING!
HM?
WHAT?
ギシ
KREAK
MY CHAIR DOESN'T WOBBLE ANYMORE!
SEKI FIXED IT FOR ME?!
I CAN ADJUST MINE, TOO?
わくわく
YAY YAY
...
THERE'S JUST A TACK STUCK INTO THE FOOT?!
HOW DARE HE CUT CORNERS?!
Hoarding the good stuff?

END

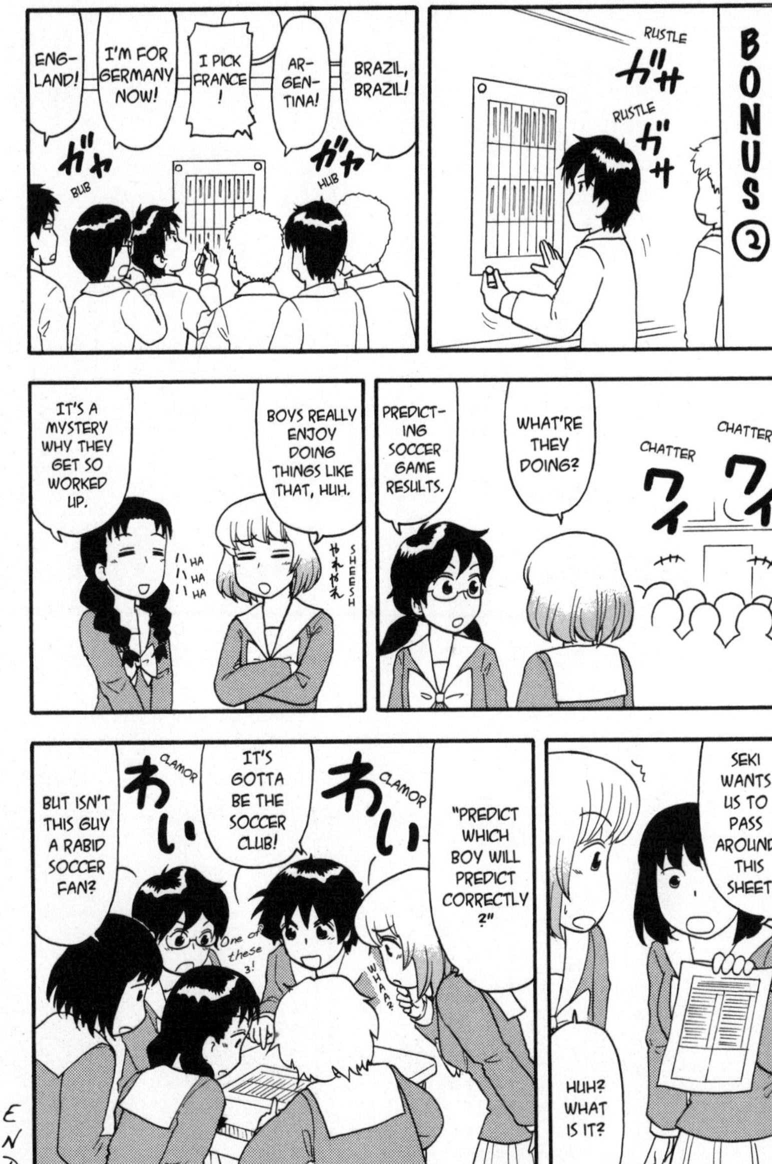
BONUS ②
RUSTLE
ガサ
RUSTLE
ガサ
BRAZIL, BRAZIL!
AR-GEN-TINA!
I PICK FRANCE!
I'M FOR GERMANY NOW!
ENG-LAND!
ガヤ
HUB
ガヤ
BUB
CHATTER
ワイ
CHATTER
ワイ
WHAT'RE THEY DOING?
PREDICT-ING SOCCER GAME RESULTS.
BOYS REALLY ENJOY DOING THINGS LIKE THAT, HUH.
やれやれ
SHEESH
IT'S A MYSTERY WHY THEY GET SO WORKED UP.
ハハハ
HA HA HA
SEKI WANTS US TO PASS AROUND THIS SHEET.
HUH? WHAT IS IT?
"PREDICT WHICH BOY WILL PREDICT CORRECTLY?"
わい
CLAMOR
IT'S GOTTA BE THE SOCCER CLUB!
わい
CLAMOR
BUT ISN'T THIS GUY A RABID SOCCER FAN?
One of these 3!
WHAA?!
END

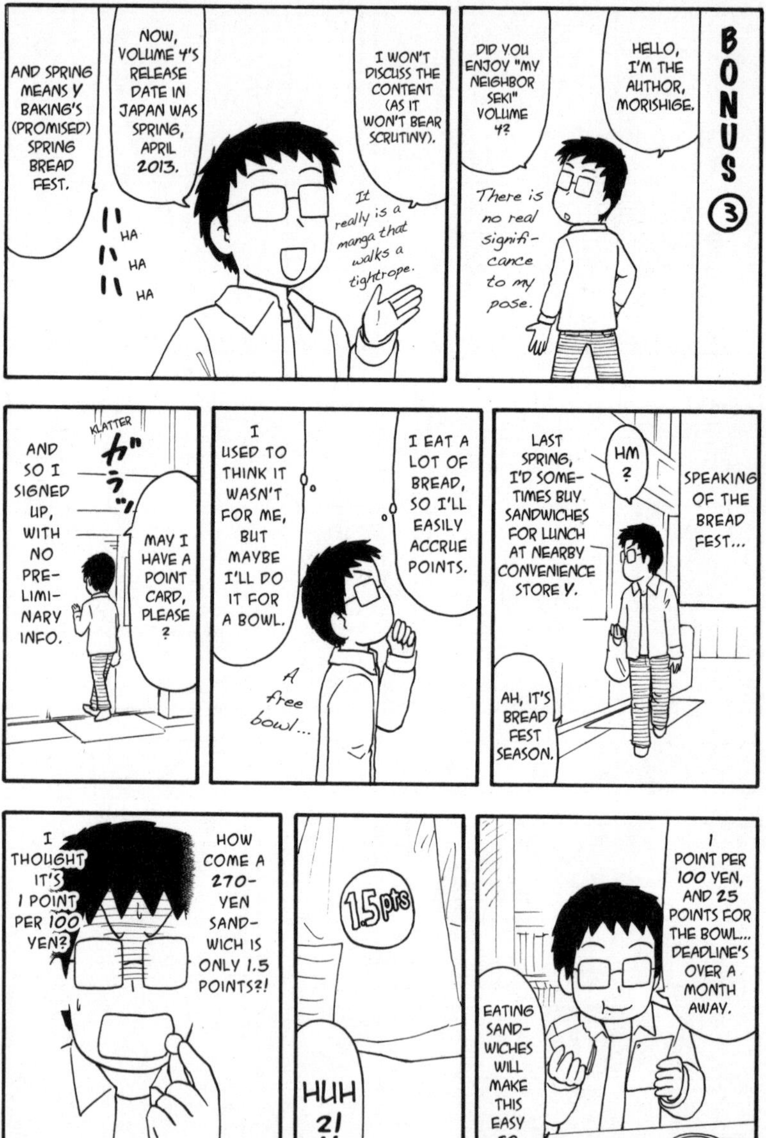
BONUS 3
HELLO, I'M THE AUTHOR, MORISHIGE.
DID YOU ENJOY "MY NEIGHBOR SEKI" VOLUME 4?
There is no real significance to my pose.
I WON'T DISCUSS THE CONTENT (AS IT WON'T BEAR SCRUTINY).
It really is a manga that walks a tightrope.
NOW, VOLUME 4'S RELEASE DATE IN JAPAN WAS SPRING, APRIL 2013.
AND SPRING MEANS Y BAKING'S (PROMISED) SPRING BREAD FEST.
HA HA HA
SPEAKING OF THE BREAD FEST...
HM?
LAST SPRING, I'D SOMETIMES BUY SANDWICHES FOR LUNCH AT NEARBY CONVENIENCE STORE Y.
AH, IT'S BREAD FEST SEASON.
I EAT A LOT OF BREAD, SO I'LL EASILY ACCRUE POINTS.
I USED TO THINK IT WASN'T FOR ME, BUT MAYBE I'LL DO IT FOR A BOWL.
A free bowl...
KLATTER
MAY I HAVE A POINT CARD, PLEASE?
AND SO I SIGNED UP, WITH NO PRELIMINARY INFO.
1 POINT PER 100 YEN, AND 25 POINTS FOR THE BOWL... DEADLINE'S OVER A MONTH AWAY.
EATING SANDWICHES WILL MAKE THIS EASY TO WIN!
1.5pts
HUH?!
HOW COME A 270-YEN SANDWICH IS ONLY 1.5 POINTS?!
I THOUGHT IT'S 1 POINT PER 100 YEN?

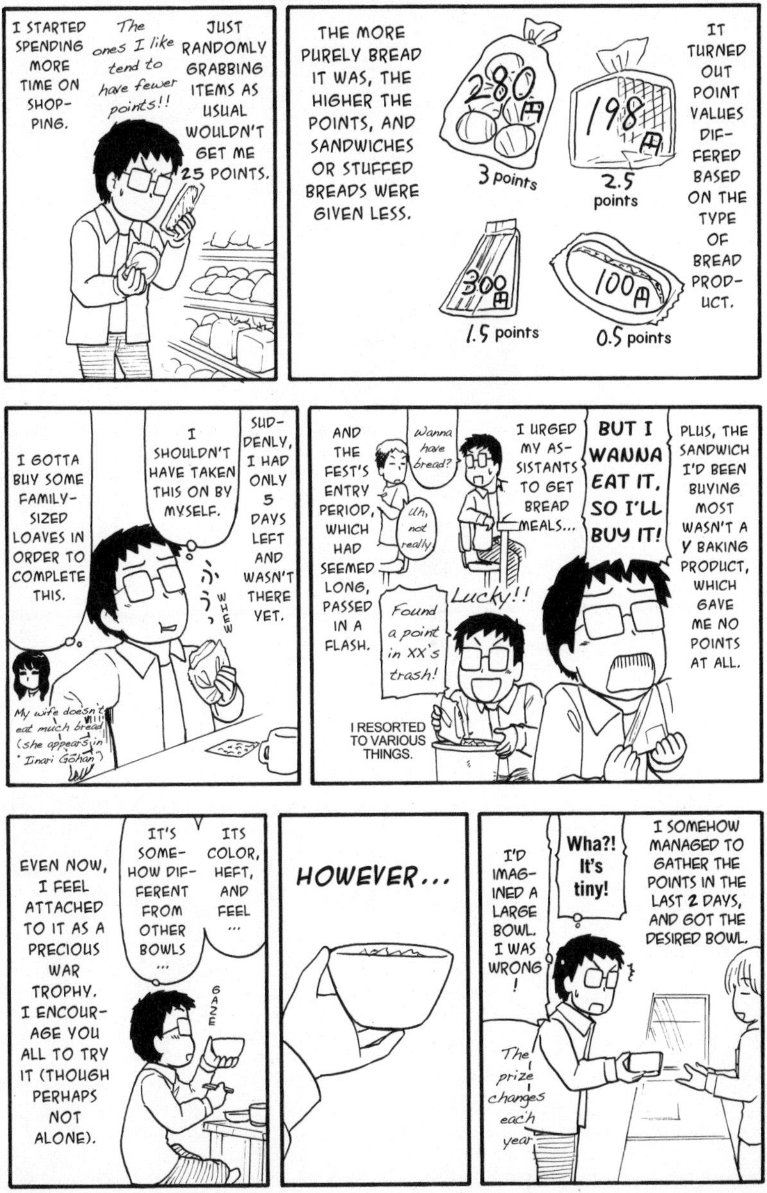

IT TURNED OUT POINT VALUES DIFFERED BASED ON THE TYPE OF BREAD PRODUCT.
THE MORE PURELY BREAD IT WAS, THE HIGHER THE POINTS, AND SANDWICHES OR STUFFED BREADS WERE GIVEN LESS.
198円
2.5 points
280円
3 points
100円
0.5 points
300円
1.5 points
JUST RANDOMLY GRABBING ITEMS AS USUAL WOULDN'T GET ME 25 POINTS.
The ones I like tend to have fewer points!!
I STARTED SPENDING MORE TIME ON SHOPPING.
PLUS, THE SANDWICH I'D BEEN BUYING MOST WASN'T A Y BAKING PRODUCT, WHICH GAVE ME NO POINTS AT ALL.
BUT I WANNA EAT IT, SO I'LL BUY IT!
I URGED MY ASSISTANTS TO GET BREAD MEALS...
Wanna have bread?
Uh, not really.
AND THE FEST'S ENTRY PERIOD, WHICH HAD SEEMED LONG, PASSED IN A FLASH.
Lucky!!
Found a point in XX's trash!
I RESORTED TO VARIOUS THINGS.
SUDDENLY, I HAD ONLY 5 DAYS LEFT AND WASN'T THERE YET.
I SHOULDN'T HAVE TAKEN THIS ON BY MYSELF.
ふう、
WHEW
I GOTTA BUY SOME FAMILY-SIZED LOAVES IN ORDER TO COMPLETE THIS.
My wife doesn't eat much bread (she appears in "Inari Gohan")
I SOMEHOW MANAGED TO GATHER THE POINTS IN THE LAST 2 DAYS, AND GOT THE DESIRED BOWL.
Wha?! It's tiny!
I'D IMAGINED A LARGE BOWL. I WAS WRONG!
The prize changes each year
HOWEVER...
ITS COLOR, HEFT, AND FEEL...
IT'S SOMEHOW DIFFERENT FROM OTHER BOWLS...
GAZE
EVEN NOW, I FEEL ATTACHED TO IT AS A PRECIOUS WAR TROPHY. I ENCOURAGE YOU ALL TO TRY IT (THOUGH PERHAPS NOT ALONE).
END

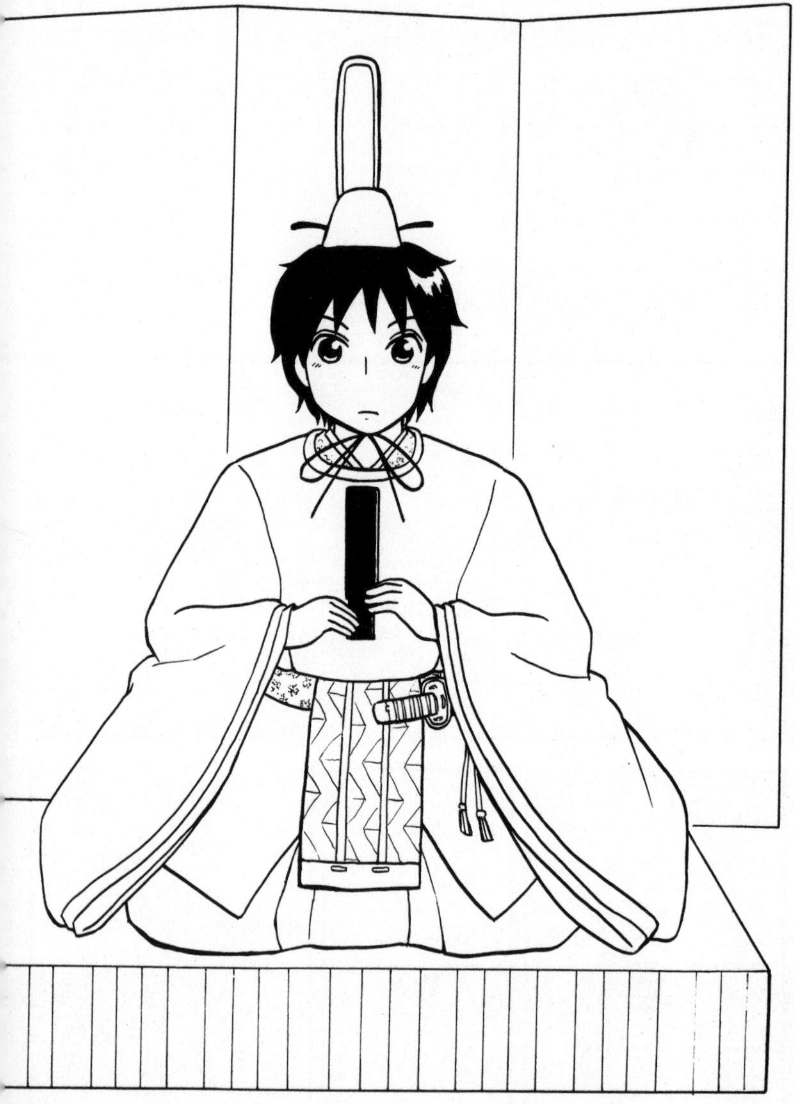

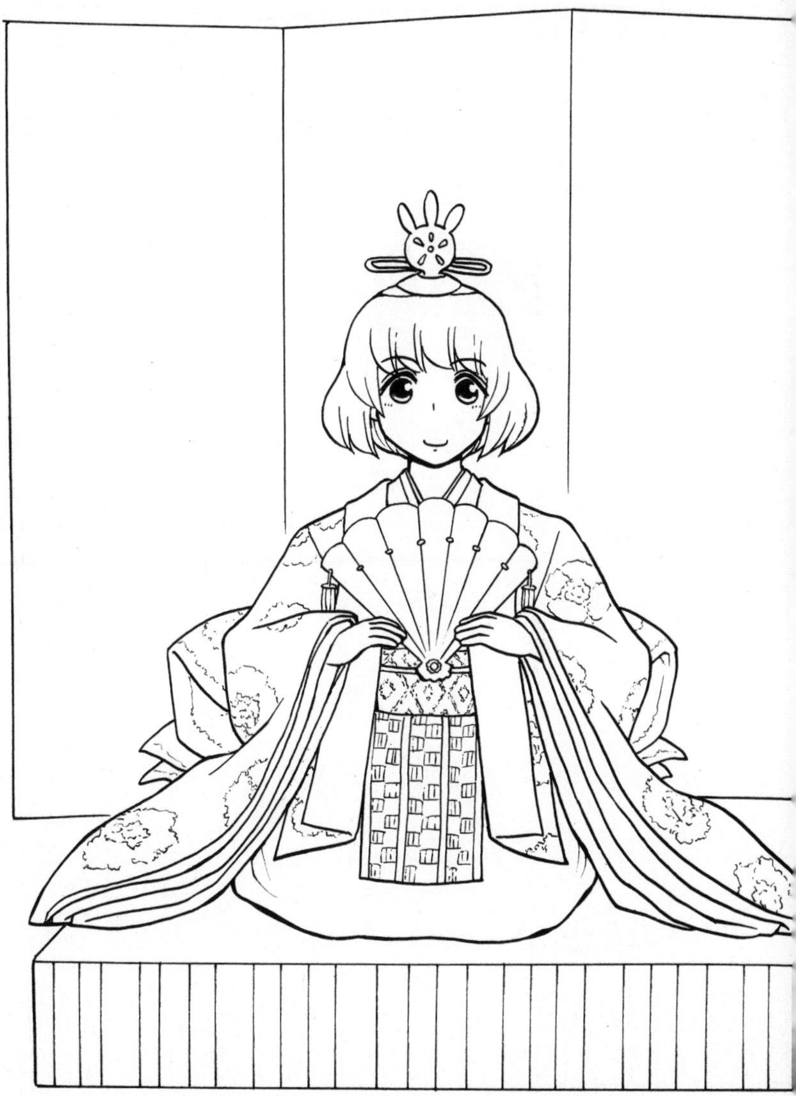

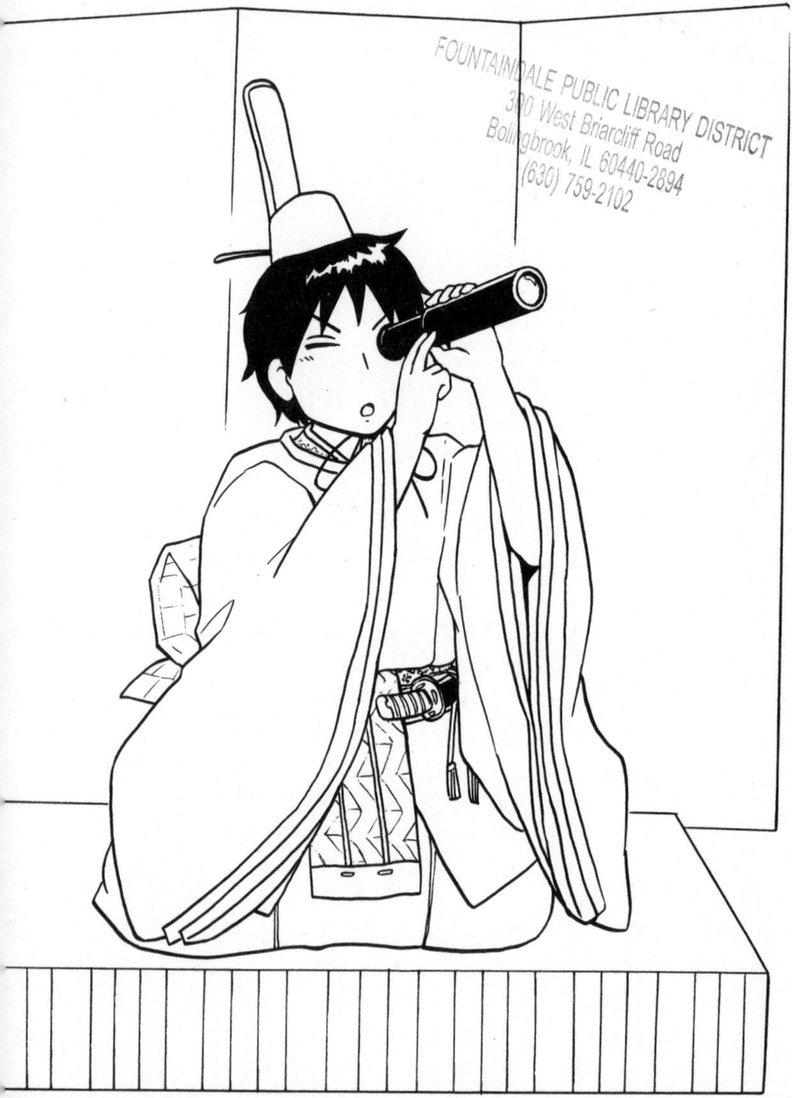

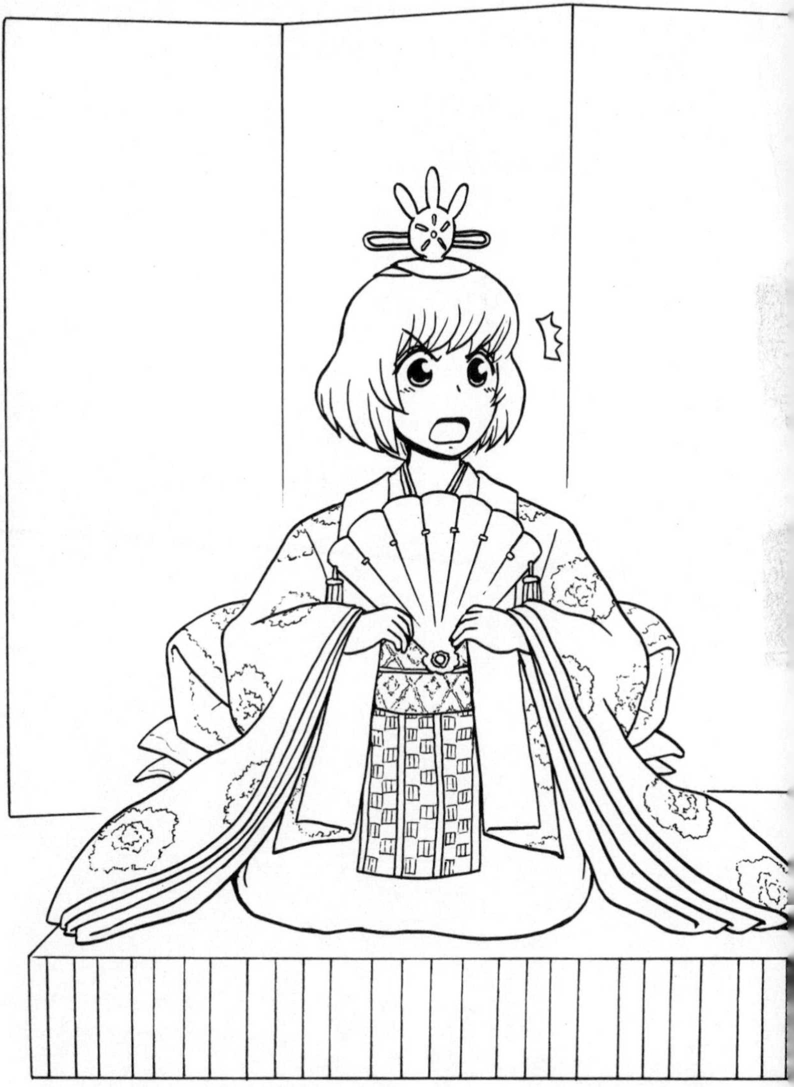

Vertical Comics!

ESP

Coming this Fall from

THERE'S A NEW HEROINE IN TOWN.

Rinka Urushiba's world is turned upside down when she wakes up one day—after falling right through the floor.

Encouraged by another ESPer who believes that Rinka's destiny is to become a hero of justice, she soon learns to use her powers for good. And not a moment too soon, as those with less-than-admirable ambitions descend on Tokyo with their own sets of superpowers. As the mysterious glowing fish flitting through the city skies gift powers seemingly at random, foes become friends and alliances are made and broken.

And what about that flying penguin?

HAJIME SEGAWA

TOKYO

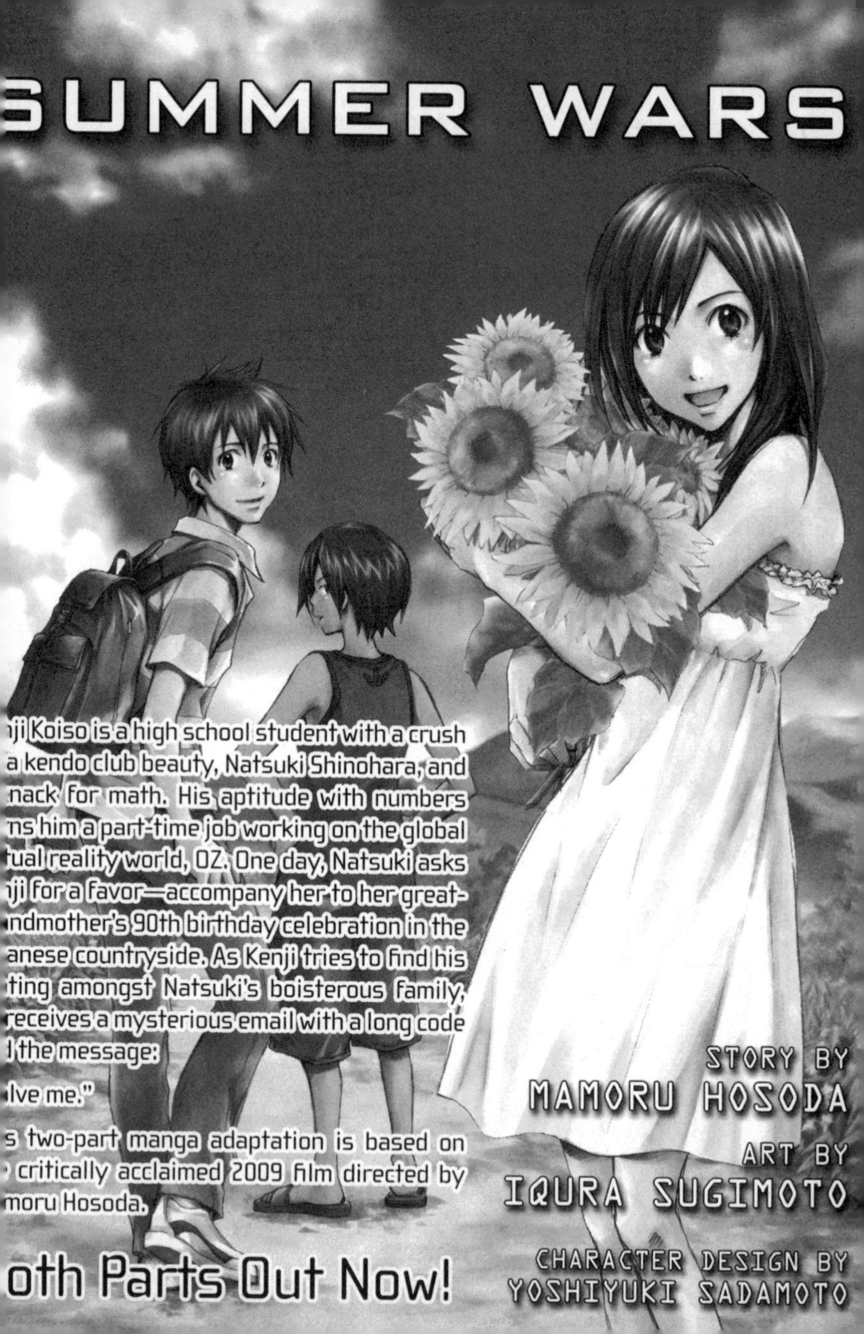
SUMMER WARS
nji Koiso is a high school student with a crush
a kendo club beauty, Natsuki Shinohara, and
nack for math. His aptitude with numbers
rns him a part-time job working on the global
tual reality world, OZ. One day, Natsuki asks
nji for a favor—accompany her to her great-
ndmother's 90th birthday celebration in the
anese countryside. As Kenji tries to find his
ting amongst Natsuki's boisterous family,
receives a mysterious email with a long code
l the message:
lve me."
s two-part manga adaptation is based on
critically acclaimed 2009 film directed by
moru Hosoda.
STORY BY
MAMORU HOSODA
ART BY
IQURA SUGIMOTO
CHARACTER DESIGN BY
YOSHIYUKI SADAMOTO
oth Parts Out Now!